Writers of English: Lives and Works

CONTEMPORARY BLACK AMERICAN POETS AND DRAMATISTS

Edited and with an Introduction by

Harold Bloom

CHELSEA HOUSE PUBLISHERS
New York   Philadelphia

Jacket illustration: Jacob Lawrence, *The Apartment* (1943) (courtesy of the Hunter Museum of Art, Chattanooga, Tennessee, purchase from the Benwood Foundation and the 1982 Collectors' Group Funds).

CHELSEA HOUSE PUBLISHERS

Editorial Director Richard Rennert
Executive Managing Editor Karyn Gullen Browne
Copy Chief Robin James
Picture Editor Adrian G. Allen
Creative Director Robert Mitchell
Art Director Joan Ferrigno
Production Manager Sallye Scott

Writers of English: Lives and Works

Senior Editor S. T. Joshi
Series Design Rae Grant

Staff for CONTEMPORARY BLACK AMERICAN POETS AND DRAMATISTS

Assistant Editor Mary Sisson
Research Robert Green
Picture Researcher Villette Harris

3 5 7 9 8 6 4 2

Library of Congress Cataloging-in-Publication Data

Contemporary Black American poets and dramatists / edited and with an introduction by Harold Bloom.
        p. cm.—(Writers of English)
    Includes bibliographical references.
    ISBN 0-7910-2213-7.—ISBN 0-7910-2238-2 (pbk.)
  1. American literature—Afro-American authors—History and criticism. 2. American literature—Afro-American authors—Bio-bibliography. 3. American literature—20th century—History and criticism. 4. American literature—20th century—Bio-bibliography. 5. Afro-Americans in literature. I. Bloom, Harold. II. Series.
PS153.N5C64 1994
810.9'896073—dc20   94-5885
[B]   CIP

Contemporary
Black American
Poets and Dramatists

▣ Contents

◈ User's Guide

THIS VOLUME PROVIDES biographical, critical, and bibliographical information on the fourteen most significant black American poets and dramatists. Each chapter consists of three parts: a biography of the author; a selection of brief critical extracts about the author; and a bibliography of the author's published books.

The biography supplies a detailed outline of the important events in the author's life, including his or her major writings. The critical extracts are taken from a wide array of books and periodicals, from the author's lifetime to the present, and range in content from biographical to critical to historical. The extracts are arranged in chronological order by date of writing or publication, and a full bibliographical citation is provided at the end of each extract. Editorial additions or deletions are indicated within carets.

The author bibliographies list every separate publication—including books, pamphlets, broadsides, collaborations, and works edited or translated by the author—for works published in the author's lifetime; selected important posthumous publications are also listed. Titles are those of the first edition; variant titles are supplied within carets. In selected instances dates of revised editions are given where these are significant. Pseudonymous works are listed, but not the pseudonyms under which these works were published. Periodicals edited by the author are listed only when the author has written most or all of the contents. Titles enclosed in square brackets are of doubtful authenticity. All works by the author, whether in English or in other languages, have been listed; English translations of foreign-language works are not listed unless the author has done the translation.

The Life of the Author

Harold Bloom

NIETZSCHE, WITH EXULTANT ANGUISH, famously proclaimed that God was dead. Whatever the consequences of this for the ethical life, its ultimate literary effect certainly would have surprised the author Nietzsche. His French disciples, Foucault most prominent among them, developed the Nietzschean proclamation into the dogma that all authors, God included, were dead. The death of the author, which is no more than a Parisian trope, another metaphor for fashion's setting of skirt-lengths, is now accepted as literal truth by most of our current apostles of what should be called French Nietzsche, to distinguish it from the merely original Nietzsche. We also have French Freud or Lacan, which has little to do with the actual thought of Sigmund Freud, and even French Joyce, which interprets *Finnegans Wake* as the major work of Jacques Derrida. But all this is as nothing compared to the final triumph of the doctrine of the death of the author: French Shakespeare. That delicious absurdity is given us by the New Historicism, which blends Foucault and California fruit juice to give us the Word that Renaissance "social energies," and not William Shakespeare, composed *Hamlet* and *King Lear*. It seems a proper moment to murmur "enough" and to return to a study of the life of the author.

Sometimes it troubles me that there are so few masterpieces in the vast ocean of literary biography that stretches between James Boswell's great *Life* of Dr. Samuel Johnson and the late Richard Ellmann's wonderful *Oscar Wilde*. Literary biography is a crucial genre, and clearly a difficult one in which to excel. The actual nature of the lives of the poets seems to have little effect upon the quality of their biographies. Everything happened to Lord Byron and nothing at all to Wallace Stevens, and yet their biographers seem equally daunted by them. But even inadequate biographies of strong writers, or of weak ones, are of immense use. I have never read a literary biography from which I have not profited, a statement I cannot make about any other genre whatsoever. And when it comes to figures who are central to us—Dante, Shakespeare, Cervantes, Montaigne, Goethe, Whitman, Tolstoi, Freud, Joyce, Kafka among them—we reach out eagerly for every scrap that the biographers have gleaned. Concerning Dante and Shakespeare we know much too little, yet when we come to Goethe and Freud, where we seem to know more than everything, we still want to know more. The death of the author, despite our current resentniks, clearly was only a momentary fad. Something vital in every authentic lover of literature responds to Emerson's battle-cry sentence: "There is no history, only biography." Beyond that there is a deeper truth, difficult to come at and requiring a lifetime to understand, which is that there is no literature, only autobiography, however mediated, however veiled, however transformed. The events of Shakespeare's life included the composition of *Hamlet,* and that act of writing was itself a crucial act of living, though we do not yet know altogether how to read so doubled an act. When an author takes up a more overtly autobiographical stance, as so many do in their youth, again we still do not know precisely how to accommodate the vexed relation between life and work. T. S. Eliot, meditating upon James Joyce, made a classic statement as to such accommodation:

> We want to know who are the originals of his characters, and what were the origins of his episodes, so that we may unravel the web of memory and invention and discover how far and in what ways the crude material has been transformed.

When a writer is not even covertly autobiographical, the web of memory and invention is still there, but so subtly woven that we may never unravel it. And yet we want deeply never to stop trying, and not merely because we are curious, but because each of us is caught in her own network of memory and invention. We do not always recall our inventions, and long before we age we cease to be certain of the extent to which we have invented our memories. Perhaps one motive for reading is our need to unravel our own webs. If our masters could make, from their lives, what we read, then we can be moved by them to ask: What have we made or lived in relation to what we have read? The answers may be sad, or confused, but the question is likely, implicitly, to go on being asked as long as we read. In Freudian terms, we are asking: What is it that we have repressed? What have we forgotten, unconsciously but purposively: What is it that we flee? Art, literature necessarily included, is regression in the service of the ego, according to a famous Freudian formula. I doubt the Freudian wisdom here, but indubitably it is profoundly suggestive. When we read, something in us keeps asking the equivalent of the Freudian questions: From what or whom is the author in flight, and to what earlier stages in her life is she returning, and why?

Reading, whether as an art or a pastime, has been damaged by the visual media, television in particular, and might be in some danger of extinction in the age of the computer, except that the psychic need for it continues to endure, presumably because it alone can assuage a central loneliness in elitist society. Despite all sophisticated or resentful denials, the reading of imaginative literature remains a quest to overcome the isolation of the individual consciousness. We can read for information, or entertainment, or for love of the language, but in the end we seek, in the author, the person whom we have not found, whether in ourselves or in others. In that quest, there always are elements at once aggressive and defensive, so that reading, even in childhood, is rarely free of hidden anxieties. And yet it remains one of the few activities not contaminated by an entropy of spirit. We read in hope, because we lack companionship, and the author can become the object of the most idealistic elements in our search for the wit and inventiveness we so desperately require. We read biography, not as a supplement to reading the author, but as a second, fresh attempt to understand what always seems to evade us in the work, our drive towards a kind of identity with the author.

This will-to-identity, though recently much deprecated, is a prime basis for the experience of sublimity in reading. *Hamlet* retains its unique position in the Western canon not because most readers and playgoers identify themselves with the prince, who clearly is beyond them, but rather because they find themselves again in the power of the language that represents him with such immediacy and force. Yet we know that neither language nor social energy created Hamlet. Our curiosity about Shakespeare is endless, and never will be appeased. That curiosity itself is a value, and cannot be separated from the value of *Hamlet* the tragedy, or Hamlet the literary character. It provokes us that Shakespeare the man seems so unknowable, at once everyone and no one as Borges shrewdly observes. Critics keep telling us otherwise, yet something valid in us keeps believing that we would know Hamlet better if Shakespeare's life were as fully known as the lives of Goethe and Freud, Byron and Oscar Wilde, or best of all, Dr. Samuel Johnson. Shakespeare never will have his Boswell, and Dante never will have his Richard Ellmann. How much one would give for a detailed and candid *Life of Dante* by Petrarch, or an outspoken memoir of Shakespeare by Ben Jonson! Or, in the age just past, how superb would be rival studies of one another by Hemingway and Scott Fitzgerald! But the list is endless: think of *Oscar Wilde* by Lord Alfred Douglas, or a joint biography of Shelley by Mary Godwin, Emilia Viviani, and Jane Williams. More than our insatiable desire for scandal would be satisfied. The literary rivals and the lovers of the great writers possessed perspectives we will never enjoy, and without those perspectives we dwell in some poverty in regard to the writers with whom we ourselves never can be done.

There is a sense in which imaginative literature *is* perspectivism, so that the reader is likely to be overwhelmed by the work's difficulty unless its multiple perspectives are mastered. Literary biography matters most because it is a storehouse of perspectives, frequently far surpassing any that are grasped by the particular biographer. There are relations between authors' lives and their works of kinds we have yet to discover, because our analytical instruments are not yet advanced enough to perform the necessary labor. Perhaps a novel, poem, or play is not so much a regression in the service of the ego, as it is an amalgam of *all* the Freudian mechanisms of defense, all working together for the apotheosis of the ego. Freud valued art highly, but thought that the aesthetic enterprise was no rival for psychoanalysis, unlike religion and philosophy. Clearly Freud was mistaken; his own anxieties about his indebtedness to Shakespeare helped produce the weirdness of his joining in the lunacy that argued for the Earl of Oxford as the author of Shakespeare's plays. It was Shakespeare, and not "the poets," who was there before Freud arrived at his depth psychology, and it is Shakespeare who is there still, well out ahead of psychoanalysis. We see what Freud would not see, that psychoanalysis is Shakespeare prosified and systematized. Freud is part of literature, not of "science," and the biography of Freud has the same relations to psychoanalysis as the biography of Shakespeare has to *Hamlet* and *King Lear*, if only we knew more of the life of Shakespeare.

Western literature, particularly since Shakespeare, is marked by the representation of internalized change in its characters. A literature of the ever-growing inner self is in itself a large form of biography, even though this is the biography of imaginary beings, from Hamlet to the sometimes nameless protagonists of Kafka and Beckett. Skeptics might want to argue that all literary biography concerns imaginary beings, since authors make themselves up, and every biographer gives us a creation curiously different from the same author as seen by the writer of a rival *Life*. Boswell's Johnson is not quite anyone else's Johnson, though it is now very difficult for us to disentangle the great Doctor from his gifted Scottish friend and follower. The life of the author is not merely a metaphor or a fiction, as is "the Death of the Author," but it always does contain metaphorical or fictive elements. Those elements are a part of the value of literary biography, but not the largest or the crucial part, which is the separation of the mask from the man or woman who hid behind it. James Joyce and Samuel Beckett, master and sometime disciple, were both of them enigmatic personalities, and their biographers have not, as yet, fully expounded the mystery of these contrasting natures. Beckett seems very nearly to have been a secular saint: personally disinterested, heroic in the French Resistance, as humane a person ever to have composed major fictions and dramas. Joyce, self-obsessed even as Beckett was preternaturally selfless, was the Milton of the twentieth century. Beckett was perhaps the least egoistic post-Joycean, post-Proustian, post-Kafkan of writers. Does that illuminate the problematical nature of his work, or does it simply constitute another problem? Whatever the cause, the question matters. The only death of the author that is other than literal, and that matters, is the fate only of weak writers. The strong, who become canonical, never die, which is what the canon truly is about. To be read forever is the Life of the Author.

◈ Introduction

THOUGH I GREATLY ADMIRE the work of Rita Dove, currently our poet laureate, I prophesy that Thylias Moss, still a young woman, will surpass Dove and will be one of the crucial American poets of our turn into the twenty-first century. A marvelously original writer, with a vision and a diction very much her own, Moss is both a superb comic poet and a radical religious visionary whose mythos is altogether new, at least to me. The comic mode and the spiritual stance so blend in Moss that I scarcely can conceive of one without the other, as here in the second section of the superb "For Those Who Can't Peel the Potatoes Close Enough," where the poet, in the Christological year of her life, compares herself to Jesus:

> Now I am thirty-three
> and sometimes unable to feel my right leg,
> a numbness threatening my feeling
> the best part of marriage, numbness
> I first felt biting through haddock
> and my lower lip until blood spurted
> and I stopped at red as I always do.
> The waitress did not and pocketed
> the bloody money.
>
> A red carpet is a tongue of blood.
> Jesus never married.
> I never French kiss.

The pungency of this is very difficult to characterize; it has little to do with mere irony, with saying one thing while meaning another. Rather, the tone is uncanny, and seems both foreign and yet familiar. It appears throughout Thylias Moss's religious poems. In the great prose-poem, "The Warmth of Hot Chocolate," Moss portrays herself as "an angel who doesn't believe in God," yet who nevertheless protects him from corruption, and maintains him as "a shadowy ever-descending brother." "The Adversary" benignly presents Satan as "the original Uncle Tom," while "A Form of Deicide" compares God both to Elvis Presley and to Santa Claus. "Renegade Angels," another extraordinary prose-poem, implicitly makes women in love represent a new breed of angels, who can either divide or double at will.

As such an angel, Thylias Moss conceives of a God not exactly faultless, as in the startling "Doubts During Catastrophe":

> No better time to recall God's fascination
> with his image. He put something of himself
> in every creation. When he was tired
> he made lazy idiots. When he had hiccups
> he made tumbleweeds. When he needed a twin
> he made Adam. And whenever he needed to
> he watched Adam seduce Eve. And when once Eve refused
> God's eyebrows raised, merged and flew off, a caracara
> seeking carrion. And there was wrath. *Vengeance*
> *is mine* he said. And then there was his seduction
> of Mary who had to submit, could not disobey the Lord.

After that marvelous catalogue, with something to offend nearly all the pious, Moss might seem to have touched a limit, but surpasses it in "Small Congregations," the title poem of her major volume to date. Here the black congregation exemplifies the saddest truth that this poetic visionary intuits about her people's intense resort to faith:

> Our shouting, our jubilation scares the ominous into
> crouching behind our ribs where it intercepts what
> would best serve us if it reached our hearts.

That is so bleak an intimation that only the masterly language saves it from being unbearable as a truth. Yeats praised Blake's poetry for its "beautiful, laughing speech"; one could say that of the best of Thylias Moss. Part Gnostic, part antic, this poetry sometimes achieves "The Rapture of Dry Ice Burning Off Skin as the Moment of the Soul's Apotheosis," which is the title of one of her grandest chants. Its opening gives us her best rhetorical question:

> How will we get used to joy
> if we won't hold onto it?

One way will be to go on reading Thylias Moss, who is capable of teaching us how to hold onto it.

—H. B.

⊞ ⊞ ⊞

Ed Bullins
b. 1935

ED BULLINS was born on July 2, 1935, in Philadelphia, the son of Edward and Bertha Marie (Queen) Bullins. He grew up in the tough black ghetto of north Philadelphia and, in spite of his mother's encouragement to finish high school, dropped out in 1952 to join the navy. After three years he returned to Philadelphia, enrolling in night school and leaving for Los Angeles City College in 1958. During this period he married and had several children, although little is known about them.

At Los Angeles City College Bullins encountered black intellectuals who encouraged his writing. It was at this time that he first experimented with playwriting, although none of his works were staged until he began attendance in the creative writing program at San Francisco State College in 1964. His first play, *How Do You Do?* (1965), reflects the absurdist drama of Samuel Beckett and Eugene Ionesco but also focuses sharply on racial issues. Many of Bullins's plays feature characters brutalized by poverty, violence, and racism, and he would later face criticism from the black community for such "negative" portrayals. Because of his uncompromising subject matter, Bullins found increasing difficulty in staging his plays, so he founded several production companies of his own and, in 1965, helped to establish Black House, a political and cultural organization that included Huey Newton, Bobby Seale, LeRoi Jones (Amiri Baraka), and others and served for a time as a base for the Black Panthers. A few years later, however, the group dissolved through internal dissension.

In the mid-1960s Bullins met a young black director, Robert Macbeth, who invited him to come to New York to participate in the newly formed New Lafayette Theatre in Harlem. Bullins did so in 1967, and the next year three of his plays (initially titled *The Electronic Nigger and Others* but later changed to the less incendiary *Three Plays*) were produced to good reviews. Bullins won the Vernon Rice Drama Desk Award for these plays, and his first collection, *Five Plays*, appeared in 1969.

1

The New Lafayette Theatre went on to stage a number of Bullins's important plays—*In the Wine Time* (1968), *Goin' a Buffalo* (1968), *The Duplex* (1970)—before it collapsed from lack of funds in 1972. Meanwhile other plays by Bullins were being put on at many other theatres in New York, including Lincoln Center. His plays continued to win awards: *The Fabulous Miss Marie* (1971) won an Obie, and *The Taking of Miss Janie* won the New York Drama Critics' Circle Award. Two further collections of his plays were published: *Four Dynamite Plays* (1972) and *The Theme Is Blackness* (1973). Bullins also issued a collection of short stories, *The Hungered One* (1971), and a novel, *The Reluctant Rapist* (1973).

Bullins has been playwright in residence at the American Place Theatre since 1973, and from 1975 to 1983 he was on the staff of the New York Shakespeare Festival. Since 1980, however, few of his plays have been performed. In 1984 he left New York and returned to San Francisco, becoming a drama instructor at the City College of San Francisco. He continues to live there with his third wife, Trixie, and their children.

▣ *Critical Extracts*

MARVIN X   MARVIN X: What about the idea of a National Black Theater? What would be its purpose, as you see it?

ED BULLINS: The purpose is that it would be a medium for communication to raise the consciousness throughout the nation, for black artistic, political, and cultural consciousness. It would keep a hell of a lot of people working—black theater people—and doing what they have to do. And it would be an institution for the black people in America who are a nation within a nation. It would be an institutional base to lay the foundation of our society and our culture and our nation. It would be an institutional form, like black schools are an institutional form, and they are becoming more apparent. The black theater would be power in a sense, power in pure terms of capitalist facilities, buildings, things, places, and power to control people's minds, to get to them and to educate them and to persuade. It would be power in the sense of welding black artists and many disciplines, because the theater is a collective effort and many arts come together to get the spirit going. And we would get unity. When you have a black theater and you have a black audience and a black artist—the idea of getting people back together is *passé*. The people *are* together and all you have to do while they are together is to tell them things which are beneficial and progressive. Those are some of the aspects of a National Black Theater. I believe, contrary to Bob Macbeth, a National Black Theater is possible at this very moment. It just takes people to get together and to commit themselves and to realize, like LeRoi ⟨Jones⟩ says, that they have the heart—and they have it—all they have to do is realize it. And they can do it. ⟨. . .⟩

MARVIN X: As a playwright, what have you gained from your association with the New Lafayette Theater?

ED BULLINS: I don't get as much from watching my plays as I used to. After I finish a play, now, I can't really read it for some months. I only start thinking about it after it's done, and then I can think about it. But from working with the New Lafayette Theater—it's the association, working with all the people, the actors, the directors—seeing how things are put together, working on Black Theater magazine, which concerns what we are doing in the theater and other black theaters across the country—that is the greatest advantage that is apparent to me right now—the association with other artists and being stimulated and growing as I am growing and knowing at least who we are working for and perceiving someway how we are working, what things we are bringing into it and what we are struggling through to get to our art to make it more consistent and correct for the needs of our people at this time. We do not want to have a higher form of white art in black-face. We are working towards something entirely different and new that encompasses the soul and spirit of black people, which is our whole experience of being here in this oppressive land. All the things that are positive in us, our music, our very strong religion, our own life-style, and incorporating it into our art on a collective basis to make us individually better artists and collectively to have a uniform positive art so that 10 years from now, the things we do now will be recognized but will be so far from where we have been. By then, I think that we will be completely different from white Anglo-Saxon Western things, and it will be totally black.

Marvin X, "Black Theater: An Interview with Ed Bullins," *Negro Digest* 18, No. 6 (April 1969): 13–14

JERVIS ANDERSON   The world of Bullins' plays is made up largely, though not exclusively, of ex-cons, hustlers, prostitutes, and young toughs; knives, guns, dope, joblessness, and people trying—by fair means or foul—to get their hands on some money; tenements and card-playing; wine-drinking and rapping on front stoops on hot summer evenings; lovers who seem to be as hostile toward each other as they are tender; old men and women who still drink and rap with style and whose heads are filled with the wisdom of the ghetto; lovely young women being hardened by life, or by their men, but full of private dreams and, despite their hardening, always vulnerable to softness and affection; and sensitive, searching young men on the threshold of being sucked into a social jungle from which they may never escape. But underlying Bullins' portrayal of this world are a genuine compassion and gentleness and love, and an ear that captures the energy and poetry of the language of the streets—for, as one critic has noted, even when Bullins' language is "rough and startlingly obscene," it "is entirely in keeping, and has a beauty all its own."

Perhaps no play is more representative of Bullins' work than *The Duplex*, which involves the residents of a southern-California rooming house. The characters, their experience, and their language run the full Bullins gamut. The play tells about the sometimes joyous, sometimes abrasive, and some-times flagellating relationships in the rooming house, and also concerns a poignant love story involving a sensitive college student named Steve Benson and the landlady, Velma Best. Velma is married to a vicious gangster, O.D., who beats her frequently and takes her money, and she turns to young Benson for understanding and affection. But their affair is doomed, for Velma, though she loathes her husband, is both afraid of him and unable to leave him. And, even when O.D. is absent, his violence and his imminent return hang like a palpable threat over the rooming house. At the end of the play, Benson has been cruelly beaten up by O.D., and the love affair has clearly been stifled; Velma will continue to hang on to a husband she both fears and detests.

Walter Kerr, after seeing the Lincoln Center production of *The Duplex*, disagreed with Bullins that it had been turned into a minstrel show. But he appeared to share the author's feeling that aspects of his intention had not been allowed to come through. The director, Kerr wrote, "failed to sense, or to nail down, the one subterranean movement in the text that seems . . . to be troubling and affecting." He went on, "The groping, rattled, uncertain love affair between the scholarly boy and the married woman who is starved for emotion works on the printed page like a night-stir in the forest, a promise that beneath all that is idle and careless and scattered by daylight, life moves somewhere, burrowing for warmth, feeling its way to a meaning."

Jervis Anderson, "Profile: Dramatist," *New Yorker*, 16 June 1973, pp. 73–74

DON EVANS   In no area is the controversy over Ed Bullins more pronounced than in the Black community's response to his plays. Often praised for his insight and skill, he is also damned for making the private issues public. At a time when the cry for Black heroes was constantly heard, Ed gave us Marco and Miss Marie; when dashikied youths walked our campuses talking of revolution and warfare, the playwright reminded us that revolutions are fought by real revolutionaries . . . not by rhetoric alone. We flew high on the beauty of Blackness, but he reminded us of the difference between potential and practice.

Ed Bullins has often been accused of being negative, of fostering negative images of Black people. His characters are men and women who don't make it, who drift through life using and abusing each other. The unerring honesty of his realistic style makes it impossible for the ugliness of their activities to be obscured or for the viewer to be comfortable. The final act of an Ed Bullins play always takes place after the fact, after the play is over and the audience has separated into individuals who must deal with their collective fate. It is over only when we have dealt with ourselves and the characters and found the distasteful elements in both. Far from being negative, Ed Bullins is concerned with those suicidal practices that render the Black man impotent; that prevent us from reaching the goals so often spoken of in the revolutionary rhetoric of the time. His concentration is on the community as it is, as he sees it now. The dilemma here, however, is that many folks assume that the playwright's stage-world represents a total view of the Black community, when he is, in truth, talking about those who are sick with very specific kinds of illnesses and pretensions. The totality of the viewpoint is relative to the totality of the social phenomena discussed and described.

Don Evans, "The 'Theater of Confrontation': Ed Bullins up against the Wall," *Black World* 23, No. 6 (April 1974): 15–16

HAROLD CLURMAN   What we see ⟨in *The Taking of Miss Janie*⟩ is a people—black, white, Jew and gentile—hung up and driven nearly mad by the fearful contradictions between ragged remnants of the American "dream" and the shameful realities of actual existence. There is a strong though fitful will to overcome the resultant disaster but no one is honest, clearheaded, steadfast, informed and disciplined enough to do so. The fanatic (in this case, a black Muslim) isolates himself from everyone, with nothing but his militantly insulting rhetoric to fortify him. The semi-educated "intellectuals" shift their vocabulary and ideology according to every change in the social climate: they take credit for everything which happens everywhere while they land nowhere. Ploys of escape escape nothing, drugs obliterate reality and lead to nonbeing, diverse brands of racism serve for slogans. Rabid affirmations and hysterical protests eventuate in frustration rather than relief. Nearly everyone is lost in a miserable flow of turbid emotion with no beneficent outlet. All are in the dark and no one is "saved"—not even those who have settled into unquiet compromise or stagnant surrender.

The play, despite its disturbing revelations, is neither mournful in tone nor tendentiously raucous. Vigorously humorous, it does not whine; it growls with a savage grin. Without pleading any special cause, it has sinew and muscle. Bold in its courageous objectivity, it is by no means depressing.

Harold Clurman, "Theatre," *Nation*, 5 April 1975, p. 414

W. D. E. ANDREWS   As a dramatist whose concern was to write from deep down in his environment, Bullins found that naturalism was an undoubtedly effective tool at hand. And it is surely the fairly conventional nature of so much of Bullins's drama which most centrally contributes to an overall impression, the conventions that I have in mind (to underline the treacherous ambiguity of the word) being those of naturalism: one is *then* aware of the incorporation of absurdist elements, implementation of the techniques of ritual theater, and the deployment of other striking dramatic means. The revolutionary nature of his theater, as he put it himself in a programmatic essay of 1965, tends not to be "of style and technique, but of theme and character." This emphasis is certainly contrary to the black theorists' insistence on the uniqueness of black nationalist theater. But black writers, when they are nationalists, find themselves in an especially difficult position. Understandably, they do not wish to associate themselves with a "white aesthetic," and yet, using English, living in America, they cannot very easily avoid the wide sweep of theatrical tradition. Even the experimental forms and devices one finds in ⟨LeRoi⟩ Jones's powerful poetic drama are also, in the widest sense, traditional. Some of them, in fact, still originate in the conventions of absurdist drama; others are stylizations of modes indigenous to black culture, yet even they (participation, song, ritual, and triumphant celebration) have antecedents in earlier Western drama.

For Bullins the black activist, naturalism may have been a compromise, but it was surely not a very serious one. What we find in his drama is that the conventional white theater form has been startlingly revitalized in the course of its interaction with an Afro-American cultural tradition. Naturalism is charged with taut black sensibility that seeks to celebrate and give full expression to the unique styles of life, rhythms, images, and idioms of contemporary black America. Not even the black middle class figures in Bullins's drama in the central way it does in Jones's: since the black bourgeoisie has devoted too much of its energy toward trying to mimic the white man, it has forsaken its blackness, and its life has ceased to be of interest.

If Jones's theater may be termed "Messianic," Bullins's may be called "Orphic," involving as it does descent into the depths of the black ghetto hell in a continual effort to reclaim whatever is precious and vulnerable in black life. For Bullins's vision embraces not just the injustices and limitations of the black experience, but a very rich humanity achieved despite these restrictive conditions. The way of viewing life, the way of feeling—the vision—that informs his plays is the vision of that unique form of black music, the blues. Common to both is the impulse to express the painful details of a brutal experience and yet, whatever the quantum of racial agony, to transcend it, to redeem it dialectically through the sheer force of sensuality, vitality, lyricism, and creativity into an almost exultant affirmation of life.

W. D. E. Andrews, "Theater of Black Reality: The Blues Drama of Ed Bullins," *Southwest Review* 65, No. 2 (Spring 1980): 179–80

SAMUEL J. BERNSTEIN   *The Taking of Miss Janie*, which is a long one-act play, is concerned with black/white relations in America. As its title suggests, the play focuses upon the rape of a white woman by a black man. Actually, it is a second sexual assault that is imminent when the play begins; Janie (or "Miss Janie," to use Monty's disparaging nickname, a throwback to slave/owner relationships) has already been raped by Monty once. In the prologue, which is angry and bitter in tone, Monty stalks Janie.

As we move into the body of the play, a flashback, we wonder whether this second sexual attack will actually take place. When we return to the rape sequence in the epilogue, the tone is of sadness and resignation in Janie and of increasing anger in Monty. Ironically, instead of showing us the completion of the second assault, the epilogue takes us to a time that is immediately prior to the first encounter. Moreover, the epilogue seems to happen both in the present (like the prologue) and in the past. This purposeful ambiguity of both time and process reflects the tone of the entire play.

Neither the extremely theatrical and sensational rape, nor even the sexual relationship of Janie and Monty per se, is of deepest concern to Bullins. Rather, Bullins uses the relationship of the couple and their relationships with the other seven characters essentially as a means for exploring black/white relations in America. It is the vividness, the power, the violence, and the social and psychological insight that makes Bullins' exploration compelling; all of these elements are then meshed with theatrical experimentalism, making the play new and excitingly different. ⟨. . .⟩

The play's surface action defies simple analysis. A black man has raped a white woman. He has waited a long time to do so and, presumably, the intervening period in their lives and the intervening occurrences in the play help us to understand this action. However, Bullins only leads; he does not explain or define. What seems likely is that Janie wanted only a platonic friendship; however, Monty, who continuously called her "Miss Janie," an insulting name, has had a need to dominate and humiliate her. Perhaps Janie represents the American ethos, to which the suppressed black has strongly ambivalent feelings. Perhaps she also represents American liberalism, with its abstract support of, yet ultimate aloofness from, the black. Since Monty, as a black American, feels that he has always been an excluded being, a second-class citizen, he has come to define his worth in terms of his ability to "make it" within, and even despite, the predominantly white cultural ethos. Although that ethos may be shallow or hollow, it must be dominated or manipulated before the black can feel triumphant.

Such attitudes, Bullins suggests, have deleterious effects on individuals and on relationships. Blacks cannot accept other blacks as desirable life partners, and true friendship between a black and a white is made difficult, if not impossible. This leads to a certain isolation for the white person who is caught in the midst of the American ethos, and a certain anger in the black who resents being riveted to the golden chains of the American dream.

It is appropriate that Bullins expresses this black/white conflict in sexual terms; miscegenation is the great fear of the racist black or white, and a false eugenics—one based on color—is the primary means by which distinction, separation, and hierarchy are maintained. Moreover, the stereotype of the vulnerable white female goddess and the supersensual black male is characteristic of American racism. ⟨. . .⟩

The Taking of Miss Janie is a flawed masterpiece. Nevertheless—in its breadth; its vivid dynamic action; its structural complexity; its unique use of time; and its effective marriage of diverse styles, rhythms, and moods—it deserves respect as one of the outstanding recent contributions to the American theatre.

> Samuel J. Bernstein, *"The Taking of Miss Janie:* Ed Bullins," *The Strands Entwined: A New Direction in American Drama* (Boston: Northeastern University Press, 1980), pp. 67–68, 77–78, 80

PETER BRUCK   *Goin' a Buffalo* opens with a chess game between Curt and his friend Rich. The first and last lines of scene 1—"I just about have you up tight, Rich"/"Checkmate, man"—symbolically introduce the notion of conflict which pervades the dramatic action. In point of fact, the whole action may be viewed as a series of attempts on the part of the characters to move each other into a position of 'checkmate'. After Art Garrison, a friend of Curt's from former days in prison, appears on the stage we witness an increasing amount of violent confrontations. Art, the archetypal hustler, who also appears in *The Fabulous Miss Marie* and *The House Party*, finally outsmarts Curt and takes possession of the two prostitutes Pandora and Mamma Too Tight.

As in most of Bullins' plays, a rather trite plot initially blurs an adequate understanding of the text. If set against the politics of hustling, however, an interesting stratification of meaning evolves. Thus the dream of the hustling couple Curt and Pandora—

> Well, I ain't no whore. . . . I'm just makin' this money so Curt
> and me can get on our feet. One day we gonna own property and
> maybe some business when we get straight . . . and out of this
> town. . . . [Curt's] a good hustler but he's givin' that up after a
> while. He can be anything he wants—

is unmasked as false, i.e., 'white', during the course of the action. The drive of the hustler to become wealthy and to attain a higher social goal is viewed here as a perverted attempt to gain a white middle-class respectability. In Bullins' dramatic universe such a dream always paves the way to self-destruction. This becomes particularly clear, if we consider the circular shape of the action. For when Art, having betrayed Curt to the police, finally takes over both Pandora and Mamma and physically abuses Pandora in the last scene, he reenacts the brutality that Curt displayed in Act I. In the parasitic world of hustling where, as Art puts it, "you look for any break you can make," nothing is ultimately changed; instead we come to realize that Art will also become the prey of others some day—which, indeed, turns out to be his fate in *The House Party*.

Goin' a Buffalo dramatizes one central aspect of black urban life under the impact of an all-engulfing white world. Such a reading becomes more obvious if we take into account the minute description of the expressionistic scene design of Acts I and III where whiteness dominates. The explicit use of this color suggests that all figures are symbolically caught in the dreams of the white man's world where they can no longer perceive, much less aspire to, a genuine black existence.

Peter Bruck, "Ed Bullins: The Quest and Failure of an Ethnic Community Theatre," *Essays on Contemporary American Drama*, ed. Hedwig Bock and Albert Wertheim (Munich: Max Hueber Verlag, 1981), pp. 128–29

GENEVIÈVE FABRE   With *Street Sounds* Bullins proceeds further in his experimentation. The forty-odd vignettes of this play are intended to make up an almost exhaustive mosaic of the black community. Here there are no arguments between characters, but isolated subjects who appear and disappear, talking about themselves. The subtitle, "Dialogues with Black Experience," emphasizes the fact that there is no real monologue in theatre: those who speak always have a listener; if not on stage, the listener is implicitly present. Also, by definition, theatre always establishes a dialogue; the message communicated through the intermediacy of a character passes from the writer-sender to the spectator-receiver.

The author's work is to find the right words to convey an aspect of black experience—made concrete through the fictional character. The theatrical discourse thus becomes an interrogation on the status of speech. The spectator's task is to identify both the speaker and the interlocutor, for dialogue exists between those voices as well as with the author or the spectator. In *Street Sounds* discourses are opposed, linked together, and reciprocally answered as in a call and response pattern: the addressee of one speech becomes the speaker of another. A woman sings her despair at being abandoned; another waits impatiently for pleasure. Here one character gets angry at the hypocrisy of most blacks without recognizing his own: there an explanatory speech from another figure reveals to him the sincerity of those he has misjudged. Here a writer abandons his creative project for a more ordered life; there a robber soon steals a neighbor's typewriter. Here a publisher congratulates himself on his successful business, there a nationalist critic gets angry about a writer's negative images of his race.

The interlocutor is at times a friend to confide in, a skeptic, an accuser before whom one justifies oneself, or an opponent who must be faced. At times he is all these at once: a dope peddler refuses to see his activity as immoral; an anguished man tells a friend his wife beats him, then suspects his confidant of being the shrew's accomplice; another refuses to be treated like a bad boy and locked up. Elsewhere, the characters are labeled by their function, occupation, or profession (Revolutionary Artist, Woman, Poet), the role they play in the discourse (The Doubter, The Explainer), or again, the function of receiver and passive object of an action (Seduced and Abandoned, Reconciled). Often the designation is ironic: thus the Liar announces he has decided to lie because the truth brings him only trouble. Or it is metaphorical: the errand boy becomes a messenger between the past and the present.

Each speaker, in his way, states a truth about black experience by discussing either his job, his political engagement, or his love life or sex life. Whatever business he is in or revolutionary slogans he pronounces, he always has some bit of wisdom to impart. Bullins orchestrates this polyphony as a single uproar rising from the street, alternately plaintive, boastful, supplicant, and accusatory. Each voice has the right to be heard, even those of Bullins' detractors who speak through the nationalist critic. Bullins thus proclaims a theatre where protagonists are placed in a position to speak, where different kinds of discourse are opposed and reconciled. He responds in this way to the voice of the audience and engages in dialogue with it through all his fictional intermediaries.

Geneviève Fabre, "Ed Bullins: The Language of the Blues," *Drumbeats, Masks and Metaphors: Contemporary Afro-American Theatre*, tr. Melvin Dixon (Cambridge, MA: Harvard University Press, 1983), pp. 188–89.

NICHOLAS CANADAY   *It Has No Choice* is another play that goes directly to the fundamental issue of black-white sexual tension. Its action is not an initial encounter between strangers, but like Baraka's *The Slave* it deals with the end of a relationship between a black man and a white woman. The title refers to a statement by Kafka that Steve, the strong black intellectual, quotes in the play:

> You do not need to leave your room. Remain sitting at your table,
> simply wait. . . . The world will offer itself freely to you to be
> unmasked, it has no choice, it will roll in ecstasy at your feet.

Grace, in this Bullins play, has no choice, rather unlike Grace, a woman with the same name, in Baraka's *The Slave*. Here the time is truncated: the Grace of *It Has No Choice* has had a relationship with Steve for only two weeks. Grace in Baraka's play repudiates Steve's counterpart, there named Walker, and takes their two daughters when she is subsequently married to a white man. That Grace leaves her black husband Walker for the same reason that Bullins's Grace says she wants to end her relationship with Steve. But Bullins's black protagonist has a much less divided personality than Walker, with much greater emotional strength. The action of *It Has No Choice* takes place in a Southern California apartment on a Sunday morning. The lovers Grace and Steve are in bed, but the sensual tranquillity is ended by Grace's declaration that she wants to end the affair. She says she is a "silly little secretary" who has enjoyed their physical intimacy but is uncomfortable with Steve's constant reading and study, his "white and black philosophy," and his view of himself as an Afro-American. There is, in short, a large part of Steve's life from which Grace is excluded. Such was exactly the Grace-Walker relationship in the earlier Baraka play: blackness has come to be perceived as an insurmountable barrier by the white female. But the significant difference between the two plays is in the resolutions. In *It Has No Choice* Steve will not let his Grace go, but instead reminds her she freely entered into the relationship and cannot reverse her decision:

> You want to go back like nothin's happened? You want to go
> back like it was before . . . so you can look through me and
> around me and never see me . . . I love *myself* too much for that.
> You're mine and if you go back, you'll go back mine.

The play ends in physical violence, with the stronger Steve dominating Grace, standing over her as she sprawls on the floor. She nods weakly, acceeding to his order to return the next day: "I think I'll enjoy making love to you tomorrow, darling." Grace has, it is clear, no choice.

Nicholas Canaday, "Toward Creation of a Collective Form: The Plays of Ed Bullins," *Studies in American Drama, 1945–Present* 1 (1986): 42–43

LESLIE SANDERS   In the real sense ⟨Bullins⟩ was then and remains now a black cultural nationalist. Yet he shuns public engagement in politics and, considering his centrality to the Black Arts/Black Power Movement, made relatively few statements which relied on the Movement's rhetoric. He sees his task as an artist as, simply, to extend people's vision of what is: Rick's cliché about reality dealing with those who confront first the realms in which they are the authors of their own unfreedom: their difficulty with love, with manhood, with the panaceas of drugs, crime, sex and violence, and romantic notions of machismo. Unless and until these abiding problems are confronted, political rhetoric, for Bullins, is meaningless, the violence Black Power proposed no more than the violence on any street corner in Harlem—and equally misdirected.

His work implies not only a comment on the rhetoric of Black Power but also on the rhetoric of the Civil Rights Movement. The non-violence King proposed is equally distant from the basic experiences of the people of whom Bullins speaks. Getting beaten up makes as little sense to him as does self-indulgent aggression. He understands fully the complexity of racial oppression, and in other plays deals with it acutely. However, that oppression is only a given in the lives of his characters, never a focus. In his major work, his eye never swerves from the self, from the black community as he sees its actual existence. The black political leader who is emblem of his beliefs is Malcolm X, but in *The Pig Pen*, in which the death of Malcolm figures, only the poet Ray and a white man, Mackman, truly mourn his passing.

Like Malcolm, Bullins' vision is urban, secular, and of the streets. It is there he finds home truths, and these are the abiding ones. Anything that deflects from dealing with them must be examined with care. Finally, Bullins queries the connection between the generalized analysis Black Power rhetoric proposed and the daily personal pain and complexity of individual existence. In suggesting that the former provided an evasion rather than a helpful understanding of the latter, he does not mean to negate the former's validity, only to test it and show where it is wanting. Bullins' mode of establishing the vision Black Power rhetoric proposed is contained rather in the phrase with which he prefaces most of his lists of characters: "The characters in this play are Black." He then proceeds to explore their world.

> Leslie Sanders, " 'Dialect Determinism': Ed Bullins' Critique of the Rhetoric of the Black Power Movement," *Studies in Black American Literature*, ed. Joe Weixlmann and Chester J. Fontenot (Greenwood, FL: Penkevill Publishing Co., 1986), Vol. 2, pp. 173–74

ARLENE A. ELDER   Bullins's list of the 'obvious elements' that should constitute black plays shows his appreciation of the spiritual or mystical dimension of traditional performance. He calls for:

> dance, as in Black life style and patterns; Black religion in its numerous forms . . . gospel, negro spiritualism to African spirit, sun, moon, stars and ancestor worship; Black astrology, numerology and symbolism; Black mysticism, magic and mythscience; also history, fable and legend, vodun ritual ceremony, Afro-American nigger street styles, and, of course, Black music.

However, Bullins still writes plays, recognisable as such by audiences formally trained in Aristotelian dramatic principles as well as those schooled in African orature and black street styles of performance. His works, then, provide the largest number of examples of that middle ground in black drama that Robert Macbeth designates 'play form rituals'. The spiritual effect of these plays depends as much upon the way they are staged as upon the texts, hence upon the director almost as much as the playwright. Director Macbeth judges his production of *In the Wine Time* and other plays at The New Lafayette Theatre as revealing the company's 'ritual point of view':

> We always try to approach [the play] from the point of view of a service, a ritual of some kind, and for that reason, because we approach them that way, our plays are a little bit different in a lot of things, the timing, the way the thing gets done, the way it's staged, how it's staged, why it's staged that way.

Speaking specifically of *In the Wine Time*, he is pleased with his staging, because it:

> includes the people in there so they understand this thing is
> between us, among us all. . . . the thing that we begin to do
> immediately includes all the people who come. So all of these
> things are orientated around, 'Welcome, sit down, Brother, we're
> gonna hold hands and sing . . .'

This statement was made in 1970. A year later, however, Macbeth admits to the possibly insurmountable difficulties in the Western dramatic form, which he calls 'really ragged' and 'very hard'; 'it doesn't serve our purposes', he realises. Of special concern is the audience's separation from the action, not just physically but also in terms of roles and responsibilities, hence, spiritual fulfilment. 'I did want you to talk back during the play', he explains to an audience member of *In the Wine Time*. 'You were supposed to get into it. But the form is limited. It doesn't really work. The Western white form is a drawing room form. They sit around and they jive. They sit there and talk to each other. Nothing really happens.' Therefore, he desires the movement to a more traditional ritual form mentioned earlier, where audience members can participate, in playwright and theorist Paul Carter Harrison's term, as 'spectator performers'.

Arlene A. Elder, "Ed Bullins: Black Theatre as Ritual," *Connections: Essays on Black Literatures*, ed. Emanuel S. Nelson (Canberra, Australia: Aboriginal Studies Press, 1988), pp. 103–4

Bibliography

How Do You Do: A Nonsense Drama. 1965.

Five Plays ⟨The Electronic Nigger and Other Plays⟩. 1969.

New Plays for the Black Theatre: An Anthology (editor). 1969.

The Duplex: A Black Love Fable in Four Movements. 1971.

The Hungered One: Early Writings. 1971.

Four Dynamite Plays. 1972.

The Reluctant Rapist. 1973.

The Theme Is Blackness: The Corner and Other Plays. 1973.

*The New Lafayette Theatre Presents Plays with Aesthetic Comments by 6 Black
        Playwrights* (editor). 1974.
The Taking of Miss Janie. 1975.
Jo Anne! 1981.

⊞ ⊞ ⊞

Rita Dove
b. 1952

RITA FRANCES DOVE was born on August 28, 1952, in Akron, Ohio, to Ray A. Dove and Elvira Elizabeth Hord. Dove was a precocious child who ranked among the top one hundred high school seniors in the country and was therefore invited to the White House as a "Presidential Scholar." After graduating from high school, Dove entered Miami University at Oxford, Ohio. In 1973 she graduated *summa cum laude*, then entered Tübingen University in what was then West Germany on a Fulbright scholarship. While in Germany, Dove actively sought out Afro-Germans in an attempt to understand their circumstances. Dove discovered that many Afro-German women suffered from the same feelings of rejection and isolation that Dove had felt in the United States. Somewhat optimistically, she wrote about the possibility of unified action among black communities worldwide—action that would inspire a revolution in world consciousness. In 1979 Dove married a German writer, Fred Viebahn, with whom she had one child.

Upon returning from Germany, Dove entered the Iowa Writers Workshop, where she received an M.F.A. in 1977. She worked principally on her poetry, which thereafter increasingly appeared in magazines and journals. In 1977 *Ten Poems*, Dove's first book of verse, appeared. It reveals her interest in the revolutionary politics of the 1960s as well as the influence of other black revolutionary poets on her work, such as Don L. Lee (Haki R. Madhubuti) and LeRoi Jones (Amiri Baraka). Many of the poems in this first small volume were reprinted along with new verses in her first full-length collection, *The Yellow House on the Corner* (1980). For the most part, the collection was poorly received. Not until the publication of *Museum* (1983) and *Thomas and Beulah* (1986) did Dove receive considerable critical praise. The latter volume also won her a Pulitzer Prize, making her only the second black poet to have won a Pulitzer Prize for poetry (the first was Gwendolyn Brooks). *Thomas and Beulah* is a long narrative poem telling the story of her family from two points of view, her grandfather's and her grandmother's. A chronology at the end of the volume provides a guide to the sometimes confusing overlap of the two stories.

More recently, Dove has published *The Other Side of the House* (1988), a set of poems to accompany photographs by Tamarra Kaida, and *Grace Notes* (1989). Her *Selected Poems* appeared in 1993. She has also written a novel, *Through the Ivory Gate* (1992), and a play, *The Darker Face of the Earth* (1994).

Dove began her teaching career as a professor of English at Arizona State University in 1981. In 1989 she became a professor of English at the University of Virginia. She was a writer in residence at the Tuskegee Institute in 1982 and has served as a member of the literature panel of the National Endowment for the Arts. Since 1987 she has been commissioner of the Schomburg Center for the Preservation of Black Culture at the New York Public Library. In 1993 she became the first black American to be appointed the United States Poet Laureate.

▦ *Critical Extracts*

PETER STITT   "Shakespeare Say" ⟨in *Museum*⟩ is linear and narrative. The moment of telling occurs during an evening when "Champion Jack Dupree, black American blues singer" (as he is identified in the note to the poem) is performing in a Munich nightclub. The mode of narration is not limited to this single period of time, however; to portray the singer's state of mind, the speaker recounts several events in sequential order, first returning to "That afternoon" when "two students / from the Akademie / showed him the town." Later in the poem, we are presented with a generalized description of the evening in question ("And tonight // every song he sings / is written by Shakespeare"), while still later we learn what happens as Champion Jack is "going down / for the third set / past the stragglers / at the bar."

The quality of this poem is evident in Dove's accuracy of description and in how she interlaces Champion Jack's songs with her narrative to flesh out his portrait:

> Champion Jack in love
> and in debt,

> in a tan walking suit
> with a flag on the pocket,
> with a red eye
> for women, with a
> diamond-studded
> ear, with sand
> in a mouthful of mush—
> *poor me*
> *poor me*
> *I keep on drifting*
> *like a ship out*
> *on the sea.*

In line with the imagery in the song he sings, Jack is described variously as looking like a ship ("a flag on the pocket"), as looking like a pirate (the "red eye" and the earring), and as sounding like an inverted Demosthenes (whereas the Greek orator, according to legend, filled his mouth with pebbles and declaimed to the sea in an effort to strengthen his voice, Jack seems to have filled his mouth with "sand," so great is his sense of sorrow).

In contrast to the narrative and linear structure of "Shakespeare Say," "The Copper Beech" is a descriptive poem in circular form (description in poetry is almost always static with regard to time). Though the poem contains twenty-five lines arranged into nine stanzas, it takes its form not from these distinguishing external features but from the progression inherent in its five sentences. The first sentence establishes setting, character, and theme: "Aristocrat among patriarchs, this / noble mutation is the best / specimen of Rococo // in the park of the castle / at Erpenberg." The second sentence delves into the past to tell how a Baroness brought the tree from South America, and the next sentence furthers interpretation: "This trailing beech became Erpenberg's / tree of grief, their // melancholy individualist, / the park philosopher."

The fourth sentence furthers the description, while the concluding provides a final description/interpretation that unites the whole:

> The aesthetic principles
> of the period: branches
>
> pruned late to heal
> into knots, proud flesh ascending
> the trunk:
>
> living architecture.

The movement of the poem is not narrative, not progressive through time, but accretive around an instance of perception; the form is therefore circular rather than linear. Rita Dove is a poet of considerable skill and promise. The poems in *Museum* are as intellectually interesting as they are attractive in rhythm and image.

Peter Stitt, "The Circle of the Meditative Moment," *Georgia Review* 38, No. 2 (Summer 1984): 403–4

LINDA GREGERSON   In *Museum*, as its title and its cover art-work announce, the author has advanced to full prominence ⟨her⟩ preoccupations with displacement and multiple frames for point of view, frames that are rather superimposed than synthesized. The book is structured and conceived with great deliberation and coherence, from its section titles and sequencing epigraphs, its attributions and its dedication: *"for nobody,"* reads a page at the front, *"who made us possible."* The book's recurrent thematics are those of light and shade, the exotic and the domestic, reticence (with its furthest limit a nearly Delphic impenetrability, like the hush in a museum) and disclosure ⟨. . .⟩ On both geographical and temporal coordinates, the sweep of the book is large: from Argos to Erpenberg to the poet's native Ohio, from the Western Han Dynasty to the nuclear age. Nor are these distances a species of lush window dressing: Dove believes in history and is capable of mining it for the lucid intersections of imagination and pragmatic ways-and-means, for the junctures where solitary virtuosity finds both its intractable limits (as Catherine of Alexandria was "deprived of learning and / the chance to travel") and its most urgent motives. And according to that other perspective on history, as captured in books or museums, Dove is concerned to render the altered status of a subject when it has been set aside for special delectation, like the fish in the archeologist's stone or like Fiammetta in Boccaccio's mind: the creature lifted to visibility by the pressure of a gaze is also partly stranded there, unsponsored even while it is wholly possessed. In technical terms—their use of the luminous image, their economics of plotting and musical phrase, their reliable modulations of syntax and levels of diction—these poems continue the same expert craftsmanship that marked Dove's earlier work. In their collective argument—and it is a profound one—they go much further.

Linda Gregerson, [Review of *The Yellow House on the Corner* and *Museum*], *Poetry* 145, No. 1 (October 1984): 47–48

HELEN VENDLER   *Thomas and Beulah* manages to keep intact the intensity of the drama and inexplicability of life and marriage. The mutual criticism of Dove's Akron couple, their enterprise and defeat, while specified to a degree that is satisfying as fiction, will remind readers of analogous episodes in the years 1900–1969 undergone by their own parents or grandparents. Dove does not suggest that black experience is identical with white experience, but neither does she suggest that it is always different. Beulah's experience of motherhood—her terror of doing it wrong, the exhaustion of having no privacy, her irritation at the grown girls—is universal. But Beulah's anger when her daughters take her to the Goodyear company picnic after Thomas's death will be personally familiar only to black readers:

> Now this *act of mercy:* four daughters
> dragging her to their husbands' company picnic,
> white families on one side and them
> on the other, unpacking the same
> squeeze bottles of Heinz, the same
> waxy beef patties and Salem potato chip bags.

Over the segregated picnickers floats the Goodyear company symbol—"a white foot / sprouting two small wings." Beulah's interior monologue, here as elsewhere, has the naturalness and accuracy of art concealing art. Dove has planed away unnecessary matter: pure shapes, her poems exhibit the thrift that Yeats called the sign of a perfected manner.

Helen Vendler, "In the Zoo of the New," *New York Review of Books*, 23 October 1986, pp. 51–52

ARNOLD RAMPERSAD   ⟨. . .⟩ with the consistently accomplished work of thirty-three year old Rita Dove, there is at least one clear sign if not of a coming renaissance of poetry, then at least of the emergence of an unusually strong new figure who might provide leadership by brilliant example. Thus far, Rita Dove has produced a remarkable record of publications in a wide range of respected poetry and other literary journals. Two books of verse, *The Yellow House on the Corner* (1980) and *Museum* (1983), have appeared from Carnegie-Mellon University Press. A third book-length manuscript of poetry, "Thomas and Beulah," is scheduled to be published early in 1986 by the same house. Clearly Rita Dove has both the energy and the sense of professionalism required to lead other writers. Most importantly—even a first reading of her two books makes it clear that she also possesses the talent to do so. Dove is surely one of the three or four most gifted young black American poets to appear since LeRoi Jones ambled with deceptive nonchalance onto the scene in the late nineteen fifties, and perhaps the most disciplined and technically accomplished black poet to arrive since Gwendolyn Brooks began her remarkable career in the nineteen forties.

These references to the sixties and early seventies are pointed. Rita Dove's work shows a keen awareness of this period—but mainly as a point of radical departure for her in the development of her own aesthetic. In many ways, her poems are exactly the opposite of those that have come to be considered quintessentially black verse in recent years. Instead of looseness of structure, one finds in her poems remarkably tight control; instead of a reliance on reckless inspiration, one recognizes discipline and practice, and long, taxing hours in competitive university poetry workshops and in her study; instead of a range of reference limited to personal confession, one finds personal reference disciplined by a measuring of distance and a prizing objectivity; instead of an obsession with the theme of race, one finds an eagerness, perhaps even an anxiety, to transcend—if not actually to repudiate—black cultural nationalism in the name of a more inclusive sensibility. Hers is a brilliant mind, reinforced by what appears to be very wide reading, that seeks for itself the widest possible play, an ever expanding range of reference, the most acute distinctions, and the most subtle shadings of meaning. ⟨. . .⟩

As a poet, Dove is well aware of black history. One of the five sections of *The Yellow House* is devoted entirely to poems on the theme of slavery and freedom. These pieces are inspired by nameless but strongly representative victims of the "peculiar institution," as well as by more famous heroic figures (who may be seen as fellow black writers, most of them) such as Solomon Northrup, abducted out of Northern freedom on a visit to Washington ("I remember how the windows rattled with each report. / Then the wine, like a pink lake, tipped. / I was lifted—the sky swivelled, clicked into place"), and the revolutionary David Walker ("Compass needles, / eloquent as tuning forks, shivered, pointing north. / Evenings, the ceiling fan sputtered like a second pulse. / *Oh Heaven! I am full!! I can hardly move my pen!!!*"). In these works and others such as "Banneker" in the later volume, *Museum*, Dove shows both a willingness and a fine ability to evoke, through deft vignettes, the psychological terror of slavery. She is certainly adept at recreating graphically the starched idioms of the eighteenth and early nineteenth centuries, at breathing life into the monumental or sometimes only arthritic rhythms of that vanished and yet still echoing age. Her poems in this style and area are hardly less moving than those of Robert Hayden, who made the period poem (the period being slavery) virtually his own invention among black poets. Dove's special empathy as a historical poet seems to be with the most sensitive, most eloquent blacks, individuals of ductile intelligence made neurotic by pain, especially the pain of not being understood and of not being able to express themselves.

> Arnold Rampersad, "The Poems of Rita Dove," *Callaloo* 9, No. 1 (Winter 1986): 52–54

PETER HARRIS   Rita Dove's *Thomas and Beulah*, winner of the 1987 Pulitzer Prize, has a distinctive, ambitiously unified design. It traces the history of two blacks who separately move North, to Ohio, meet and get married in the 1920's, and go on to raise four girls, enduring many vicissitudes before their deaths in the 1960's. Arranged serially and accompanied by an almost essential chronology, the poems, we are told in a note beforehand, are meant to be read in order. Much as Michael Ondaatje has done in his poem-like novel, *Coming through Slaughter,* Dove reconstructs the past through a series of discontinuous vignettes which enter freely into the psyches of the two main characters.

It is important that the poems are arranged chronologically because we often need all the help we can get in clarifying many of the references. Even with chronology as a guide, the poems sometimes seem unnecessarily obscure and cryptic. More often, however, the difficulty of the work is justifiable because the insights are exactly as subtle as they are oblique. In exploiting the virtues of ellipsis, Dove evidently has faith we will have gumption enough to stare a hole in the page until our minds leap with hers across the gaps. For example, in the opening poem, "The Event," Thomas dares his drunken friend, Lem, to jump off a riverboat and swim to a nearby island. Lem jumps and drowns. Later in the volume, we find out that Thomas is haunted by Lem's death for the rest of his life. But in the opening poem, the aftershock goes unmentioned:

> Thomas, dry
> on deck, saw the green crown shake
> as the island slipped

under, dissolved
in the thickening stream.
At his feet

a stinking circle of rags,
the half-shell mandolin.
Where the wheel turned the water

gently shirred.

Given Dove's reticent lyricism, we can't be completely sure from this description that Lem had drowned; we can only guess. That leaves us uncertain and, therefore, vulnerable, which is quite appropriate because the world we are entering with Thomas is fraught with deceptive beauty and danger. Even the shirring of roiled water can indicate death. ⟨. . .⟩

⟨. . .⟩ The psychic cost of suffering makes itself keenly felt in *Thomas and Beulah*, a blues book that aims, through music and sympathy, to reach an affirmative answer to the question posed by Melvin B. Tolson, which Dove includes as the epigraph to the volume:

Black Boy, O Black Boy,
is the port worth the cruise?

Peter Harris, "Poetry Chronicle: Four Salvers Salvaging: New Work by Voigt, Olds, Dove, and McHugh," *Virginia Quarterly Review* 64, No. 2 (Spring 1988): 270–73

STEVEN SCHNEIDER   SS: How does it feel to be the first black woman poet since Gwendolyn Brooks to win the Pulitzer Prize?

RD: My first reaction was quite simply disbelief. Disbelief that first of all there hasn't been another black person since Gwendolyn Brooks in 1950 to win the Pulitzer Prize in poetry, though there certainly have been some outstanding black poets in that period. On a public level, it says something about the nature of cultural politics of this country. It's a shame actually. On a personal level, it's overwhelming.

SS: Did you feel you had written something special when you completed *Thomas and Beulah?*

RD: I felt I had written something larger than myself, larger than what I had hoped for it to be. I did not begin this sequence as a book; it began as a poem. The book grew poem by poem, and it wasn't until I was about a third of the way through that I realized it would have to be a book. So

I grew with it and I had to rise to it. I started with the Thomas poems because I wanted to understand my grandfather more—what he was like as a young man, how he grew up and became the man I knew. To do that though, I realized pretty early on that I could rely neither on my memories of him nor on the memories of my mother or her sisters or brothers, but I had to get to know the town he lived in. What was Akron, Ohio like in the '20s and '30s? It was different from the Akron I knew. That meant I had to go to the library and read a whole bunch of stuff I never counted on researching to try to get a sense of that period of time in the industrial Midwest. On other levels, I had to enter male consciousness in a way which was—well, I knew I could do it for one or two poems but this was an extended effort. I was really, at a certain point, very very driven to be as honest as I could possibly be. Also, I didn't want to impose my language or my sensibility upon their lives. And things got—

SS: Things got very complicated?

RD: That's right.

SS: Did you have a different kind of satisfaction about finishing this book than your other two books?

RD: It was different. I am not going to say I was more satisfied; I don't think I have a favorite book of mine. But there was a feeling of relief because I had made it through.

> Steven Schneider, "Coming Home: An Interview with Rita Dove," *Iowa Review* 19, No. 3 (Fall 1989): 112–13

ROBERT McDOWELL   Rita Dove has always possessed a storyteller's instinct. In *The Yellow House on the Corner* (1980), *Museum* (1983), and *Thomas and Beulah* (1985), this instinct has found expression in a synthesis of striking imagery, myth, magic, fable, wit, humor, political comment, and a sure knowledge of history. Many contemporaries share Dove's mastery of some of these, but few succeed in bringing them together to create a point of view that, by its breadth and force, stands apart. She has not worked her way into this enviable position among poets without fierce commitment.

Passing through a graduate writing program (Iowa) in the mid-1970s, Dove and her peers were schooled in the importance of sensation and its representation through manipulation of The Image. The standard lesson plan, devised to reflect the ascendancy of Wallace Stevens and a corrupt revision of T. S. Eliot's objective correlative, instructed young writers to renounce realistic depiction and offer it up to the province of prose; it promoted subjectivity and imagination-as-image; it strangled a generation of poems.

How and why this came to pass is less important, really, than admitting that it is so. Literary magazines are gorged with poems devoid of shapeliness and scope. Imagistic, cramped, and confessional, they exist for the predictably surprising, climactic phrase. A historically conscious reader, aware of literary tradition, might understandably perceive an enormous cultural amnesia as the dubiously distinguishing feature of such poems. Such a reader will rue the fact that the writing and interpretation of poetry has diminished to a trivial pursuit, a pronouncement of personal instinct. If this is the dominant direction of a discouraging Moment, then Rita Dove distinguishes herself by resolutely heading the other way.

Unlike the dissembling spirit indicated above, Dove is an assembler who gathers the various facts of this life and presents them in ways that jar our lazy assumptions. She gives voice to many positions and many characters. Like the speaker/writer of classic argumentation, she shows again and again that she understands the opposing sides of conflicts she deals with. She tells all sides of the story. Consider the titles of her books, their symbolic weight. The personal turning point *House on the Corner* evolves, becoming the public Museum (symbol of preserved chronology); that, in turn, gives way to the names of two characters whose lives combine and illustrate the implicit meanings of the personal House and the public Museum.

Robert McDowell, "The Assembling Vision of Rita Dove," *Conversant Essays: Contemporary Poets on Poetry*, ed. James McCorkle (Detroit: Wayne State University Press, 1990), p. 294

JOHN SHOPTAW   At the beginning of Rita Dove's arresting new volume of poetry ⟨*Thomas and Beulah*⟩, we are given directions for reading that turn out to be true but impossible to follow: "These poems tell two sides of a story and are meant to be read in sequence." The impossibility is not physical, as in the instructions prefacing John Ashbery's long double-columned poem, *Litany*, which tell us that the columns "are meant to be read as simultaneous but independent monologues"; rather, the impossibility in reading the two sides of Rita Dove's book—Thomas's side (I. "Mandolin," 23 poems) followed by Beulah's side (II. "Canary in Bloom," 21 poems)—is biographical and historical. The lives of Thomas and Beulah, whether considered together or individually, lack what would integrate them into a single story. The events in *Thomas and Beulah* are narrated in strict chronological order, which is detailed in the appended chronology. The subjection of story time to historical time, unusual in modern narratives, gives Dove's sequence a tragic linearity, a growing sense that what is done cannot be undone and that what is not done but only regretted or deferred cannot be redeemed in the telling. The narrative runs from Thomas's riverboat life (1919) to his arrival in Akron (1921) and marriage to Beulah (1924), to their children's births, his jobs at Goodyear, his stroke (1960) and death (1963). Then the narrative begins again with Beulah: her father's flirtations, Thomas's flirtations and courtship (1923), their marriage (1924), a pregnancy (1931), her millinery work (1950), a family reunion (1964), and death (1969). In the background, the Depression and the March on Washington mark respectively the trials of the couple's and their children's generation.

The sequence of *Thomas and Beulah* resembles fiction more than it does poetic sequence—Faulkner's family chronicles in particular. Dove's modernist narrator stands back paring her fingernails like an unobtrusive master or God. The cover shows a snapshot, of Thomas and Beulah presumably, and the volume may be considered as a photo album, or two albums, with only the date and place printed underneath each picture. Thomas and Beulah are probably Rita Dove's grandparents; the book is dedicated to her mother, Elvira Elizabeth, and the third child born to Thomas and Beulah is identified in the chronology as Liza. But whether the couple is actually Rita Dove's grandparents is less important than the fact that all evidence of their relation has been removed. Any choice of genre involves an economy of gains and losses. Objective, dramatic narration—showing rather than telling—has the advantage of letting the events speak for themselves and the disadvantage of dispensing with the problematics of narrative distortion and a camera-eye or God's eye view. *Thomas and Beulah* tells it like it is and assumes it is like it tells us.

John Shoptaw, "Segregated Lives: Rita Dove's *Thomas and Beulah*," *Reading Black, Reading Feminist: A Critical Anthology*, ed. Henry Louis Gates, Jr. (New York: Meridian, 1990), pp. 374–75

BONNIE COSTELLO   The discipline of writing *Thomas and Beulah*, a family epic in lyric form, required Rita Dove to focus, as never before, her talent for compression. How to get years of her grandparents' joy and anguish into spare lines without presuming to sum up for them; how to telescope distances of place, background, dreams, without narrating—these were some of the problems she solved so brilliantly in that book. The past shed its patina as bits of voice and image shone through to bespeak whole epochs and regions. The book moved us by its understatement, the major ally of compression, and by its sympathetic imagination, that refused to make Thomas and Beulah stereotypes, the mere objects of our pity or nostalgia.

In *Grace Notes* Dove returns to the range of subjects and settings that characterized her first two books (she is remarkably broad in the scope of her references without ever being showy). All the features we have grown to appreciate in this poet arise here in their finest form: descriptive precision, tonal control, metaphoric reach within uncompromising realism. Moreover, she had brought these talents to bear upon a new intimacy and moral depth, served by memory and imagination working together.

The first poem of *Grace Notes*, set off as a kind of prologue, establishes the tone and terms of the volume. "Summit Beach, 1921" presents a girl of courtship age, refusing to join in the festive abandon of young dancers on the beach and choosing to sit by the fire instead. Within 25 lines we learn the history of this girl's stance and come to know her motives and desires even while we never know her name or her relation to the poet. A scar on her knee is the consequence of her childhood fantasy of flying off "Papa's shed." Yet she still "refused / to cut the wing," advised by her father to preserve angelic innocence ("you're all you've got") and waits, instead, for love's "music skittering up her calf." The dreams of this young woman, her "parasol and invisible wings" are in one sense betrayed by the reality around her, the limits imposed because of gender and race—this is a "Negro beach"—and more universally because of gravity and mortality. The winking scar on her knee is the constant reminder of the real world's pull. Yet the poet clearly admires the resilience of this dreamer and her spirit—scarred but winged—pervades the poems of *Grace Notes*. All of Dove's books have been marked by their thoughtful arrangement and *Grace Notes*, divided into five sections, marks out several distinctive areas of reflection, united by the dual images of wounds and wings, themes of pain and the will to resist one's limits, which she introduces in this first poem.

Bonnie Costello, "Scars and Wings: Rita Dove's *Grace Notes*," *Callaloo* 14, No. 2 (Spring 1991): 434–35

EKATERINI GEORGOUDAKI   Although conditions were more hospitable for black women writers after the Black Power/Black Arts Movement of the 1960s and the Feminist Movement of the 1970s, the ideologies of class, gender, and race still persisted in American society in the 1980s, when Rita Dove started publishing her work. She therefore shares certain dilemmas and concerns with previous Afro-American women poets, such as their feelings of displacement, fragmentation, and isolation, and their distaste for conventional stereotypes, hierarchies, divisions and boundaries. She also continues their search for wholeness, balance, connection, continuity, reconciliation with the self and the world, as well as their efforts to redefine the self and history, and to renew cultural values.

As a black person living in the predominantly white societies of the Old and New World, having entered an inter-racial and inter-cultural marriage (her husband is a German writer), and trying to forge an autonomous female poetic voice against the background of a male dominated Euro- and Afro-American literary tradition, Dove has often crossed social and literary boundaries, violated taboos, and experienced displacement, i.e. living "in two different worlds, seeing things with double vision," wherever she has stayed (USA, Germany, Israel). Talking to Judith Kitchen and Stan Sanvel Rubin about her European experiences which inspired her second book, *Museum* (1983), Dove admits that she had a sense of displacement while she was in Europe, and that she expressed this sense through various characters and situations in *Museum*. She remarks, however, that her stay in Europe broadened her world view and contributed to her personal growth as a person and an artist:

> When I went to Europe for the first time—that was in '74, way before I had thought of this book—it was mind boggling to see how blind I'd been in my own little world of America. It had never dawned on me that there was a world out there. It was really quite shocking to see that there was another way of looking at things. And when I went back in '80–81 to spend a lot of time, I got a different angle on the way things are, the way things happen in the world and the importance they take. Also as a *person* going to Europe I was treated differently because I was American. I was Black, but they treated me differently than people treat me here because I am Black. And in fact, I often felt a little like Fiammetta; I became an object. I was a Black American, and therefore I became a representative of all of that.

And I sometimes felt like a ghost, I mean, people would ask me
questions, but I had a feeling that they weren't seeing *me*, but a
shell. So there was that sense of being there and not being there,
you know. Then because you are there you can see things a little
clearer sometimes. That certainly was something, I think, that
informed the spirit of *Museum*.

Dove's complex experiences in the USA and abroad (Europe, N. Africa,
Israel) have affected both her vision and her poetic method. Although she
deals with the problems of racism and sexism, she does not adopt the
polemical voice of either a black nationalist or a feminist poet, and therefore
she does not let indignation, anger, and protest control her verse. Although
she focuses on the black experience in many of her works she goes beyond
the definition of black literature which reflected the black ideal that pre-
vailed since the late 1960s: "Black literature BY blacks, ABOUT blacks,
directed TO blacks. ESSENTIAL black literature is the distillation of black
life."

Ekaterini Georgoudaki, "Rita Dove: Crossing Boundaries," Callaloo 14, No. 2 (Spring
1991): 419–20

KIRKLAND C. JONES   In Dove's poems, dramatic monologue
and compressed narrative are the primary contexts through which the language of the people is presented. In her short stories, though they are often
very brief, the dialogues and musing of her characters are set forth in
authentic speech patterns. Moreover, Dove has a keen sense of history. She
links the past and the present through her characters' names and through
the appropriateness of their speech, revealing Dove's brilliant cross-cultural
perceptivity, as her characters' voices move in and out of the centuries,
simultaneously transcending the local and the mundane. "Catecorner," an
expression found in ⟨*Fifth Sunday's*⟩ title story, is a folksy way of describing
the site of the church building, along with the phrase "let loose," meaning
to set free. And the language of the black church adds enough flavoring to
join the generations of worshippers with their inherited family and community traditions—"the junior ushers," "the junior choir," as they stand up to
sing, "their blue silk robes swaying slightly as they rocked to the beat." The
marching choir, the little-girl "gleaners," the fat officious women in white,

all fit the story's "Fifth Sunday" language, modern enough to be Methodist and familiar enough to impart a quality of agedness and blackness.

Aunt Carrie, in the story that bears her name, speaks long dramatic monologues, and her speech is almost correct enough to match her assumed primness, allowing her to communicate with her young niece to whom she recounts more than one interesting story. Aunt Carrie is the type of matron who sprinkles her addresses with "dear." But she lapses occasionally into the remembered language of her parents and grandparents—"Don't go apologizing to me . . . makes me blush," she exclaims, and later in a much more relaxed, more confiding tone, she admits to her niece, "I didn't think about nothing at all." But on a whole, dialect is more subtle in the prose vignettes than in the author's most representative poems.

Kirkland C. Jones, "Folk Idiom in the Literary Expression of Two African American Authors: Rita Dove and Yusef Komunyakaa," *Language and Literature in the African American Imagination*, ed. Carol Aisha Blackshire-Belay (Westport, CT: Greenwood Press, 1992), pp. 152–53

▦ *Bibliography*

Ten Poems. 1977.

The Only Dark Spot in the Sky. 1980.

The Yellow House on the Corner. 1980.

Mandolin. 1982.

Museum. 1983.

Fifth Sunday. 1985.

Thomas and Beulah. 1986.

The Other Side of the House (with Tamarra Kaida). 1988.

Grace Notes. 1989.

Through the Ivory Gate. 1992.

Selected Poems. 1993.

The Darker Face of the Earth: A Verse Play in Fourteen Scenes. 1994.

Nikki Giovanni
b. 1943

NIKKI GIOVANNI was born Yolande Cornelia Giovanni, Jr., on June 7, 1943, in Knoxville, Tennessee. Her father, Jones Giovanni, was a social worker and her mother, Yolande Cornelia Watson, was an employee of the Welfare Department; they had one other child, Nikki's older sister Gary. Giovanni entered Fisk University in 1960, was tossed out, and re-entered in 1964, when she became serious not only about her studies but also the growing black political movements. She also began to write at this time. She attended the Fisk Writers Workshop directed by John Oliver Killens and graduated from Fisk *magna cum laude* in February 1967. In that same year, she participated in the Cincinnati Black Arts Festival. Giovanni continued her education at the University of Pennsylvania School of Social Work with the help of a Ford Foundation Grant and, later, a National Foundation for the Arts Grant.

At an early age, Giovanni expressed doubts about the traditional institution of marriage. Her alternative, independent, and politically active life led to her decision to become an unwed mother. In 1971 her son Tommy was born and she balanced her literary and political pursuits with an unfailing devotion to her son.

Giovanni's increasing interest in black identity and black history is revealed in her first two published books, *Black Feeling, Black Talk* (1968) and *Black Judgement* (1968). They are somewhat homogeneous in theme but varied in form, style, and tone (which ranges from militant to nostalgic). Many of the poems in these two collections touch upon political events, such as the assassinations of Martin Luther King, Jr., President Kennedy, and Malcolm X. These two books, initially published by a small press, were reissued in one volume in 1970.

A third collection of verse, *Re:Creation* (1970), continued along similar lines. But in 1971 Giovanni's first volume of children's verse appeared. *Spin a Soft Black Song: Poems for Children* is indeed much softer in tone, but much of her political vigor remains in these children's poems. She later published two more collections of children's verse: *Ego-Tripping and Other Poems for Young People* (1973) and *Vacation Time: Poems for Children* (1980).

When she returned to writing for adults, Giovanni revealed a marked difference in theme and construction. Her next four collections of verse, *My House* (1972), *The Women and the Men* (1975), *Cotton Candy on a Rainy Day* (1978), and *Those Who Ride the Night Winds* (1983), show a greater interest in personal concerns and a broader, less militant, and more humanistic approach.

Giovanni experienced unexpected success with *Truth Is on Its Way* (1971), a sound recording on which she reads her poetry against a backdrop of gospel music. As a result, she found herself a celebrity attracting much public attention. She has issued several other recordings of her poetry readings. Giovanni has also written an autobiographical sketch entitled *Gemini: An Extended Autobiographical Statement on My First Twenty-five Years of Being a Black Poet* (1971), and a collection of essays, *Sacred Cows—and Other Edibles* (1988). Recently she has devoted attention to celebrating the intellectual and emotional heritage of the elderly, compiling the anthologies *Appalachian Elders* (1991; with Cathee Dennison) and *Grand Mothers* (1994).

Giovanni has taught and lectured at a variety of colleges and universities, including Queens College, Rutgers, and Ohio State; since 1987 she has been professor of English at Virginia Polytechnic Institute and State University in Blacksburg, Virginia.

Critical Extracts

NIKKI GIOVANNI   I like all the militant poems that tell how we're going to kick the honkie's backside and purge our new system of all honkie things like white women, TV, voting and the rest of the ugly, bad things that have been oppressing us so long. I mean, I wrote a poem asking, "Nigger, can you kill?" because to want to live under President no-Dick Nixon is certainly to become a killer. Yet in listening to Smokey and the Miracles sing their *Greatest Hits* recently, I became aware again of the revolutionary quality of "You Can Depend on Me." And if you ask, "Who's Loving You?" just because I say he's not a honkie you should still want to know if I'm well laid. There is a tendency to look at the Black experience too narrowly.

The Maulana has pointed out rather accurately that "The blues is counter-revolutionary," but Aretha is a voice of the new Black experience. It's rather obvious that while "Think" was primarily directed toward white America, Ted White could have taken a hint from it. We must be aware of speaking on all levels. What we help to create we will not necessarily be able to control.

The rape of Newark in the 1968 election was criminal. If revolutionaries are going to involve themselves in politics, they should be successful. And while I'm sure poems are being written to explain the "success" of the Newark campaign, and essays and future speeches are being ground out on brand-new Scot tissues in living color blaming the Black community for not supporting the United Brothers, I would imagine the first problem the United Brothers encountered that they were unable to overcome is that they were not united. ⟨. . .⟩

Revolutionary politics has nothing to do with voting anyway. But if we enter electoral politics we should follow the simple formula that every Black person is a potential vote and must be welcomed and treated as such, with or without dashiki, with or without natural.

Nikki Giovanni, "Black Poems, *Poseurs* and Power" (1969), *Gemini: An Extended Autobiographical Statement on My First Twenty-five Years of Being a Black Poet* (Indianapolis: Bobbs-Merrill, 1971), pp. 106–8

DON L. LEE   Nikki Giovanni has published two thin volumes of poetry, *Black Feeling, Black Talk* and *Black Judgement,* which reflect her awareness of the values of Black culture as well as her commitment to the revolution. In "The True Import of Present Dialogue" she asks the Black male/warriors to "kill the nigger" in themselves, to let their "nigger mind die," to free their black hands and "learn to be Black men." Like many of us, Miss Giovanni is concerned that Black men have been sent out of the United States to kill other "colored" peoples of the world when the real enemy is here. She expresses this same concern in "Of Liberation," where she points out that there is an international bond between all peoples of color. Stress is placed on unity, the need to work together for mutual progress.

"Poem (No Name No. 3)" mentions leaders of the Black revolution who have been either silenced permanently or at least hampered seriously in their efforts to increase the awareness and involvement of our people and help them to effect a means to cast off the chains. Cautioning, warning the apathetic, Miss Giovanni states: "if the Black Revolution passes you bye its for damned sure / the white reaction to it won't."

In the autobiographical "My Poem," the poet tells us that she has been robbed, that because of her involvement in the movement she expects at any time a deliberate, planned attack on her very person. In spite of harassment and personal danger, however, she expresses her conviction that the killing/silencing of one revolutionary will not stop the onward movement of our people ⟨. . .⟩

Nikki writes about the familiar: what she knows, sees, experiences. It is clear why she conveys such urgency in expressing the need for Black awareness, unity, solidarity. She knows how it was. She knows how it is. She knows also that a change can be effected. ⟨. . .⟩

Nikki is at her best in the short, personal poem. She is definitely growing as a poet. Her effectiveness is in the area of the "fast rap." She says the right things at the right time. Orally this is cool, but it doesn't come across as printed poetry. We eagerly await her new book, *Re: Creation*, and hope that the sister has slowed down and tightened up her lines.

Don L. Lee, *Dynamite Voices: Black Poets of the 1960's* (Detroit: Broadside Press, 1971), pp. 68, 70, 74

PETER BAILEY   There are black artists—those in what is called "the black power literary establishment"—who are convinced that Nikki's emergence as a "star" will hinder her development as a *black* poet. Says one member of that group: "In the beginning I thought that Nikki was going to be one of the stabilizers in the black cultural scene; one who could be counted on to maintain her integrity. Unfortunately, she is off on an ego trip. That might be alright in and of itself, but her talent doesn't match her reputation. She needs to retire for a while and develop her talent rather than continue the quest to be a personality. What is happening to her happens to many committed black people when they get status, money and recognition. They start ego-tripping." The critic makes it clear that the success and acceptance of her album is important. "It is important because it reaches many new people. Black people respond to oral works and that makes it extremely important. That's why she must not get into the wrong bag." ⟨. . .⟩

Nikki listens carefully as these criticisms are related to her. Sometimes she smiles. Sometimes she blurts a four-letter comment. Sometimes there is no response at all. About the "black power literary establishment," she says its members are "as dumb and as decadent as their white counterparts." She accuses them of "trying to tell everyone what to do and telling people that 'if you do what we say, we will make you famous.' That's some s   ." She blasts on: "Furthermore, there are only two black publishing houses and they mostly publish their friends and that's the god's truth. They select just who and what they will publish. I resent them always telling people what to do. They say, 'Don't publish with whitey; don't go on white TV shows,' yet everytime you look around there's one of them on the David Frost Show or something."

Nikki also rejects the notion that the black artist has a responsibility to provide possible solutions for black people in their liberation struggle; that black artists should not merely "tell it like it is" but also should tell it like it *can* and *should* be. "I'm not about telling people what they should do," she says. When asked if this is not an easy cop-out, an avoidance of responsibility, she replies: "Definitely not. People are going to do what they want to do. If a young brother came to me and told me that he had decided to go and have a rumble with a cop, I wouldn't try to stop him. I'd just ask him if he wanted to eat before he leaves." Even if he had only a brick and the cop had a gun? she is asked. "That's right. It's his decision to make."

Peter Bailey, " 'I Am Black, Female, Polite . . .' " (1972), *Conversations with Nikki Giovanni*, ed. Virginia C. Fowler (Jackson: University Press of Mississippi, 1992), pp. 35–37

JUNE JORDAN   One more essay ⟨in *Gemini*⟩ must be mentioned, her last: "Gemini—A Prolonged Autobiographical Statement on Why." This will prove particularly interesting to everyone familiar with the author's poems. When you compare the poetry with the ambivalence and wants expressed in this essay, it becomes clear that a transition is taking place inside the artist.

She has written in one poem: "Nigger / Can you kill. . . . Can we learn to kill WHITE for BLACK / Learn to kill niggers / Learn to be Black men." Now, in this final essay she is a woman writing: "I don't want my son to be a warrior. . . . I don't want my son to be a George or a Jonathan Jackson. . . . I didn't have a baby to see him be cannon fodder." Whatever the depth of the transition, the uncertainties are real and plainly spoken: "Perhaps Black people don't want Revolution at all. That too must be considered. I used to think the world needs what I need. But perhaps it doesn't." And, the final two lines of the book: "I really like to think a Black, beautiful, loving world is possible. I really do, I think."

To be sure, that is a puzzling conclusion. Is it the black part, or the beautiful, or the "loving world" part, that leaves her unsure—or all of them? Maybe that was the goal, to raise more questions about herself, at the age of 27, than she would or could answer. At 27, that might seem fair enough, and a lot less surprising than an honest-to-God autobiography.

> June Jordan, [Review of Gemini], New York Times Book Review, 13 February 1972, p. 26

CLAUDIA TATE   CLAUDIA TATE: The black revolutionary fervor of the sixties seems to be gone. We no longer even hear the rhetoric. Does this suggest that the revolution is over?

NIKKI GIOVANNI: I bought three new windows for my mother's basement. Have you ever bought windows for your mother's basement? It's revolutionary! It really is.

I have a problem I think I should share with you. For the most part this question is boring. We're looking at a phenomemon as if it were finished. Everyone says, "Well, what happened to the revolution?" If you want to deal with states [dialectical transitions] you have to deal with Marx. But I'm not into that. From where I am, I see a continuous black revolution going on for the last four hundred years in America. There has been a continuous revolution of black people for the last two thousand years. And it's not letting up.

When you look at the decade from 1954 to 1964, you're forced to say black Americans won their objectives. We didn't like the segregated buses. We didn't like the segregated schools. We didn't like the way we were treated in stores. We didn't like the housing patterns. We didn't like our lack of professionals. We won. But looking at the late seventies, there's no way you can consider the Bakke decision to be favorable. It was 5–4. It was really a bad decision. Close cases make bad law. There's no question Bakke should have come in 9–0 either way, if it's going to be definitive. Then you would have had a law. You don't have a law now.

I'm looking for a riot. I'm living in a city that kills cops like people kill flies. Cincinnati, Ohio is leading the nation in the number of policemen killed. We're number one. The black community seems to be saying, "Well, you can play Nazi, but we ain't playing Jew." And black folks have been shooting back. We're saying, "Wait a minute. Who do you think you're playing with?" Nobody's going back to 1954. No matter what the rollback is. It's not even going back to '64. No matter what "let's take the breather" is.

When people start to say "What happened to the sixties," we've got to remember, "Hey, this is the eighties and what are we going to do now?" Where are we going because it's going to continue. My generation didn't start the bus boycotts. But we decided where they should go. Now it's time again to decide on a direction. We weren't the first generation to say "This ain't right." But we were the first to know we had to fight in terms of our bodies. We recognized we were going to have to go to jail, and we were going to get beaten; our houses were going to get bombed. But we went on the line. I mean bodies, a lot of bodies. I'm not the first poet, neither is Carolyn Rogers nor Gwen Brooks, to say, "Hey, this is intolerable." Neither was Langston Hughes, nor Claude McKay. We're talking about a struggle for freedom that keeps going on and on. People are tending to approach the whole problem like, "Oh! Wow! It's all over. It's been done." This is not a movie!

Claudia Tate, "Nikki Giovanni," *Black Women Writers at Work* (New York: Continuum, 1983), pp. 61–62

JEAN GOULD   Nikki Giovanni forged her own identity painfully perhaps, but with great determination. She had left home with her infant son to set up her own household in New York City when she was offered a job as a consultant and contributing editor to *Encore* magazine by publisher-editor Ida Lewis, who became her close friend. The poet's success, once she had been launched, was phenomenal. In ten years she produced thirteen books—a variety of writing that includes poetry, autobiography, "raps" with James Baldwin and Margaret Walker (released also on records), besides extensive travel for readings and lectures. In all she did she took into consideration her son.

She early established a regime for herself that would be backbreaking for a far more robust body than hers appeared to be. When Tommy was small, she would be up in their three-bedroom apartment on the Upper West Side of Manhattan by six a.m., get him off to school nearby, do her household chores or shop until late morning, and then write most of the afternoon, at least until Tommy came home from school. After he went to bed she might work until dawn, depending on her deadlines. When she is on tour her son stays with a secretary, but from the time he was a small boy she took him with her to visit her parents, who had been aghast at the idea of their daughter, an "unwed mother," trying to bring up a child by herself, but they soon saw that she was entirely capable of parenthood as she had learned from them both the positive and negative aspects of it. One morning when she and Tommy were going toward the elevator, he stopped halfway there and said, "Carry me." Switching her constantly carried briefcase from her right arm to the left, Nikki picked him up. But she warned him, smiling, "If you aren't a good father, I'll brain you." Ida Lewis, who wrote the foreword to My House, Giovanni's second volume, noted that Nikki never said good husband or good provider, but "broke it down to a basic," as Ida wrote. Tommy had responded complacently by putting his thumb in his mouth; he was used to his mother's hyperbole; from infancy he had been given the security of her loving care. The two were partners in meeting life's challenge.

Jean Gould, "Nikki Giovanni," Modern American Women Poets (New York: Dodd, Mead, 1984), pp. 335–36

WILLIAM J. HARRIS   Giovanni is a frustrating poet. I can sympathize with her detractors, no matter what the motives for their discontent. She clearly has talent that she refuses to discipline. She just doesn't seem to try hard enough. In "Habits" she coyly declares:

> i sit writing
> a poem
> about my habits

which while it's not
a great poem
is mine

It isn't enough that the poem is hers; personality isn't enough, isn't a substitute for fully realized poems. Even though she has created a compelling persona on the page, she has been too dependent on it. Her ego has backfired. She has written a number of lively, sometimes humorous, sometimes tragic, often perceptive poems about the contemporary world. The best poems in her three strongest books, *Black Feeling, Black Talk, Black Judgement, Re:Creation*, and *Cotton Candy*, demonstrate that she can be a very good poet. However, her work also contains dross: too much unrealized abstraction (flabby abstraction at that!), too much "poetic" fantasy posing as poetry and too many moments verging on sentimentality. In the early seventies, after severely criticizing Giovanni's shortcomings, Haki Madhubuti said he eagerly awaited the publication of her new book, *Re:Creation;* he hoped that in it she would fulfill the promise of her early poetry. Even though it turned out to be one of Giovanni's better books, I find myself in a similar situation to Madhubuti's. I see that not only does Giovanni have promise, she already has written some good poems and continues to write them. Yet I am concerned about her development. I think it is time for her to stand back and take stock of herself, to take for herself the time for reflection, the vacation she says Aretha deserves for work well done. Nikki Giovanni is one of the most talented writers to come out of the Black sixties, and I don't want to lose her. I want her to write poems which grow out of that charming persona, not poems which are consumed by it. Giovanni must keep her charm and overcome her self-indulgence. She has the talent to create good, perhaps important, poetry, if only she has the will to discipline her craft.

William J. Harris, "Sweet Soft Essence of Possibility: The Poetry of Nikki Giovanni," *Black Women Writers (1950–1980): A Critical Evaluation*, ed. Mari Evans (New York: Anchor Books/Doubleday, 1984), p. 228

MARGARET B. McDOWELL   The most significant development in Giovanni's career has been her evolution from a strongly committed political consciousness prior to 1969 to a more inclusive consciousness which does not repudiate political concern and commitment, but which regards a revolutionary ethos as only one aspect of the totality of Black experience.

Her earlier political associates and favorable reviewers of the late 1960s often regarded her development after 1970 with consternation, as representing a repudiation of her racial roots and of political commitment, without perhaps fully understanding the basis for her widened concerns and interests. Giovanni's shift in interest from revolutionary politics and race as a collective matter towards love and race as they affect personal development and relationships brought strong reviewer reaction. (The shift to less favorable criticism, which is apparent in the reviews of My House, is also evident in the late notices of Gemini, Giovanni's most widely reviewed book.) The problems involved in studying the relationship between this shift in her poetry and the somewhat delayed shift from favorable to less favorable criticism, as her artistry grew, are complex. And they are further complicated by the fact that, at the very time the negative reviews of her poetry markedly increased, her popularity with readers surged dramatically ahead. Witness the late sales of Gemini (1971) and Black Feeling/Black Talk/Black Judgement (1970), the new sales of My House (1972), and the record-breaking sales of her two early albums of recorded poetry. Her audiences around the country grew markedly in size and enthusiasm in 1972, and feature articles and cover stories on "the Princess of Black Poetry" appeared in over a dozen popular magazines in 1972 and 1973.

Studying the relationships between the positive and negative reviews and between the opinions of reviewers and popular audiences is made more difficult by an anomaly presented by Giovanni's Black Feeling/Black Talk/ Black Judgement: two-thirds of the poems in this 1970 volume are brief, introspective lyrics which are political only in the most peripheral sense—that they mention a lover as someone the speaker met at a conference, for instance. The remaining third, poems which are strongly political and often militant, received practically all the attention of reviewers. Critics ignored almost completely the poems that foreshadow nearly all the poetry Giovanni was to write in the next thirteen years. In short, the wave of literary reviews that established Giovanni's national reputation as a poet also established her image as a radical. Yet, by the summer of 1970, when these reviews began to appear, Giovanni had been writing solely non-political, lyric poetry for a year. The label "the poet of the Black revolution" which characterized her in the popular media was already a misnomer in 1970, when it began to be popularly used.

Margaret B. McDowell, "Groundwork for a More Comprehensive Criticism of Nikki Giovanni," Studies in Black American Literature, ed. Joe Weixlmann and Chester J. Fontenot (Greenwood, FL: Penkevill Publishing Co., 1986), Vol. 2, pp. 143–44

MARITA GOLDEN   In *Sacred Cows and Other Edibles*, Nikki Giovanni—poet, personality, social critic, iconoclast and raconteur—exhibits
the best and the worst uses of the essay as a vehicle for expression, verbal
performance and exploration of the mundane and the special. ⟨. . .⟩

The problem with *Sacred Cows and Other Edibles* ⟨. . .⟩ is that it falls short
precisely because Giovanni's glib, wise-cracking, overly conversational style
(which has made her poetry so popular) is ill-suited to the intellectual
requirements of the essay. These pieces mildly entertain more than they
probe; more often than not, the reader is merely reminded of what is obvious
rather than introduced to another way of seeing things.

Giovanni is at her best in the selection titled "Reflections on My Profession" and "Four Introductions"—pieces dedicated to writers, among them
Paule Marshall and Mari Evans. In "An Answer to Some Questions on
How I Write" Giovanni asserts, "I don't have a lifestyle. I have a life,"
which made me want to cheer this hearty refutation of categories and
oversimplification of the human equation. And puncturing the vague pom-
posity of the current hot cliché, the "role model," Giovanni says: "When
people do not want to do what history requires, they say they have no role
models. I'm glad Phillis Wheatley did not know she had no role model and
wrote her poetry anyway." And she sums up the job of the writer with a
feisty confidence saying, "We write because we believe that the human
spirit cannot be tamed and should not be trained." This is Giovanni at her
best—sparkling *and* thoughtful.

Marita Golden, "Tennis, Termites, Game Shows and the Art of Writing," *Washington
Post Book World*, 14 February 1988, p. 3

MARTHA COOK   ⟨. . .⟩ Giovanni displays a new sense of herself
as a poet in *Those Who Ride the Night Winds*. In "A Song for New-Ark"
and also in "I Am She," Giovanni seems confident of the role she has
chosen for herself, secure in her place in society. As she says in the latter
poem, "I am she . . . who writes . . . the poems. . . ." Again the ellipses give
the sense of openness, of more to come from this poetic talent. While the
poems in this volume seem to reflect Giovanni's own feeling that she has
reached maturity as a poet, there are still indications of the necessity of
coping with the demands of modern life. She acknowledges the presence
of loneliness, not as she did through the poems in the volume *Cotton Candy*

on a Rainy Day, where loneliness seemed to be a problem for which she could at the time see no solution, but in a way that indicates the strength of her inner resources. In the poem, "The Room with the Tapestry Rug," she creates a persona who confronts loneliness by seeking out "the room . . . where all who lived . . . knew her well. . . ." The room holds memories of the past, symbolized by a garment created by a member of her family who was important in her childhood, used in a literal and metaphorical way to keep out the cold.

But Giovanni moves beyond this fairly traditional symbol, refusing to let the room be only a place of confinement and protection from the larger world; it becomes a place where she can also find comfort in the cool air from outside, while luxuriating in the security of her own space:

> If it was cold . . . she would wrap herself . . . in the natted blue sweater . . . knitted by a grandmother . . . so many years ago . . . If warm . . . the windows were opened . . . to allow the wind . . . to partake of their pleasure . . .

The closing paragraph of the poem indicates the resources of the persona beyond her memories of the past: "Her books . . . her secret life . . . in the room with the tapestry rug. . . ." Here she shows not only the need for but the fact of control over the places in her own life.

In the 1970s, such poems as "My House" conveyed an important theme of the development of a strengthening identity as a single woman; in the 1980s, such poems as "The Room with the Tapestry Rug" and "I Am She" illustrate not only the strength but also the depth and range of that identity. It is appropriate that a volume that so strongly exhibits Giovanni's talents as a writer should also attest to the importance of literature and art in her life, an importance reflected as well in her continued involvement in efforts to bring people and the arts together. ⟨. . .⟩

Looking at Giovanni's poetry in the context of Southern literature expands rather than limits the possibilities for interpretation and analysis. In fact, this approach reveals that within the body of her work lies a solid core of poems that do not rely on political or personal situations for their success. Rather, they develop universal themes, such as coming to terms with the past and with the present so that one may move into the future—again, themes that have been and continue to be of particular significance in Southern poetry. These themes mark her work as a contribution to the canon not just of Southern poetry, of black poetry, of feminist poetry, but also of contemporary American poetry. However, Giovanni's response to any generalization, any categorization, would probably echo the closing line of her poem "Categories," from *My House*. Emphasizing her uniqueness as an individual, she might well proclaim, "i'm bored with categories."

Martha Cook, "Nikki Giovanni: Place and Sense of Place in Her Poetry," *Southern Women Writers: The New Generation*, ed. Tonette Bond Inge (Tuscaloosa: University of Alabama Press, 1990), pp. 298–99

VIRGINIA C. FOWLER   As a poet who emerged during the 1960s ⟨. . .⟩ Giovanni has consistently believed in a connection between art and action, a central impetus of the Black Arts Movement; in Larry Neal's words, "It is a profound ethical sense that makes a Black artist question a society in which art is one thing and the actions of men another. The Black Arts Movement believes that your ethics and your aesthetics are one." Although we have seen that Giovanni objected to the prescriptiveness that eventually would destroy the Black Arts Movement, her poetry, both early and late, reflects the kind of ethical concerns described by Neal. As she goes on to explain to ⟨Claudia⟩ Tate, the "militant stance" prescribed by adherents of a black aesthetic was as repugnant to her as any prescriptiveness; but beyond this, it also lost its usefulness: "What are we going to do with a stance? Literature is only as useful as it reflects reality." Ironically, prescriptive assumptions of just this sort are evident in Tate's question. Had Giovanni's poetry continued to be "extroverted, militant, arrogant" (if one accepts Tate's terms) in the 1970s and 1980s, it would have ceased to "reflect reality." The "shift" to which Tate refers is not, Giovanni's answers make clear, the result of a decision to write a different kind of poetry. Instead, as the social and political realities of her world changed, both she— who is "a part of the body politic"—and her poetry—which deliberately attempts to "reflect" the world—also changed.

Elsewhere Giovanni identifies some of the changing realities that her poetry reflects. "I started as a writer concerned about the black situation in America and have grown to be a writer concerned about the black situation in the world. I have come to realize that gender bias is a real problem. It's difficult to be a woman, but being black and female produces a double bind." In addition to this kind of expansion in her awareness and focus, she points to the implications that space exploration has for human beings: "A lot has happened. I don't want anybody to think it's just me. It's all of us. It has to do with the way we conceptualize the world. We are earthlings. When Viking II took off we became earthlings. Nobody knows what an earthling is, and how an earthling relates to other earthlings." Our world, in other words, looks very different now than it did in 1968 when Giovanni began her career as a poet. And her poetry will inevitably reflect those differences because they give shape to who she is.

Virginia C. Fowler, Nikki Giovanni (New York: Twayne, 1992), pp. 127–28

▨ *Bibliography*

Black Feeling, Black Talk. 1968.

Black Judgement. 1968.

Black Feeling, Black Talk/Black Judgement. 1970.

Re:Creation. 1970.

All I Gotta Do. 1970.

Night Comes Softly: An Anthology of Black Female Voices (editor). 1970.

Poems of Angela Yvonne Davis. 1970.

Gemini: An Extended Autobiographical Statement on My First Twenty-five Years of Being a Black Poet. 1971.

Spin a Soft Black Song: Poems for Children. 1971.

My House. 1972.

A Dialogue (with James Baldwin). 1973.

Ego-Tripping and Other Poems for Young People. 1973.

A Poetic Equation: Conversations between Nikki Giovanni and Margaret Walker. 1974.

The Women and the Men. 1975.

Cotton Candy on a Rainy Day. 1978.

Vacation Time: Poems for Children. 1980.

Those Who Ride the Night Winds. 1983.

Sacred Cows—and Other Edibles. 1988.

Appalachian Elders: A Warm Hearth Sampler (editor; with Cathee Dennison). 1991.

Conversations with Nikki Giovanni. Ed. Virginia C. Fowler. 1992.

Grand Mothers: Poems, Reminiscences, and Short Stories about the Keepers of
        Our Traditions (editor). 1994.
Knoxville, Tennessee. 1994.
Racism 101. 1994.

Michael S. Harper
b. 1938

MICHAEL STEVEN HARPER was born on March 18, 1938, in Brooklyn, New York, the son of Walter Warren and Katherine Johnson Harper. Harper's maternal grandfather practiced medicine, and from an early age Harper was encouraged to study medicine. In spite of poor health, he excelled at the Susan Miller Dorsey High School, although he did relatively little creative writing there. He entered Los Angeles City College in 1956, receiving an A.A. in 1959. He then entered Los Angeles State College of Applied Arts and Sciences (now California State University at Los Angeles) still intent on pursuing medicine, but a professor dissuaded him from this profession in the belief that blacks could not succeed in medical school; accordingly, Harper opted for a degree in English literature, gaining it in 1961. Shortly thereafter he was accepted into the Iowa State Writers Workshop, where he worked primarily on poetry and earned the nickname the Padre—apparently because he wore two hats around campus. He received the M.F.A. in 1963.

Harper began his teaching career in 1964 at Contra Costa College in San Pablo, California. He subsequently taught at Lewis and Clark College (Portland, Oregon) and California State College before coming to Brown University in 1971, where he is now the I. J. Kapstein Professor of English and director of the writing program. He has been a visiting professor at Reed College, Harvard, Yale, Carleton, and elsewhere.

Harper's poems began appearing in various literary journals in the late 1960s, and in 1970 *Dear John, Dear Coltrane*, his first collection of poems, was published; it was nominated for a National Book Award. This volume reveals Harper's longstanding interest in music (especially jazz and blues), to which he was exposed at an early age.

The poems in *Dear John, Dear Coltrane* celebrate not only Coltrane and other musicians, but also the general relationship between music and poetry. Harper has claimed that his poetry is most effective when read aloud. It is not unusual for a black American writer to be influenced by jazz and blues, but Harper's themes have not been limited to the black American experi-

47

ence. Indeed, he finds it somewhat baffling that various critics, both black and white, have denied the influence of non–black American literature and British literature on black American artists. Harper's poetry is generally narrative and much of it seeks to reclaim the various historical influences that have shaped the black American community.

Much of Harper's prolific poetic output is explicitly concerned with history: *History Is Your Own Heartbeat* (1971), *Photographs: Negatives: History as Apple Tree* (1972), and *Images of Kin: New and Selected Poems* (1977). Yet the history Harper is concerned with is not only communal history but also personal history, and the relationship between the two. Among his more recent poetry volumes are *Healing Song for the Inner Ear* (1985) and *Songlines: Mosaics* (1991). Harper has also compiled the important critical anthology, *Chant of Saints* (1979; with Robert B. Stepto), and, with Anthony Walton, a volume of modern black American poetry, *Every Shut Eye Ain't Asleep* (1994).

Harper has received many awards and honors for his poetry, including a National Institute of Arts and Letters Creative Writing Award (1972), a Guggenheim Fellowship (1976), a National Endowment for the Arts grant (1977), and a Massachusetts Council Creative Writing Award (1977). He married Shirley Ann Buffington in 1965; they have three children. Harper continues to teach and write at Brown University.

▓ *Critical Extracts*

EDWIN FUSSELL   Naively (good intentions; generous editor), I set out to write an omnibus essay-review, insufficiently aware of how many laminations and concentricities inform Michael S. Harper's complex and coherent *oeuvre*. ⟨. . .⟩ This is very likely the finest poetry now being written in a woe-begotten and woe-begone country—perhaps the best since John Berryman—and the serious reader had better buy or at least read all of it at once. Most of my remarks are perforce addressed to the latest volume ⟨*Nightmare Begins Responsibility*⟩, though I shall glance at others. First, a clarification and an admonition. Clarification—Harper is a black poet; Harper is an American poet. Asked if he saw any contradiction in terms, he replied: "None at all. They are two aspects of the same story." In the same interview he spoke of his responsibility (calling, vocation) to connect "black idioms and black traditional motifs" with "American institutions, the American lexicon, the American landscape." Beyond that, Harper writes toward "a totally new aesthetic, a totally new world-view" not yet existing, and a place never before conceived. In other words, "a poet has a responsibility to his people. And when I say people, I mean all people." To start with, Harper wants to re-create America, substituting for the Declaration of Independence ("a document written for a handful of men to protect their interests and commodities") what he calls "the democratic Promise." Like John Coltrane, Harper makes his way by "extension and overextension." (Abraham Chapman, "An Interview with Michael S. Harper," *Arts in Society*, 11 [1975], 463–71, *passim*.) ⟨. . .⟩

"Nightmare Begins Responsibility" is again Harper at his absolute best. It is also an extremely difficult poem to understand, though not in the least difficult to feel, and so I once again avail myself of the poet's informal statement. "The poem was meant to crystalize the breaking out of these compartments into a more unified vision . . . politics here defined as power relationships rather than the more narrow conception." Like many poems by black American poets, it is (partly) formed on black-white metaphorical contrasts. Unlike many black American poets, Harper refuses the cheap and easy dualism, and instead explores the linguistic resources of the language for many and delicate nuances. "Photographs: *Negatives*" (published separately, and then included in *Song: I Want a Witness*) is an obvious example of what I mean. In "Nightmare Begins Responsibility," the agonized father watches his infant son die, unavoidably putting his trust in everything white to be found in a hospital, the oxygen tent, for example, or, in metaphor, *"white-doctor-who-breathed-for-him-all-night."* Each reader will have to decide for himself how successfully Harper has broken out of his "compartments," toward unity. The answer can only be found in the music of the poem, where Harper lets himself all the way out, blending a great variety of styles, early and late, blues, jazz, refrain, syncopation (omitted words), technological-medical-jargon satire, and sheer elegance. ⟨. . .⟩ The epigraph of *Song: I Want a Witness* and of *Debridement*:

> When there is no history
> there is no metaphor;
> a blind nation in storm
> mauls its own harbors;
> spermwhale, Indian, black,
> belted in these ruins.

Through such "belting" metaphors as these Harper makes American history now and for generations still to be born. He is also remaking American history from *its* origins. I discriminate, as I think Harper does, between the *past*, which simply exists as unalterable fact, and *history*, or our ongoing appropriation of it. The major metaphor holding the five sections of this latest book together is historical, the dialectic of nightmare and kin, responsibility and development. Not luck, but high art and honor, led Harper to this trope. It is the only real one to be had.

> Edwin Fussell, "Double-Conscious Poet in the Veil (for Michael S. Harper)," *Parnassus: Poetry in Review* 4, No. 1 (Fall–Winter 1975): 5–6, 22–24

ROBERT B. STEPTO   In the Reuben/Michael poems, the allusions to jazz and, through Du Bois, to Afro-American letters place the lost sons in art full of ancient theme, allusion, and archetype, and are thereby another kind of "bandage" healing memories of loss and recurring nightmare. Above all, they tell us something of the poet's role and responsibilities in creating kinship. By finding the allusions and metaphors and placing them in a historical continuum it is he who makes experience sufficiently compassable for the survivors (including himself) not merely to survive but also pursue a responsible life full of loving moral action. In "Ruth's Blues," these ideas are recast and renewed in the final poem "Here Where Coltrane Is," where in simply declaring ". . . I play 'Alabama' . . ." the poet claims not only to bring the true America to Ruth, and hence to America, but also that he brings himself.

This assertion is hardly audacious or novel. It is part of a heritage and at least as old (in America) as Du Bois' stirring words of eighty years ago:

> Will America be poorer if she
> replace her brutal dyspeptic
> blundering with light-hearted
> but determined Negro humility?
> or her coarse and cruel wit with
> loving jovial good-humor? or her
> vulgar music with the soul of the
> Sorrow Songs?

"I play 'Alabama' " restates DuBois' language as a coded image. It is a call for "modal songs" redeeming and reconstructing (the true Reconstruction) the "illiterate halls" which are variously Ruth's Victorian house and "rural goldmine" landscape and America as a whole. As the poem and series end, however, Harper places the artist's role as a redeemer in a certain perspective:

> For this reason Martin is dead;
> for this reason Malcolm is dead;
> for this reason Coltrane is dead;
> in the eyes of my first son are the browns
> of these men and their music.

While honoring his son Roland by placing him in the continuum, much as the dead sons ascended to kinship with the four black girls for whom he wrote "American History" and Coltrane composed "Alabama," Harper at the same time re-sings his son's song, *"Ungie, hi Ungie,"* which, in its regenerative and modal qualities, is both the paradigmatic lyric of Ruth's Blues and the reason why Roland may share the "brown eyes" of the great. Modality, for which kinship is the prevailing metaphor, is not the exclusive province of the master articulators, although we may first come to perceive it through them: "Alabama" and Roland's song are but a few of the infinite dimensions of moral conscience transformed into tonal metaphor.

Robert B. Stepto, "Michael S. Harper, Poet as Kinsman: The Family Sequences," *Massachusetts Review* 17, No. 3 (Autumn 1976): 486–87

DAVID IGNATOW   As a vision of America, *Images of Kin* could have been the epilogue to Hart Crane's masterpiece, *The Bridge*—were Crane alive today to see the country in less than glorious light. Michael Harper has been publishing his poetry since 1970, and by now it is more than obvious that he has been writing steadily on one theme. He is passionately identified with the history of his people. As it was for Crane, history is, for Mr. Harper, a personal matter, but he, as a black man, carries in him the burden of the past enslavement of his race and, unlike Crane, who wrote to celebrate this country, for Mr. Harper the problem is to relieve himself of his burden. It is the storm center of his poems and it has made for a writing that could not have come easily.

Like Crane, who also had his knotted passages, Mr. Harper has objectified and made painfully vivid what in any other mode could have been simple crying for mercy or sententious talk. It is Mr. Harper's achievement to have

projected his most difficult and complex insights and feelings through the
epical manner, yet at the same time carried us along to identify with him.

In the section of the new poems called "Healing Songs," he begins looking
for his own personal resolution and ease, as if he had found himself at last
in tune with his society. There is a guarded reaching out for tenderness
with others, and some measure of amusement, too, as for instance in the
second part of the third stanza from "Dining from a Treed Condition, An
Historical Survey":

> I look out the Tower window over the sun-dial
> of Etienne's savage memory carved in blue spruce
> and the rainbowed cypress hearing Christmas prayers
> of Barhyte's slaves, Thom Campbell, his wife, Nancy
> quartered in clear pieces of Bear Swampground
> southeast of the Rose Garden, conjuring amused
> comic tales of Tom Camel's unself episodes
> of tree-climbing and masquerade.
>
> Told to saw off a limb on Mr. White's place
> he sat on the limb vigorously sawing the obstructing
> branch; dazed after a loud crack, on the ground
> Tom cried to Mr. White: "Oh, no Sah! I had the good
> fortune to land on mah head."

Of course it is an amusing poem, and is so intended, even in its references
to the master-and-slave relationship. The fact that Mr. Harper has created
this new perspective for himself, without bitterness or loss of dignity to
himself, speaks volumes about a whole new advance in Mr. Harper's career.

David Ignatow, "Three Poets," *New York Times Book Review*, 5 March 1978, p. 14

JOHN F. CALLAHAN   For Michael Harper the mission of poetry
is bound up with eloquence and the magic of the spoken word, the oral
tradition. Harper is a poet whose vision of personal and national experience
is worked out in the Afro-American grain—that tradition of pain and
rejuvenation expressed in the sorrow songs, and the blues, and folktales,
the whole range of Afro-American oral tradition, a tradition, it is important
to remember, which also touches formal American/Afro-American rhetorical patterns, from Abraham Lincoln and Frederick Douglass in the nineteenth century to Martin Luther King in the nineteen-fifties and -sixties.

Harper is alert to the possibilities of rhetoric and the complexities of that ancient and American rhetorical tradition whose purpose was to challenge, vex, please, persuade, and, at last, illuminate the audience. He is a poet not of paradox but of the paradoxical, of simplicity in the midst of complexities, affirmation in the midst of tragedy—but affirmations so aware of the incongruities of eloquence that his voice intensifies the sense of tragedy and devastation.

Make no mistake about Harper's allegiance to a single complex, diverse tradition. Much as he recognizes and heeds points of departure between American and Afro-American cultural patterns, Harper is a major American poet for the same reasons and in the same work that he is a major Afro-American poet. His stance is deliberately chosen, and defiant toward any who try to subordinate either the American or Afro-American aspect of his tradition, experience, or language. Harper's purpose, like Du Bois's at the turn of the century, is to turn the notion (and fact) of double-consciousness, of racial and cultural polarity, into a strength, an energy, a source of wholeness. Like Du Bois, Harper wishes nothing to be lost in the passage to a "better and truer self."

At forty, Harper has written a dozen or more extraordinary poems, poems long-lived and stunningly original, poems that transform his stance as an American/Afro-American poet into a reality with the power of illumination.

John F. Callahan, "The Testifying Voice in Michael Harper's Images of Kin," Black American Literature Forum 13, No. 3 (Fall 1979): 89

SOLLACE MITCHELL   *Chant of Saints* documents a change in black poetry from the rhetorical mode of the 1960s and 1970s, exemplified by the work of Amiri Baraka (né Leroi Jones) and the Black Arts Movement he led, to an aesthetic mode that owes more to the trope than the slogan. What is rejected is the language of domination often associated with the race of oppression in America, whose idiom is heard thus by Michael Harper:

> these fatherless whites
> come to consciousness
> with a history of the gun—
> the New World, if misery had
> a voice, would be a rifle cocking.

The writers and poets whose work is represented in *Chant of Saints* do not by any means comprise the whole of the Afro-American literary community, but they do make up a group whose commitment to craft is at least as strong as commitment to colour (which comes out explicitly in the interviews with Ralph Ellison and Derek Walcott). In this respect the collection is reminiscent of Alain Locke's *The New Negro*, which marked a similar blossoming of black arts and letters in the 1920s, the Harlem Renaissance. Besides work from and interviews with Ellison and Walcott, Toni Morrison, Robert Hayden, Gayl Jones, and Leon Forrest are also represented; and to round out the volume there are several critical essays on the roots of contemporary black culture in Africa, slavery, and the blues. ⟨. . .⟩

Each of the many contributors seems to wish to move on from, without disowning, the nationalist voice that erupted, strong but shrill, during the Black Power movement. The issue of how best to influence a black readership remains vital, as Baraka's recent attack on Ellison and the editors (in *Black American Literature Forum*) testifies. The nationalist period was unquestionably the humus for the 1970s harvest, for it was the nationalists who consolidated the position of strength from which black poets now have the luxury to speak.

> Sollace Mitchell, "From Slogans to Tropes," *Times Literary Supplement*, 30 May 1980, p. 626

MICHAEL S. HARPER   I wrote about my "Grandfather" because he was a hero in the highest sense, though he waited tables in white clothes. He taught me to study Sugar Ray's left-hook technique, to step inside someone's sense of time, of theatre, of the stage and arena, and to floor show to one's own tune. Ellison called it *antagonistic cooperation;* Wright called it the switchblade of the movie-screen. Language and rhetoric is essential power. Why else were the slaves prohibited from reading, from learning to pen their own sagas? All great art is finally testamental, and its technical brilliance never shadows the content of the song. Deliver the melody, make sure the harmony's correct, play as long as you like, but play sweet, and don't forget the ladies.

A final note on the blues is that they always say yes to life; meet life's terms but never accept them: "been down so long that down don't worry me / road so rocky, won't be rocky long." Johnny Hodges must have said this to Duke on tour: "you run them verbs (the key of G), I'll drive the thought (the rabbit on his own rainbow)."

I'll make a coda on the American audience, which is vast potentially. "I wish you'd buy more books," said Huck to Tom—meanwhile Jim was bringing his family to freedom. The landscape of the poem is the contour of the face reading the Declaration of Independence. How many White Jeffersons are there in this country, anyway? When I was interviewed for my present duty at Brown University, all that slave trade money came back to haunt me once again, a man yelled out from the genteel back of the room that I was an impostor borrowing from musicians. Couldn't I do something about my accent? People were embarrassed for him. He was quickly ushered out, and the East Side returned to normal, good old Providence with its old money and the mafia flair. I remembered that Douglass had been run out of Providence to New Bedford after an abolitionist meeting, and it's rumored that John Brown (the fanatical one) came all the way from Oberlin, Ohio, to meet the best gunsmith in town, a Black infantryman from the Black Regiment of Rhode Island.

> Michael S. Harper, "My Poetic Technique and the Humanization of the American Audience," *Black Literature and Humanism*, ed. R. Baxter Miller (Lexington: University Press of Kentucky, 1981), pp. 30–31

JOSEPH A. BROWN   As a human being, Harper believes that "life's terms" must be met; and as a poet, Harper argues that the existing techniques and traditions of poetry must be confronted. It is enough to master the forms, because in mastery the artist demonstrates power. But something must be added to nature, to life, to the "available realistic or legendary material." The world in which Michael Harper lives is not significantly different from the world of Paul Laurence Dunbar or John Coltrane. That world is the real and legendary *America*, a world where the souls of black folk are continually threatened with dreams which turn into nightmares. For Harper, technique is natural, the easy part of poetry. What he wrestles with in his poetry is what he sets out for himself in his declaration of intentions: understanding the conscience. Harper's methodology derives from the music of his maturity. If the dream becomes a nightmare, if the legend is a lie, say so; confront the wall head-on, swallow the fire straight, with no soothing "chaser":

> Human beings are capable of all kinds of possibility, combination, and diversity. But if one has a vision of history as myth as lie, one has a closed, reductive view of things. Of course the fantasy of white supremist America with its closed myths has always been a fantasy of a white country. Out of that kind of fantasy came genocide, Indian massacres, fugitive slave laws, manifest destiny, open-door policies, Vietnam, Detroit, East Saint Louis, Watts, the Mexican War, Chicago and the Democratic Convention of 1968.

Harper considers the nightmare and finds it suffocating; the walls of reality close in. The alternative to this closed, reductive view of things is, obviously, an open-ended breaking through of "what seems to be," thereby giving precedence to the *effort* involved in taking life straight. In describing his concept of effort, Harper invokes the presence and example of John Coltrane:

> One of the things that is important about Coltrane's music is the energy and passion with which he approached his instrument and music. Such energy was perhaps akin to the nature of oppression generally and the kind of energy it takes to break oppressive conditions, oppressive musical structures, and oppressive societal structures.

Harper finds relevance in the performer, as much as in the performance. This is true of his comments on Coltrane and it is equally true of all his poetic subjects. Therefore, it makes sense to search through Harper's poems for examples of how he reflects upon his own growing awareness of the poet-as-performer. In the interview just quoted, Harper says, "It's my responsibility to articulate." He dwells upon this point in his poetry by centering on the moment when words fail him, at the moment when his experiences seem most constricting. *Death* in all its manifestations is the subject matter of Michael Harper's poetic career. How he has fought a way for himself out of the tomb, the temptation to eternally reside in nightmares; how he wills himself to construct a ladder of saints as a way of remembering those who instructed him in open-ended, "modal" living; how, finally, he offers his performance as a sign of hope and encouragement to his readers—all of these place Michael Harper where he wants to be: the child of the great performing blues artists.

Joseph A. Brown, "Their Long Scars Touch Ours: A Reflection on the Poetry of Michael Harper," *Callaloo* 9, No. 1 (Winter 1986): 210–11

NICCOLÒ N. DONZELLA   The first time I saw Michael Harper he was on the back of a Coltrane album, looking fierce amidst a page of passages from *Dear John*. The next time I saw him was at Brown. I had driven up from Bridgeport to introduce myself the Spring before I was to report there as a student in the Graduate Writing Program. For about fifteen minutes I stood in the hall outside his office, listening to his thunderous rage on the other side of the door. When at last he opened the door, it wasn't so much a man in a room I saw, as a man wearing a room. He was big; he was mad; I started thinking about Iowa.

I also started thinking, "Why is this man so angry?"

I saw a lot of him during the next two years, mostly in his office during the late afternoon. I was his research assistant. He'd save up that rage all day and then, generously, pour it out for me.

That rage could take you places. It could take you away from whatever you had had the temerity to think you knew about poetry, literature, or life. But more than that, it could take you to America; not just the corner of America you had glimpsed growing up, but the transcendent America that few of us are fortunate enough to see and still fewer of us are gifted enough to describe.

The transcendent America was the America he insisted you see and then come to terms through what he described as its sacred literature—the sum of our best visions about ourselves. He taught the America of Jefferson, Tubman, Lincoln, and King; the America of first and second and third chances; the America of public schools and private courage. He would have you absorb its courage in a poem about his grandfather defending his house from rioters, let you hear its music in a sonnet by Hayden, make you reason with it in an essay by Ellison. It was a hard place sometimes, but a shining place, too. In the end, he made you know that you belonged in it and, more importantly, that you owed it your allegiance so long as you remained on its shores.

Niccolò N. Donzella, "The Rage of Michael Harper," *Callaloo* 13, No. 4 (Fall 1990): 805

KYLE GRIMES   In a poem called "Deathwatch" (from *Dear John, Dear Coltrane*), Harper writes about the hospital death of his newborn son. The poem shares with *Debridement* a concern with the tension between clinical particulars and the outrageous distortions of cultural myth. "Death-watch" ends with three lines which could well be taken as a key to the discursive texture of *Debridement*:

> America needs a killing.
> America needs a killing.
> *Survivors will be human.*

In *Debridement* Harper, at the risk of his own poetic voice, arranges the various cultural myths which infiltrate the sequence in such a way that they annihilate one another's pretensions to authority. America needs a killing. In so doing, though, Harper at least suggests a "survivor" of sorts— a language of open-ended myth which is capable of articulating the brutal particulars of human experience, the "human essentials" upon which a valid history of Vietnam might be founded.

Kyle Grimes, "The Entropics of Discourse: Michael Harper's *Debridement* and the Myth of the Hero," *Black American Literature Forum* 24, No. 3 (Fall 1990): 438–39

ROBERT DALE PARKER   Song takes us back to music. Harper's poems evoke traditions, including musical traditions, in a *language* of many musics, including jazz, blues (see especially the longer version of "Last Affair: Bessie's Blues Song" in *Images of Kin*), call and response (e.g., "Dear John, Dear Coltrane"), oratory (e.g., "Martin's Blues"), medical technocracy (e.g., "Debridement"). Perhaps the musical notes are among the most distinc-tive, but sometimes we let them drown out the specifically literary and poetic musics, whereas so much of the wonder in Coltrane or Harper comes in the medley of more sounds at once than any one metaphor can name. And so, while admiring the musical music, I want to testify also to the literary and poetic musics in Harper's work, as in the great title poem of *Nightmare Begins Responsibility*, which revises Yeats's epigraph to *Responsibili-ties*—"In Dreams Begin Responsibility," or, in the same volume, the last section of tributes culminating with "Alice," Harper's moving homage to Alice Walker and Zora Neale Hurston, which he was reading to audiences, as I recall, that in 1973 or '74 mostly included people who had never heard of Walker or Hurston. To have a tradition, he suggests, it needs to be testified to. Testimony becomes pedagogy, and pedagogy becomes prophecy.

Robert Dale Parker, "Poetry and Pedagogy: A Memory of Michael Harper Teaching," *Callaloo* 13, No. 4 (Fall 1990): 812

JOHN S. WRIGHT   Much of the prevailing book on Michael fixes on his credentials as a jazz poet and a narrative poet—on the allusive frequency with which the healing song of African-American musicians shapes his verse, and on the storylined sequences of poems that seem to mark him as an interpreter of historic events. Well enough. Oliver Jackson, longest tongue and sharpest eye of the Iowa blood brotherhood, knew early that the Padre's High Modes are John Coltrane's more than Northrop Frye's. And Robert Hayden once remarked approvingly the narrative power that Harper won from devastating personal experiences.

But the seeking eye has a home in this rock, too, don't you see; and to it, history is collage, not cause or chronos. Jack the Bear, whose buggy jiving Michael still keeps close at hand, admonishes us that a jazz sensibility summons the whole body, mimes it, and therefore that diagnosing the inner eye might well lead to therapies for the inner ear. After all, the blind eye does separate music from its makers, denigrifies it, to be precise; and jazz is inconceivable without a seeing "picture history" of its faces, places, codes, and family ties. Two-fisted wielder of photomechanical gizmos that he is, Michael has accordingly put his own cyclops eye to reintegrative musical purpose: the result, an eight-volume in-progress jazz-scored cyclorama of otherwise invisible portraits of African America—"negatives" he called some of them early on—counter-images of family and community units, their celebrations and grievings and unseen commentaries on the public weal and woe. Analogues appear in Michael's cyclorama to the camera eyes of James Der Zee, Gordon Parks, Roy DeCarava, where images unstuck from the sweet flypaper of black life fuse a poet's spirit with a lensmaster's ocular acuity and where the unrecognized romance of obscured lives emerges from darkroom shadow.

Trane would approve. McCoy Tyner—pianist left-hand visionary and regular Harper confrere—already has. Michael's "book on Trane," like McCoy's, locates a universe and a new way of thinking in Trane's modal improvisations, music which is always about relationships, about unity, about summoning "magara"—life-force—and the counter-Cartesian spirituality Trane experienced in the sound of an Indian *shenai*, an Arabian *zoukra*, a West African *baloo*. The only abstractions here are in the telling. The music and the poetry become modal only in the doing—for Michael, as father, son, husband, brother, teacher, poet, friend. The love supreme that opened Trane to the freedom principle in the great modal musical cultures of the non-Western world briefs Michael's explorations into the intensely personal experience of unnamed intimates that figures so prominently in his poetic labors, and that frustrates those readers both addicted to confessional lyric and unattuned to the aesthetic values of reticence. Here, in answer to the culture of narcissism and the cult of personality, Michael's counter-confessional mode of revelation has been the microcosmic metaphor—History as the singular heartbeat, as the private persona, as the politic body of the solitary soul, as family album—and it organizes *modally* the visual imagery of much of his finest work. Political retreat and solipsism are the obverse of such a strategy. Almost invariably in Michael's poems it is a means of *making* and *feeling* connections between the otherwise disseevered realities that are the signs of our social and psychic disunity, and the obstacles to healing action.

John S. Wright, "A Photoplate for the Padre," *Callaloo* 13, No. 4 (Fall 1990): 818–19

◈ *Bibliography*

Dear John, Dear Coltrane. 1970.

History Is Your Own Heartbeat. 1971.

Photographs: Negatives: History as Apple Tree. 1972.

Song: I Want a Witness. 1972.

Debridement. 1973.

Nightmare Begins Responsibility. 1975.

To an Old Man Twiddling Thumbs. 1975.

Images of Kin: New and Selected Poems. 1977.

Chant of Saints: A Gathering of Afro-American Literature, Art, and Scholarship
        (editor; with Robert B. Stepto). 1979.

Homage to the New World. 1980.

Rhode Island: Eight Poems. 1981.

Healing Song for the Inner Ear. 1985.

Songlines: Mosaics. 1991.
The Beauty Shell. 1992.
Mr. Knowlton Predicts. 1994.
Every Shut Eye Ain't Asleep: An Anthology of Poetry by African Americans Since 1945 (editor; with Anthony Walton). 1994.

June Jordan
b. 1936

JUNE JORDAN was born in New York on July 9, 1936. Her parents, who were immigrants from Jamaica, wanted their daughter to be a doctor and sent her to the Northfield School, an exclusive girls' school in Massachusetts. One of the few black students in her class, Jordan graduated in 1953 and entered Barnard College in New York City that fall. Two years later she married a Columbia graduate student, Michael Meyer, and abandoned her own studies to take care of their son.

After moving with her husband to Chicago, Jordan returned to Harlem around 1960 and began working on Frederick Wiseman's film about life in the ghetto, *The Cool World*. Around this time she became interested in city planning and met R. Buckminster Fuller, with whom she devised plans for the revitalization of Harlem. In 1969 Fuller nominated Jordan for the Prix de Rome in Environmental Design, which she won. She spent the next year studying at the American University in Rome. Her marriage ended in 1965, and she continued to work as a freelance journalist, writing poetry in her spare time. A long poem titled *Who Look at Me* was published in 1969. It reflects the racial and political concerns that mark much of her poetry.

Since *Who Look at Me* appeared in 1969, Jordan has published seven more volumes of poetry, including *Some Changes* (1971), *New Days* (1974), and *Things That I Do in the Dark: Selected Poetry* (1977). *Passion* (1980) and *Living Room* (1985) gather the poems she wrote between 1977 and 1984, while *Lyrical Campaigns* (1989), *Naming Our Destiny* (1989), and *Haruko/ Love Poetry* (1993) present selections of her best poetic work. Jordan has also written several plays, including *The Issue* (1981) and *Bang Bang Uber Alles* (1986), which have been performed but not published.

In 1971 her first novel, *His Own Where*, was nominated for a National Book Award. This young adult book is written in dialect, referred to as Black English, which aroused much protest from parents who felt that their children should not be guided toward nonstandard English models of writing and dialogue. The case was decided in the Michigan courts, where a judge ruled that Black English was a viable alternative to standard English and could not be banned in public schools. Jordan continued writing fiction for children: the novels *Dry Victories* (1972), *New Life: New Room* (1975), and *Kimako's Story* (1981), and the biography *Fannie Lou Hamer* (1972). She has also published several collections of essays: *Civil Wars* (1981), *On Call* (1985), *Moving towards Home* (1989), and *Technical Difficulties* (1992). These essays, like much of her poetry, express Jordan's challenging and uncompromising views on political, literary, and social issues.

Jordan has held teaching positions at various colleges, including City College of the City University of New York, Connecticut College, Sarah Lawrence, and the State University of New York at Stony Brook. Since 1989 she has been a professor of Afro-American studies and women's studies at the University of California at Berkeley.

◈ *Critical Extracts*

JAMES A. EMANUEL   Opposite the title page of *Who Look at Me* is a painting simply entitled "Portrait of a Gentleman." The gentleman is black. June Jordan's book suggests all black Americans are as unknown as the anonymous early 19th-centuury artist and his subject.

"We do not see those we do not know," she writes. "Love and all varieties of happy concern depend on the discovery of one's self in another. The question of every desiring heart is, thus, 'Who Look at Me?' In a nation suffering fierce hatred, the question—race to race, man to man, and child to child—remains: 'Who Look at Me?' We answer with our lives. Let the human eye begin unlimited embrace of human life."

By intermixing 27 paintings of black Americans from colonial times to the present with an original, understated but intense poem that comments indirectly on the paintings and enhances their meaning, she has given children a splendid opportunity to "begin unlimited embrace of human life."

James A. Emanuel, [Review of *Who Look at Me*], *New York Times Book Review*, 16 November 1969, p. 52

LOUIS L. MARTZ   June Jordan's book, *Some Changes*, inaugurates the new "Black Poets Series" edited by Julius Lester, who provides a brief introduction to the volume, where he says: "For some, her poetry may not qualify as 'black poetry' because she doesn't rage or scream. No, she's quiet, but the intensity is frightening. Her poetry is highly disciplined, highly controlled." It is indeed the skill of her control that is at a first reading most impressive about this volume ⟨. . .⟩ At the same time, the temper of the volume is tough-minded. There is a harsh poem in memory of Martin Luther King; there is a bitter rejoinder to L.B.J.:

> He lost the peace so
> he can keep the peril he
> knows war is nothing like please.

Louis L. Martz, "New Books in Review," *Yale Review* 59, No. 4 (June 1970): 561–62

SARAH WEBSTER FABIO   This book ⟨*His Own Where*⟩ begins: *"You be different from the dead. All them tombstones tearing up the ground, look like a little city, like a small Manhattan . . . Cemetery let them lie there belly close. . . ."*

Whose where? Why cemetery? How sex? At what early age? Between the first and last pages, for Buddy Rivers, 16-year-old protagonist, and his first love, Angela, the only progression is the short sleep in the cemetery, time for her young dream. The story of their trials, the immediacy of their physical attraction is told in flashback and dream flashes, filling the pages of the chapters from one to 17.

June Jordan, author and poet (*Who Look At Me* and *Some Changes*) knows the abandonment of this age. It is a limbo between childhood and young adult, where the void is so great as to be unbearable. It is true here that the mind often stammers for language and the heart only responds to song— to the radio, which you use like a compass on a music map. Angela, at 14, trying to understand Buddy, tells him, "Tune the dial to what you want." There must be bridges if we are to reach our young. *His Own Where* promises to be one. ⟨. . .⟩

Buddy's immediate problem is his father's hospitalization. This, when coupled with his mother's earlier desertion, creates alienation. Although his father has taught him how to fend for himself; how to clean, build, plant, draw plans, he still needs adult contact. At school, he agitates for free and healthy sex, contraceptives, a turned-on lunchroom, coeducational classes in anatomy; his principal suspends him from school and he is told not to return without a parent. Complications arise when he becomes involved with Angela, recognizing her imprisonment and seeing himself as the force of her liberation. Her cab-driving father, who drinks heavily, and her overworked mother, who is a nurse at the hospital, are united in their suspicion of her evilness. She is humiliated and beaten daily to keep her straight. This ends when she is beaten unmercifully; the parents are investigated for child abuse; the home is shattered. ⟨. . .⟩

Buddy sees himself as a man of action. In dream flashes, we see him attending to emergency room patients, liberating Angela from St. Margaret's, a Catholic Home for Girls, filling empty skyscrapers with children who need space to breathe. Finally, he moves with runaway Angela to the cemetery to create, even for a moment, "His own where, own place for loving made for making love."

Sarah Webster Fabio, [Review of *His Own Where*], *New York Times Book Review*, 7 November 1971, pp. 6, 28

JASCHA KESSLER   June Jordan assembles *Some Changes* out of the black experience, and she does so coherently. Her expression is developed out of, or through, a fine irony that manages to control her bitterness, even to dominate her rage against the intolerable, so that she can laugh and cry, be melancholic and scornful and so on, presenting always the familiar faces of human personality, integral personality. She adapts her poems to the occasions that they are properly, using different voices, and levels of thought and direction that are humanly germane and not disembodied rages or vengeful shadows; thus she can create her world, that is, people it for us, for she has the singer's sense of the dramatic and projects herself into a poem to express its special subject, its individuality. Of course it's always her voice, because she has the skill to use it so variously: but the imagination it needs to run through all her changes is her talent. Moreover she seems not to have rejected on principle what has been available to poets in the way of models; in other words, you can see all the white poets she has read, too. She has been assimilating their usages of phrase and stanza; she sees with her own eyes through them, speaks them with her own voice, which is another way of remarking that she is interested in poetry itself. No matter how she will use her poems, and most of them are political in thrust, she has the great good sense, or taste, not to politicize her poetry. There is a difference, even in love poetry, nature poetry, and she has some of that sort, between speaking as yourself and editorializing for others. She is both simple and strong; she is clear in the head, besides. Her compassion and suffering for others is put into lyrical statement, and not into poems which are weapons. I can't shield myself against her, and have no wish to do so, let alone feel myself forced to deliver counter-blows, forced to feel gratuitous pain, gratuitous outrage. It may be because Jordan is a woman, that even her anger and despair are kept within the bounds of the humane, where poetry is too. That is the circle I draw round myself, though it is often broken into, or broken out of, as the case may be. ⟨. . .⟩

When June Jordan goes through her changes, she does it; she doesn't talk about doing it. For us there is pleasure in that, because we can go through them with her. And that means she has poetry near her.

Jascha Kessler, "Trial and Error," *Poetry* 121, No. 5 (February 1973): 301–3

JUNE JORDAN   *The Black Poem . . . Distinctively Speaking.* What is it? Quite apart from individual volumes of Black poetry, I have learned that I hold decidedly different expectations of a Black Anthology, as compared to any other kind. If the single poem, or if the anthology qualifies as distinctively Black, then, as compared to a "white anthology" or a "white poem," I expect the following:

> *A striving for collective voice, or else its actual, happy accomplishment. Even if the person proceeds in the 1st person singular, I expect a distinctively Black poem to speak *for me*-as-part-of-an-*us*, a bounded group that the poem self-consciously assumes as an integral, guiding factor in her/his/their individual art.
>
> *From a reaching for collective voice, as a self-conscious value, it follows that a distinctively Black poem will be accessible to random readers, rather than "hard," or arrantly inaccessible. (This does not mean that prolonged/repeated study will not yield new compulsion. But it does mean that the first time around, which may be an only time, the poem has to "hit" and "stick," clearly, and openly, in a welcoming way.)
>
> *Collective voice necessarily refers to spoken language: Distinctively Black poems characteristically deal memories and possibilities of spoken language, as against literary, or written,

language. This partially accounts for the comparative *directness*
and force of Black poetry; it is an intentionally collective, or
inclusive, people's art meant to be shared, heard and, therefore,
spoken—meant to be as real as bread.

   *Sound patterns, rhythmic movement and change-ups often
figure as importantly as specific words, or images, in distinctively
Black poetry. (Even if the poet says nothing especially new, I can
expect to take pleasure in the musical, textural aspects of the
poem; they will be as intrinsic to the work, as the words.)

To conclude this second point: Distinctively Black poetry adheres to
certain, identifiable values—political and aesthetic—that are open to adop-
tion, enjoyment by anyone. Overriding everything else is the striving and
respect for collective voice. These distinctive values also constitute the
main sum of what I look for, and prize, in The Black Poem.

   June Jordan, "The Black Poet Speaks of Poetry," *American Poetry Review* 3, No. 3
   (May–June 1974): 50

DORIS GRUMBACH   In the *American Poetry Review* issue for May/
June 1974 there are a number of interesting contributions, not the least of
which, to my biased mind, is June Jordan's "The Black Poet Speaks of
Poetry." Her thesis is that "white people/white editors, of major/nationwide
magazines and publishing houses simply do not read and do not value and
do not publish what I would call The Black Poem." There follow citations
of who those major/nationwide magazines are and lo, *The New Republic*
leads all the rest: "Although *TNR* regards itself as a political journal, when
have you seen a political poem published there?"

   You will note that the black poem, in the course of a few sentences, has
transmuted itself to something called the *political* black poem. When I wrote
to her to point out the notice *TNR* has taken of black poets and writers,
she made this distinction: "The kind of poetry I am referring to is Distinctly
Black/Political poetry." Disclaiming my citations of Alice Walker, Sterling
Brown, Barbara Smith, Michael Harper, Ishmael Reed, Ivan Webster as
examples of writers whom *TNR* either has published, is about to publish,
or has dealt with critically, she said none of them qualified under her
stringent definition, which by now had acquired a new word, "Distinctly."
She accused *TNR* of "having been offered, and has steadily refused to publish
Distinctly Black/Political Poetry many times in the last several years" (capital

letters are all hers). My response was that I had no way of knowing for certain from the ms. that the DBP poetry *was* black, or was by a black. So it was entirely possible that, for reasons other than racist, I or my predecessor *had* returned the poetry offered to us by DBP poets. Our correspondence went on in this fashion, she accusing me of "patronizing response" that is "so apparently the nature of your immediate reaction to criticism by Black People."

This drove me not so much to anger as to June Jordan's own poetry, the only DBP poet she cited in her letter as having been rejected by us. (I am constrained to add that when I wrote telling her the names of other noted poets—*white*—whose poems I had rejected she suggested we discontinue our correspondence because she could not read my handwriting.) Her newest book is called *New Days*, published in September of this year by Emerson Hall publishers. It contains some very admirable poems, some very angry ones (clearly what she would call Political), but an even greater number that I would call love poems, or poems of exile and return in her words in which neither the color of the poet nor her politics are apparent. ⟨. . .⟩ There are other very good ones, some I like somewhat less, though they are not necessarily the Distinctly Black Political ones, and a few I liked not at all, convincing me that *TNR* or the other media she accuses—*NY Times, New Yorker, NY Review of Books, American Review, Harper's, Atlantic,* and a number of publishing houses—may have rejected poets for a number of reasons besides racism, among them, the private esthetic of the literary editor, the poetic value of the submitted poem, the state of things at the publishing house at the moment (some publications, like ours, are stocked for a year or more with accepted poetry) and, God help us, space limitations.

Doris Grumbach, "Fine Print," *New Republic*, 9 November 1974, p. 44

NTOZAKE SHANGE   To be in exile & be a poet is to be turned in on oneself / more than to be free of the trauma / there is a case that the whole nation of us who are African are in exile / here in this english-speakin place / but the collections of poems by june jordan ⟨*New Days*⟩ / & joseph jarman ⟨*Black Case*⟩ steer us away from a sense of dislocation / these are exiles returned / & more ourselves than many of us who stayed durin the holocausts & frenzy of sixties / illusions grow in newark & paris / whatever we have stepped outta cycle / outside ourselves / ⟨. . .⟩ aside from

confrontin the vast disarray that is the contemporary world / circlin on
itself / maybe swallowin us / loosin us in the momentum / less we do as
jarman chants:

> can you look at your black skin
> your black self if you got one
> and then do itit is
> time
> say do it yes
> go sing
> the sound the music it is *fire*.

& jordan incants:

> YOUR BODY IS A LONG BLACK WING
> YOUR BODY IS A LONG BLACK WING

we shall twist in despair & distortion / in conceits & wrong information
same as those jarman's ODAWALLA moved through 'the people of the
Sun' teachin through 'the practice of the drum and silent gong' / or jordan's
"Gettin Down to Get Over":

> momma momma
> teach me how to kiss
> the king within the kingdom
> teach how to t.c.b. / to make do
> an be
> like you
> teach me to survive my
> momma
> teach me how to hold a new life
> momma
> help me
> turn the face of history
> *to your face*

movin back in on ourselves / to discover all that is there / is not lovely
worth holdin / but necessary to know / what is real / who we are / jordan &
jarman examine mercilessly their own dilemmas / which become / all of
ours

Ntozake Shange, [Review of *New Days: Poems of Exile and Return*], *Black Scholar* 8,
No. 5 (March 1977): 53–55

DARRYL PINCKNEY   "Passion" is an appropriate title for this gathering of 51 new poems. Miss Jordan, in the preface, calls for a "people's poetry," hailing Walt Whitman and Pablo Neruda as notable examples. It is impossible to accept her charge that there is a "vendetta" against Whitman in America. Even before recent scholarly work that sympathetically discusses the homoerotic in Whitman's sensibility, there was Randall Jarrell's important essay. It is also difficult to understand why the quest for a "New World" poetry must entail the rejection of T. S. Eliot, Robert Lowell, Wallace Stevens or Elizabeth Bishop, four of the finest poets in the language. There is no contradiction in admiring *The Waste Land* as well as lyrics from the streets. One can learn from any tradition.

The poems in *Passion,* mostly in free verse, share many of the themes of the essays. These poems are confidently within an oral tradition, and although the oral can often mean the merely rhetorical, Miss Jordan serves the tradition well, with a sensitive ear for the vernacular, for the ironic tone. ⟨. . .⟩

The energy and seriousness of these poems are impressive and, like the essays, they are the work of a writer of integrity and will.

> Darryl Pinckney, [Review of *Civil Wars* and *Passion*], *New York Times Book Review*, 9 August 1981, p. 26

PETER ERICKSON   Those who come to June Jordan's poetry because of her reputation as a strictly political poet will be surprised at the large number of love poems and of her constant recourse to this genre. Setting aside political concerns, the poet indulges her erotic longing: "I can use no historic no national no family bliss / I need an absolutely one to one a seven-day kiss" ("Alla Tha's All right, but," *Passion*). What is here a raucous assertion and celebration of sexual need has earlier—more often than not—been an expression of intense vulnerability in love. Jordan's first collection of poetry, *Some Changes* (1971), is divided into four untitled sections, the implicit rationale for section two being love. This second section, arguably the richest in the volume, has an important long-term effect on Jordan's overall poetic development, thus providing a key to that development.

An atmosphere of deep malaise—interrupted by occasional, though still muted, bursts of erotic release of self-affirmation—dominate section two of

Some Changes. The last poem of section one, "I Live in Subtraction," makes the transition to the next section by firmly setting a dejected tone. Though "I" is the first word and subject of every line, the action of the poems is to reduce rather than enlarge this self, the continual subtracting effect culminating in the contemplation of suicidal gesture: "I can end a dream with death." We are not told how this psychological state came about, though we might guess the poet has been hurt by love when she says that she has forgotten or directs herself to "forget you name." Her demoralization is presented as a given, its origin and cause left a mystery.

Nor are we told the reason for the sadness in "My Sadness Sits Around Me." This title is reiterated in the poem's first and last lines, creating a literal enclosure which represents the emotional isolation that envelops the poet. We are forced simply to note and to accept this sadness which the poems gingerly explore without explaining more precisely. The same image of being cut and sealed off is reproduced in "Nobody Riding the Roads Today," where the last stanza can only repeat the first: "Nobody riding the roads today / But I hear the living rush / far away from my heart." The formal circularity mimics and heightens the poet's desolation.

The troubled mood of these poems can be usefully associated with the general background of Jordan's life during this period, so long as we do not insist on a one-to-one correspondence by which the life is supposed to explain the poetry. The two crucial events of which the reader needs to be aware are, in successive years, Jordan's divorce from her husband (1965) and her mother's suicide: first with a brief mention in *Civil Wars* (p. xvii), then at length in her second address at Barnard College. In the latter, Jordan presents her recollection of the suicide with such vivid immediacy that it is almost as if it were occurring in the present rather than fifteen years ago, as if Jordan must relive her confused feelings in order finally to attain expiation.

> Peter Erickson, "The Love Poetry of June Jordan," *Callaloo* 9, No. 1 (Winter 1986): 223–24

SARAH BENTON   The threat of annihilation by white America is the pulse of June Jordan's writings. This makes hers a rare voice in the refined world of the political essay. From her account of a riot in Harlem in 1964 to her oration for the death of ⟨Jesse⟩ Jackson's Presidential bid in

1988 she measures all political movement against this irreducible standard: does it combat the likelihood of death by violence, by suffering or by suicide? With her fingers on this fear, she keeps herself in the bloodstream of the peoples to whom she feels herself thrice kin: blacks, women and the third world. For unlike them, June Jordan has earned an audience through her work as poet, public speaker and academic. ⟨. . .⟩

When she sees the world in simple black and white she jeopardises the fragile alliance for which she speaks, as in her attack on a group of Hassidic Jews. But she is again rare in her efforts to describe the conflicts between black, and women's and third world movements. Rarer still in seeing the solution in love, as in: "It is against such suicide, and is against such deliberate strangulation of the possible lives of . . . powerless peoples . . . everywhere that I work and live, now, as a feminist, trusting that I will learn to love myself well enough to love you . . ." The vulnerability of a form of writing that does not investigate, or write directly from, the lives of the oppressed, is that it can fall into a sententious moralism. Most of the time, the power of her words carries her argument through.

Sarah Benton, "A Rare Voice" [Review of *Moving towards Home* and *Lyrical Campaigns*], *New Statesman and Nation*, 7 April 1989, p. 46

MARILYN HACKER   June Jordan's new book ⟨*Naming Our Destiny*⟩ is an anthology of causes won, lost, moot, private and public, forgotten and remembered. Anyone who doubts the relevance and timeliness of poetry ought to read Jordan, who has been among the front-line correspondents for almost thirty years and is still a young and vital writer. So should anyone who wants his or her curiosity and indignation aroused, or wants to read a voice that makes itself heard on the page. ⟨. . .⟩

What makes politically engaged poetry unique, and primarily poetry before it is politics? Jordan's political poetry is, at its best, the opposite of polemic. It is not written with a preconceived, predigested agenda of ideas and images. Rather, the process of composition is, or reproduces, the process of discovering how events are connected, how oppressions are analogous, how lives interpenetrate. Jordan's poems are strongest when they deal with interior issues, when she begins with a politics of the personal, with the articulate and colloquial voice of, if you will, "a woman speaking to women" (and to men) and ranges outward to illustrate how issues, lives and themes are inextricably interconnected. ⟨. . .⟩

How can a white critic say that a black poet has a spectacular sense of rhythm? Modestly, or courageously. Jordan writes (mostly) free verse. Many writers of free verse produce a kind of syntactically disjointed prose, expecting line breaks to provide a concentration and a syncopation not achieved by means of language. In Jordan's best poems there is a strong, audible, rhythmic counterpart to the line breaks, a rhythm as apparent to the reader as it is to the auditor who hears the poet deliver them. This is true of her poems that have been set to music by Bernice Reagon of the a cappella group Sweet Honey in the Rock ("Alla Tha's All Right, but" and "A Song of Sojourner Truth"), but it's equally true of dramatic monologues like "The Talking Back of Miss Valentine Jones" and "Unemployment Monologue," and of the interior monologues evolving into public declaration, like "Poem About My Rights."

The fluid speech-become-aria quality of Jordan's free verse poems also makes them difficult to quote, though never difficult to remember. They are not made of lapidary lines and epigrammatic stanzas. They gather momentum verbally, aurally. Most often, the effects of the voice and the statement are cumulative.

Why is this important? Because it fixes the poems in the reader's memory; because it makes these poems, even those on the most serious subjects, paradoxically fun to read. It is a reason for these texts to be written in verse, to be poetry. They are not fiction, journalism, essays or any other form of prose, even when they share qualities with these other genres. When Jordan's poems are unambiguous and straightforward, as well as when they are figurative, ironic or complex, her words create a music, create voices, which readers must hear the way they were written. Her poems read themselves to us.

Marilyn Hacker, "Provoking Engagement," *Nation*, 29 January 1990, pp. 135–36

DAVID BAKER   The issues of race and self-reliance (artistic and otherwise) are not the only political topics to which Jordan returns persistently. She speaks searingly in behalf of the hitherto silenced or subjugated: women, the poor and hungry, the imprisoned, the politically tyrannized in Nicaragua, the enslaved in Manhattan. I can think of very few contemporary

American poets who have been so willing to take on other people's troubles; decidedly, this is not the poetry of a sheltered, introspective confessional, not the work of a tidy scholar or a timid dormouse. Jordan's variety of poetic stances enacts her drive to connect and represent, for in addition to her principal mode of delivery—the poet talking directly to an audience—she also speaks through a number of other characters in persona poems, giving sympathetic articulation to lives, idioms, and concerns beyond her own. Like Carl Sandburg, she makes public art out of public occasion and the available word, and she does so with confidence and conviction.

David Baker, "Probable Reason, Possible Joy," *Kenyon Review* 14, No. 1 (Winter 1992): 154–55

ADELE LOGAN ALEXANDER   *Technical Difficulties* is a book about America—subtitled, as it is, "The State of the Union." This is America observed and found both noble and nurturing, brutal and malformed—often at the same time—by a brilliant and mature African American scholar who has looked at our country with her own unique clarity of vision and focus. Her subjects include affectionate tributes to her own Jamaican heritage ("For My American Family") and that of those other immigrants, not the Poles, Russians, Irish, or Germans but the too-often invisible and darker-skinned newcomers whose journeys through New York harbor, past the Statue of Liberty and Ellis Island, have been largely overlooked in our romantic imaging of the American melting-pot. 〈. . .〉

Jordan tackles and dissects familiar themes: family, race, neighborhood ("two-and-a-half years ago," she writes, "I . . . returned to my beloved Brooklyn where, I knew, my eyes and ears would never be lonely for diversi-fied, loud craziness and surprise"), the love of men, women and children, the mutable American Constitution, education, creativity and politics (of nations and of sexuality, the "correct" and the "incorrect"). For many years she has been a teacher and writer, with several books of essays, including *Civil Wars, Moving towards Home* and *On Call*, to her credit, as well as collections of poetry, including the less well-known *Who Look at Me*— poems for children about African American artists and their work. These new essays, though they cover a variety of topics, come together into a unified and consistent whole. Adapting the Cubists' technique of viewing a subject from many different perspectives at once, Jordan sees all sides and then reassembles the fragments into a consistent, if multifaceted, whole. One should not say *Technical Difficulties* is "better" than what preceded it, but it is surely "more," and though a little of Jordan's well-muscled prose goes a long way, in this case it is also true that "more is better." ⟨. . .⟩

Jordan vigorously rants at our familiar "emperors," from George Washington to Ronald Reagan. She reminds us of the meaty, but non-mainstream, substance that has been deliberately omitted and obscured from our educational, cultural and political lives. I look to her not only to rail at the way things have been ("if you're not an American white man and you travel through the traditional twistings and distortions of the white Western canon, you stand an excellent chance of ending up *nuts*," she says) but to knock our white, male-centered world cockeyed from its moorings and provide more of the revised visions that we need.

Adele Logan Alexander, "Stirring the Melting-Pot," Women's Review of Books 10, No. 7 (April 1993): 6–7

Bibliography

Who Look at Me. 1969.

The Voice of the Children (editor; with Terri Bush). 1970.

Soulscript: Afro-American Poetry (editor). 1970.

Some Changes. 1971.

His Own Where. 1971.

Dry Victories. 1972.

Fannie Lou Hamer. 1972.

Poem: On Moral Leadership as a Political Dilemma (Watergate, 1973). 1973.

New Days: Poems of Exile and Return 1970–1972. 1974.

New Life, New Room. 1975.

Niagara Falls. 1977.

Things That I Do in the Dark: Selected Poetry. 1977.

Unemployment: Monologue. 1978.

Passion: New Poems 1977–1980. 1980.

Kimako's Story. 1981.

Civil Wars. 1981.

Living Room: New Poems. 1985.

On Call: Political Essays. 1985.

Bobo Goetz a Gun. 1985.

Naming Our Destiny: New and Selected Poems. 1989.

Moving towards Home: Political Essays. 1989.

Lyrical Campaigns: Selected Poems. 1989.

Technical Difficulties: African-American Notes on the State of the Union. 1992.

Haruko/Love Poetry: New and Selected Poems. 1993.

Etheridge Knight
b. 1931

ETHERIDGE KNIGHT was born on April 19, 1931, in Paducah, Kentucky, in a large family that included four sisters and two brothers. Poverty was an ever-present factor in his youth, and as an adolescent Knight learned more from the men with whom he congregated in bars and poolrooms than from the two years he spent in high school before dropping out. At that point, when he was fourteen, he ran away from home and developed an addiction to narcotics. Later, at age seventeen, he joined the army.

Knight spent the years 1947–51 in the army as a medical technician, being sent first to Korea and then to Guam. He suffered some unspecified injury, either physical or psychological, that caused a continuance of his addiction to drugs. Knight's life seemed virtually over when, in seeking money to support his habit, he was convicted in 1960 of robbery in Indianapolis and sentenced to ten to twenty-five years at the Indiana State Prison in Michigan, Indiana. This experience, however, proved the source of a new phase of his existence.

As a boy Knight had been taught "toasts," oral narrative poetry in rhymed couplets dealing largely with sex, crime, and violence and employing figures out of black folklore and street slang. While in prison, where he spent eight years, Knight refined these toasts into poetry and by 1963 was submitting his work for publication. At the time of his release in 1968, Knight had developed friendships with other important black writers and publishers, including Gwendolyn Brooks, Sonia Sanchez, and Dudley Randall. Randall published Knight's first book, *Poems from Prison* (1968), with his Broadside Press; Brooks wrote an introduction to the volume; and Knight married Sanchez upon his release.

Knight's first volume—as well as an anthology he assembled, *Black Voices from Prison* (1970), first published in an Italian translation as *Voce negre dal carcere* (1968)—reveals an unmistakably male orientation and an uncompromising anger at the oppression of black people, but it is leavened with moving paeans to black political and literary figures (including Malcolm X and Langston Hughes) as well as sensitive poems to lovers and family members. Knight uses his prison experience as a wide-ranging metaphor for the imprisonment of all black Americans in a racist society.

For several years after leaving prison, Knight served as writer-in-residence at various universities, including the University of Pittsburgh (1968–69), the University of Hartford (1969–70), and Lincoln University in Jefferson City, Missouri (1972). He was also the recipient of several awards and grants, including one by the National Endowment for the Arts and a Guggenheim Fellowship. His personal life, however, continued to be plagued by turbulence and drug addiction. He divorced Sonia Sanchez and in 1973 married Mary Ann McAnally, with whom he had two children; after another divorce he married Charlene Blackburn, with whom he had one child.

Knight issued *Belly Song and Other Poems* in 1973; it was nominated for both the Pulitzer Prize and the National Book Award. This volume develops many of the themes found in his first volume; some of the poems utilize rhythms and other techniques Knight learned when spending a summer in Nigeria with Wole Soyinka. By the late 1970s Knight had moved to Memphis, Tennessee, and in 1980 *Born of a Woman* was released by Houghton Mifflin; it was Knight's first important publication by a major trade publisher. This volume represented the height of Knight's fame; since then he has published relatively little, although a further selection of his work, *The Essential Etheridge Knight*, appeared in 1986. Nevertheless, Knight's reputation as a poet whose work is both accessible and stylistically rich is assured.

▣ *Critical Extracts*

JEWEL C. LATIMORE   "Vital. Vital," says Gwendolyn Brooks in the preface ⟨to *Poems from Prison*⟩—and truth is there. Urgent are his words. And strong. And hard. Etheridge Knight brings the strength and hardness of black existence through his poetry to his people.

One does not look for the white aesthetic of universalism in this poetry. Mr. Knight asked in an earlier issue of this publication ("Black Writers' Views on Literary Lions and Values," Jan. 1968), "Where is the universality of the human situation?" Indeed, black experience has never been a "universal" one encompassing all humanity, but, rather, experience spawned of Western pseudo-society, long endured by, and peculiar to, black people—

> ... No universal laws
> Of human misery
> Create a common cause
> Or common history
> That ease black people's pains
> Nor break black people's chains.

It is this peculiar experience that Mr. Knight has used to create his art ⟨...⟩

Etheridge Knight's poetry is just that—poetry. And as such, it is art, and a living experience for the reader.

> Jewel C. Latimore, [Review of *Poems from Prison*], *Negro Digest* 17, No. 9 (July 1968): 82, 84

PATRICIA LOGGINS HILL   Etheridge Knight's prison poetry, by means of its temporal/spatial references and movements, liberates the minds and spirits of his readers, and of his people as a whole. At times, the poet leads the reader from a concrete definition of space into a space that refuses definition. And he controls time with the same fluidity. Space can be a movement which is defined through time, as in "The Idea of Ancestry"; and time can be, as the poem "He Sees through Stone" demonstrates, a movement defined through space. In "The Violent Space," these patterns regularly reverse, yet the reader is never lost inside the structure of Knight's poems because, at one point or another, the poet offers a concrete reference grounded in either time or space. In "The Violent Space," for example, the poet says, in the third stanza, "You are all of seventeen and as alone now / In your pain as you were ..."; in "He Sees through Stone," the reader knows where the old man is sitting; and, in "The Idea of Ancestry," the poet stares at his prison cell wall. The poet's constant use of such references and time/space movements serve an important function: They allow him to merge his consciousness with the consciousness of his people. As a result, his prison experiences become a microcosm of the collective experiences of Black people.

That Knight means for his prison experiences to serve as a microcosm of the freedomless void that his people are experiencing is made clear in the "Preface" to his anthology *Black Voices from Prison:*

> From the time the first of our fathers were bound and shackled
> and herded into the dark hold of a "Christian" slaveship—right
> on up to the present day, the whole experience of the black man
> in America can be summed up in one word: prison . . . and it is
> all too clear that there is a direct relationship between men
> behind prison walls and men behind myriad walls that permeate
> society.

While Knight was "inside" prison, he was constantly aware that other Blacks resided in the "larger prison outside." The "inside" and "outside" prison experiences become interchangeable within the structure of Knight's poems by means of his concrete references and temporal/spatial movements. These references and movements allow the poet to lead his reader, via the heightened experience of good poetry, to a mythic consciousness in which all space is "the violent space" and all time is eternal. Knight imparts this consciousness, its time and its space, to his people as a unifying force. The human being's particular way of experiencing time and space is his only way of knowing life itself. It *is* life for him, it *is* vital. If this conception of time and space is held in common by a people, they achieve a group identity.

Knight brings this conception of group identification to the new Black aesthetic. Yet, ironically, it is this conception that sets him apart from the other new Black poets. While Baraka, Madhubuti, and Major see themselves as poets/priests—as leaders, teachers, and/or spokesmen of the Black revolutionary movement of the 1960s and '70s—, Knight sees himself as being one with Black people. Whereas Major, Madhubuti, and Baraka seem to share W. E. B. Du Bois's vision of the social structure of the Black community—that a "talented tenth," a Black intelligentsia, must lead and uplift the masses of Black people—, Knight identifies closely with the folk. While the new Black poets see themselves functioning much like the "old black one" with "the secret eyes," the shaman and the teacher of ritual and tradition in Knight's poem "He Sees through Stone," Knight sees himself as one of the "black cats" in the circle of ritual. He is one with the other participants, his race as a whole. Knight's reliance on various time/space elements for group identification is successful: His poetry functions as a vital, liberating force for the new rites. As Gwendolyn Brooks has said of

Knight's poetry in her preface to his *Poems from Prison*, the writing embodies "a Blackness that is at once inclusive, possessed and given, freed and terrible and beautiful." This is the particular way of living Blackness that Etheridge Knight expresses.

> Patricia Loggins Hill, " 'The Violent Space': The Function of the New Black Aesthetic in Etheridge Knight's Prison Poetry," *Black American Literature Forum* 14, No. 3 (Fall 1980): 119–20

DARRYL PINCKNEY   The poems brought together in *Born of a Woman* are, for the most part, simple to the point of being facile, even crude.

> Poets are naturally meddlers. They meddle in other people's lives and they meddle in their own, always searching and loving and questioning and digging into this or that. Poets meddle with whores—they meddle with politicians, zen, the church, god, and children; they meddle with monkeys, freaks, soft warm lovers, flowers, whiskey, dope and other artists—especially jive-assed doctors.

Knight takes a very funky posture in his Preface and this posture is the depressing thing about this collection. Knight's subjects include the loneliness of prison cells, women leaving, trying to kick drugs, black musicians, family feeling, Malcolm X, politics—a wide range of experience and admirable concerns. That is not the problem. Anything can be the occasion for a poem. But not just anything on the page makes for a poem. Etheridge Knight writes in a loose, funky style associated with the Sixties and black militancy, a period that was loud and noisy with talk against the tyranny of so-called white poetics. ⟨. . .⟩

The world Knight portrays in his poems is often harsh and brutal. He aspires to a language that will remain true to these experiences, words that will not give any falsifying distance. It makes for a very vigorous and immediate style that is often successful. ⟨. . .⟩ Far too often, however, the poems evince that uninteresting tendency to feel that a *rap* is all that need be offered. ⟨. . .⟩ A rap is not enough, however true, politically, the message is taken. Raps that are trying to pass for poems have a strange redundant quality: we feel we know all this already and not much is going on in the poem to make us see or feel this in a new way. The ordinariness of the imagery makes the poems degenerate into sentimentality, which is a disservice to Knight's capacity for tender expression. "Our love is a rock against the wind, / Not soft like silk or lace." Another danger of the rap is that it dates quickly.

Darryl Pinckney, "You're in the Army Now," *Parnassus: Poetry in Review* 9, No. 1 (Spring–Summer 1981): 310–11

CRAIG WERNER   Knight's aesthetic as reflected both in his metrics and his imagery ⟨. . .⟩ always balanced the demands of Poet, Poem, and People, granting equal attention to the aesthetic demands of the language and to the impulse toward self-expression. This synthetic approach raised questions from the beginning of Knight's career. Even while identifying *Poems from Prison* as a "major announcement," Haki R. Madhubuti (then writing as Don L. Lee) questioned the propriety of Knight's allusions to Euro-American culture. Rather than abandoning such allusions, Knight soon relinquished the emphasis on a separate black aesthetic. Even while altering his stance, however, he maintained a strong sense of the black populist heritage: "Our poetry will always speak mainly to black people, but I don't see it being as narrow in the 70s as it was in the 60s." Extending this argument, Knight proposed a version of universalism based on shared emotional experience, rather than of specific images or forms: "My poetry is also important to white people because it invokes feelings. . . . The feelings are common, whether or not the situations that create the feelings are common . . . I might feel fear in a small town in Iowa. You might be afraid if you get off the subway in Harlem. It's the same fear, but the situations are different." This widening of the definition of the People to include any reader capable of responding to his emotional impulse in no way entails a movement away from populism. The lasting contribution of the Black Aesthetic to Knight's poetics lies precisely in his continuing commitment to the People: "I pay attention only to the people in the audience. If they don't dig it, then it ain't nothing no way."

This commitment to the People, even when "it is lonely . . . and sometimes / THE PEOPLES can be a bitch" ("A Poem to Galway Kinnell"), defines Knight's poetic achievement throughout his career. As the structure of *Born of a Woman* indicates, Knight has approached this commitment from a variety of perspectives. Part I, titled "Inside-Out," focuses on Knight's awakening in prison and his dawning awareness of his relationship with an outside world. Part II, "Outside-In," concentrates on his self-exploration—the Poet is one-third of Knight's aesthetic trinity—once released. Part III, "All About—And Back Again," reemphasizes that, whatever his explorations, the Poet Knight ultimately returns to the base he finds in the People and expresses in the Poems.

> Craig Werner, "The Poet, the Poem, the People: Etheridge Knight's Aesthetic,"
> *Obsidian* 7, Nos. 2–3 (Summer–Winter 1981): 9–10

HOWARD NELSON   "The Idea of Ancestry" is a poem about what it means to belong to a family—not just a nuclear family, but a large weaving of people that spreads out to include several branches and generations—and what it feels like to be isolated from it. The poem is in two parts. It begins with the poet lying on his prison bunk gazing at the forty-seven photographs of relatives he has taped to his wall. Looking at them, he gives a series of small catalogues of connectedness: "I know / their dark eyes, they know mine. I know their style, they know mine . . . / I have at one time or another been in love with my mother, / 1 grandmother, 2 sisters, 2 aunts (1 sent to the asylum) . . . / I have the same name as 1 grandfather, 3 cousins, 3 nephews, / and 1 uncle. . . ." The pictures and his thoughts make him feel part of a vital human flow—the ongoing, complex, living thing a family that has a sense of itself can be—but at the same time sharpens his loneliness. This is particularly so because the uncle at the end of the last list, it turns out, has long since vanished: "disappeared when he was 15, just took / off and caught a freight (they say)." He is at once a part of the family and "an empty space." Year after year he has been discussed by the family, especially by the ninety-three-year-old matriarch of the clan who is the keeper of the family Bible and the symbol of family roots and tradition. "There is no / place in her Bible for 'whereabouts unknown.'" The uncle's absence is a presence when the family gathers, and the poet, alone in his cell, ripped out of the fabric by a prison sentence, is haunted by the feeling that he has more in common with his uncle than a name.

The second section of the poem is a flashback to a family reunion which took place a year earlier. Both parts of the poem are set in fall, the season when the poet's yearning to get back to the family is always strongest—

appropriate because of Thanksgiving as well as more subtle mortal reasons. With his characteristic vivid conciseness, Knight describes the longing to get back among family and family places—as basic as the instinctual drive of a migrating salmon—and the pleasure and ease of finally being on home ground again. But this time too he was pulled away from the family, in this case by a narcotics habit which forced him to leave and in turn led to his imprisonment. Then the poem returns to the present and the cell with its silent "47 black faces." The poet's thoughts have made him very restless: he paces, flops down on his bed—torn by his double sense of connectedness and isolation. He repeats a sort of invocation of the lone individual to the family spirit, spoken earlier as well—"I am all of them, / they are all of me, I am me, they are thee"—, then closes with another specter of loneliness and the breakdown of his life-lines within the family: ". . . and I have no children / to float in the space between." In these last two statements the poem follows its fundamental curve, away from abstract formulation of an "idea of ancestry" into definition in terms of a field of emotions grounded in concrete situations and images. The idea may remain unparaphrasable, but when Knight has finished his poem it has become a solid, subtle, moving thing.

Howard Nelson, "Belly Songs: The Poetry of Etheridge Knight," *Hollins Critic* 18, No. 5 (December 1981): 6–7

UNSIGNED   Etheridge Knight became and has remained best known as a prison-poet, whose settings discover an ultimate metaphor for the condition of being a black male in the United States. The typing is crude but valid: Knight's work is truly subterranean, tense with the hardness, paranoia, and bitter humor that have characterized criminal poets since Villon. But Knight is more than simply a talented psychopath, and his poetry develops a remarkable range. Once one has discarded the inevitable, programmed poems of propaganda, there remains a substantial body of work that is distinguished both for subject matter and technique. There is, for instance, a scattering of striking haiku—

> Eastern guard tower
> glints in sunset. Convicts rest
> like lizards on rocks.

—and there are some surprisingly subtle and interesting experiments with internal rhyme. There are intensely painful love poems, hallucinations, blue raps, folk narratives, and meditations upon ancestry that assume naturally a biblical pace and diction. The theme is freedom, the need of the spirit for the wind and the sea, and Knight usually invokes it ironically—by the definition of his world as both physical and psychological prison. He has distinguished his voice and craftsmanship among contemporary poets, and he deserves a large, serious audience for his work.

Unsigned, [Review of *Born of a Woman*], *Virginia Quarterly Review* 57, No. 1 (Winter 1981): 27

H. BRUCE FRANKLIN   *Born of a Woman* offers a good introduction to the achievements of modern black prison poetry, for Knight has been one of its leaders in developing a powerful literary mode based on the rhythms of black street talk, blues, ballads, and "toasts." The volume includes such now classic poems as "Hard Rock Returns to Prison from the Hospital for the Criminal Insane," "The Idea of Ancestry," "For Freckle-Faced Gerald," and "It Was a Funky Deal" from his *Prison Poems* of 1968 ⟨. . .⟩ as well as the best of *Belly Song and Other Poems* (1973). Knight compresses the essential difference between the situations of black and white prisoners into a brilliantly ironic jewel of a poem, "The Warden Said to Me the Other Day," in which he assumes an old slave stance while outfoxing the master:

> The Warden said to me the other day
> (innocently, I think), "Say, etheridge,
> why come the black boys don't run off
> like the white boys do?"
> I lowered my jaw and scratched my head
> and said (innocently, I think), "Well, suh,
> I ain't for sure, but I reckon it's cause
> we ain't got nowheres to run to."

H. Bruce Franklin, "Hard Cell," *Village Voice*, 27 July 1982, p. 37

ETHERIDGE KNIGHT   *Interviewer* ⟨Steven C. Tracy⟩: Some critics have distinguished your poetry from some of your contemporaries, specifically some of the early Broadside poets, by pointing to the personal reflection and perhaps introspection in some of your poems that was absent in some of the other poets. In other words, some of your poems probe inner conflicts and turmoils of the individual, while many of the other poets spoke for the collective. But you've also suggested that the Black artist must "perceive and conceptualize the collective apsirations, the collective vision of Black people, and through his art form give back to the people the truth he has gotten from them." Do you agree with what the critics have said about you in deference to your other contemporary poets? And how do you reconcile the individual with the collective aspirations—the exploration of the inner conflicts with presenting the collective aspirations of Black people?

Knight: Well, you listen. You pay attention to what's going on outside of you and what's going inside of you, and if you pretty much tell the truth, express in such a way that your audience recognizes it's valid and recognizes those same feelings. Again, the poetry is evocative, and then you know that you're generally speaking the truth. You know, we might react differently but if a three-headed bird flew in this window, I'm going to get scared, you know you might keep a cool face, you know. I might jump up and say "aah." If I know myself pretty well, I know you scared too. I operate from that point. I believe that one has to move from the "I," subjective, through the verb, to the "we." If I verbalize, see, I am a Black male in this country and if I, through my own self-examination, expressed that, I bet you I'm pretty much going to be hitting what most other Black males feel. A poet should speak only for himself; the "I." That's what always gets me when I hear some of the critics talking about "I've read this book objectively." There ain't no such thing. As soon as I hear this word "objectively" I throw it away because I know they're bullshitting. There is no way you can approach art objectively. Art is not an objective thing, you know, but in our language now when one says I'm being objective, that's as if to say I'm being truthful. That's a lie. The truth is more in subjectivity than objectivity.

Interviewer: Back in the late 60's and early 70's Black writers shared a common purpose, a common objective: to use their art as a vehicle toward social, political, moral revolution. Many seem to have spoken as a collective, but now there are many voices addressing many and varied issues. What do you feel accounts for the changes that have occurred among Black writers over the last decade and a half; or do you think it has changed?

Knight: I think it's changed somewhat and one of the reasons is America's ability to co-opt. Some Black poets, like any other poets, were simply protesting. And all that you have to do when someone is protesting is to satisfy what it is they are protesting. Poetry in the world, all art, is essentially revolutionary because it essentially appeals to freedom. And art cannot exist in an oppressive society and the more oppressive the society, the louder the artist will work, you know, whether it's a poet or painter or what. Sometimes they will escape. It happened in America especially among a lot of the whites, they expatriated. Take Pound and Eliot; rather than become revolutionary they retreated into the past, into Europe, history, and their vision became narrow. They had no vision of a bright future. Some of them jump off bridges, some find some kind of retreat into the past—Hemingway, for instance. All of that whole time of expatriating of American artists was because of the oppressiveness. We were a country who was concerned more with the material than the immaterial. This country is very culturally deprived. I often laugh when they say minority children are being culturally deprived. Bullshit! You know, when their lives are filled with art, with music, song and dance and sight. Somebody made a statement about critics and their evaluation of art and how they always seem to "be objective" in a vacuum, and art does not exist in a vacuum. Art exists within a context, a political, economic, and social context and the only real critics of any artist is that artist's audience. You know what I mean. Really.

Etheridge Knight, "A *MELUS* Interview: Etheridge Knight," *MELUS* 12, No. 2 (Summer 1985): 16–17

RAYMOND R. PATTERSON   Many of the twenty-eight poems first published in *Poems from Prison* ⟨. . .⟩ appear in *The Essential Etheridge Knight*. They are placed among work drawn from two later collections, *Belly Songs and Other Poems* (1973) and *Born of a Woman* (1980), followed by a section of recent poems. While *Poems from Prison* opens with "Cell Song," a grim statement of alienation ("I alone / tread the red circle / and twist the space / with speech") softened by earthy humor ("Come . . . sprinkle / salt on the tail / of a girl"), *The Essential Etheridge Knight* opens with a bit of flim-flam: "Split my skin / with the rock / of love old / as the rock / of Moses / my poems / love you" ("Genesis"). But once inside the book, we encounter the familiar gallery of doomed prison inmates: Hard Rock, "known not to take no shit," until "the doctors . . . bored a hole in his head, / Cut out part of his brain, and shot electricity / Through the rest"; the aged

convict who "sees through stone," "who under prison skies / sits pressed by
the sun / against the western wall"; the raped Freckled-Faced Gerald, "sun-
kissed ten thousand times on the nose / and cheeks . . . Pigmeat / for the
buzzards to eat." We meet again the doomed of society's larger prison: the
streetwalker and her impotent lover in "As You Leave Me"; the ineffectual
brother in "The Violent Space"; the almost-saved prodigal in "The Idea of
Ancestry"; the patriotic Flukum, the soldier home from war, "shot in his
great wide chest, bedecked with good / conduct ribbons" ("A Poem for
Black Relocation Centers"). Here, too, are the elegies for Langston Hughes
and Dinah Washington, and four poems for Malcolm X, one addressed to
Gwendolyn Brooks: "The Sun came, Miss Brooks. / And we goofed the
whole thing." So much doom, frustration, and failure redeemed by poetic
fears of visual and psychic accuracy, such poignant detailing of loss: "In the
August grass / Struck by the last rays of sun / The cracked teacup screams."
The essence of Etheridge Knight? ⟨. . .⟩

Dedicated to members of the poet's family, *The Essential Etheridge Knight*
closes with "Rehabilitation & Treatment in the Prisons of America," a
parable that casts prison administration as a mechanism for destroying blacks,
based on their acknowledgment of identity: "He was black, so he rushed—
ran—through that door—and fell nine stories to the street." It is significant
that Knight dedicated *Poems from Prison,* his first book, to "all the other
black cats everywhere." Black cats, folk belief has it, have nine lives and
always land on their feet. Indispensable Etheridge Knight? "Can there
anything / good come out of / prison" asks the poet of "Cell Song." To
read *The Essential Etheridge Knight* leaves no doubt.

    Raymond R. Patterson, "Black Cats," *American Book Review* 9, No. 4 (September–
October 1987): 1

REGINALD GIBBONS   Hard Rock, along with Gerald, Flukum,
Shine, Pooky Dee and others, here ⟨in *The Essential Etheridge Knight*⟩ rise
side by side out of Knight's anti-Spoon-River. Some would call the power
of Knight's poetry "raw"; it is certainly, on many occasions, "political," in
the sense of voicing repeatedly the violence to body and spirit of the history
of racism. What a reading of this selection of poems most reveals is that while
the feeling in Knight's poems is characteristically strong and uninhibited, his
vision of the life he puts into his poems is complicated, and his poetics

capacious. His technical prowess ranges from blunt harshness to sudden, very surprising shifts toward rhetorical tropes of subtlety. This is apparent even in the famous "Hard Rock," which blends a compressed representation of street and cell talk with a fourteener couplet:

> "Ol Hard Rock! man, that's one crazy nigger."
> And then the jewel of a myth that Hard Rock had once bit
> A screw on the thumb and poisoned him with syphilitic
>   spit.

The strength of this is not that Knight may have studied some earlier English poetry and adapted an odd sort of line with historical precedent—like a jazz musician quoting in the midst of the blues a classic and surprising show-tune. It's rather that Knight's work, for all its features that arise from black speech and song, remains open to so many other possibilities of language and therefore of poetry in English. His work is not narrow. And his utilization of poetic precedent is unusual—perhaps something that only a black American poet is likely to be able to do. That is, although he has taken freely what he has needed from that Anglo-American poetic tradition as we have it in our available texts, he has not suppressed the language of his own social being.

Reginald Gibbons, [Review of *The Essential Etheridge Knight*], *TriQuarterly* No. 71 (Winter 1988): 222–23

◈ *Bibliography*

Poems from Prison. 1968.

2 Poems for Black Relocation Centers. 1968.

Voce negre dal carcere (with others). 1968, 1970 (as *Black Voices from Prison*).

For Black Poets Who Think of Suicide. 1970.

A Poem for Brother/Man: After His Recovery from an O.D. (with others). 1972.

Belly Song and Other Poems. 1973.

Born of a Woman: New and Selected Poems. 1980.

The Essential Etheridge Knight. 1986.

Genesis. 1988.

Audre Lorde
1934–1992

AUDRE GERALDINE LORDE was born on February 18, 1934, in New York City, to Frederic Byron and Linda Belmar Lorde. She attended public schools in Manhattan and, at an early age, began to write poetry. In 1951 she enrolled at Hunter College, working at a number of odd jobs to support herself and graduating in 1959. In 1954 she spent a year studying at the National University of Mexico.

Shortly after graduation Lorde entered a library science program at Columbia University, receiving the M.L.S. degree in 1961. During the next seven years Lorde worked at Mount Vernon Public Library and the Town School Library in New York City. In her spare time she wrote poetry and in 1968 her first collection, *The First Cities,* appeared. This volume received little attention but was praised for its originality of language. In that same year Lorde received a National Endowment for the Arts grant, resigned her position as librarian, and became poet-in-residence at Tougaloo College in Mississippi. Tougaloo presented Lorde with her first reprieve from urban life. The city, however, is a significant influence in Lorde's poems, being generally a place of confinement and deterioration.

Lorde's second book of poetry, *Cables to Rage* (1970), was published in England but distributed in America by the Broadside Press. The poems, like those in *The First Cities,* largely focus around human relationships. With *From a Land Where Other People Live* (1973; nominated for a National Book Award), the evolution of Lorde's concerns became evident. Unlike many of her contemporaries, Lorde's themes progressed from personal awareness toward a larger societal vision. Her vision of the world somewhat resembled her description of the city: it is a place of oppression, large and uncaring, walled in by racism and injustice. In *The New York Head Shop and Museum* (1974), Lorde's politics became more explicit. She also adopted much of the militant black rhetoric of the radical black poets of the 1960s.

Lorde, however, came to be known primarily as a lesbian feminist poet. She had become involved in the Greenwich Village "gay-girl" milieu as early as 1955, and although she married an attorney, Edwon Ashley Rollins, in 1962 and had two children with him, she was divorced in 1970. From that time onward, Lorde's efforts to win respect for lesbians were unremitting. Many of the poems in such collections as *Coal* (1976), *The Black Unicorn* (1978), *Chosen Poems, Old and New* (1982), *Our Dead Behind Us* (1986), and *The Marvelous Arithmetics of Distance* (1993), as well as the autobiographical novel *Zami: A New Spelling of My Name* (1982), examine such issues.

Lorde also published two collections of essays, *Sister Outsider* (1984) and *A Burst of Light* (1988), as well as *The Cancer Journals* (1980), an account of her fight against breast cancer. She helped found the Kitchen Table: Women of Color Press, a black feminist publisher, and Sisters in Support of Sisters in South Africa.

Audre Lorde taught at several universities, including the City University of New York, John Jay College of Criminal Justice, and, from 1978, at Hunter College, where she was Thomas Hunter Professor of English. She died of liver cancer on November 17, 1992, in St. Croix in the U.S. Virgin Islands.

▩ *Critical Extracts*

ANTAR SUDAN KATARA MBERI   There are many poems ⟨in *Coal*⟩ such as "Coal," "Summer Oracle," "Generation," "Poem for a Poet," "Hard Love Rock," "Bridge through My Window," and "Conversations in Crisis" which are good to excellent poems. At the same time, there is a marked, uneven and sometimes ambiguous character to the book. The long poem "Martha" is extremely reflective of this. It seems an unwieldy attempt to convey poetically an accident, the victim, in relationship to life and the crucifixion. The idea is not a bad one in itself, but despite the occasional insights, the narrative fails badly; is dead. The poem itself in its persona almost borders on the neurotic and is not always clear; this may be its justification and intent but I am not convinced.

Coal is not as strong and well-knit a collection as the aforementioned collection ⟨*From a Land where Other People Live*⟩ which won a National Book Award nomination. Yet there is this argument to be made in its behalf. What comes through is the "stretchingness" of Audre Lorde's poetry into new poetic vistas of the Afro-American and general human experience. This book almost seems a transition, a harbinger of an entire new world and way of defining it.

Antar Sudan Katara Mberi, "Poetic Vistas of Afro-American Experience," *Free-domways* 16, No. 3 (Third Quarter 1976): 195

R. B. STEPTO   In contrast to ⟨Maya Angelou's⟩ *And Still I Rise*, Audre Lorde's seventh volume of poems, *The Black Unicorn*, is a big, rich book of some sixty-seven poems. While *The Black Unicorn* is as "packaged" as *And Still I Rise* (the prominent half-column of authenticating commentary from Adrienne Rich constitutes much of the wrapping), it really does not need this promoting and protecting shell. Perhaps a full dozen—an incredibly high percentage—of these poems are searingly strong and unforgettable. Those readers who recall the clear light and promise of early Lorde poems such as "The Woman Thing" and "Bloodbirth," and recall as well the great shape and energy of certain mid-1970s poems including "To My Daughter the Junkie on a Train," "Cables to Rage," and "Blackstudies," will find in *The Black Unicorn* new poems which reconfirm Lorde's talent while reseeding gardens and fields traversed before. There are other poems which do not so much reseed as repeople, and these new persons, names, ghosts, lovers, voices—these new I's, we's, real and imagined kin—give us something fresh, beyond the cycle of Lorde's previously recorded seasons and solstices.

While *The Black Unicorn* is unquestionably a personal triumph for Lorde in terms of the development of her canon, it is also an event in contemporary letters. This is a bold claim but one worth making precisely because, as we see in the first nine poems, Lorde appears to be the only North American poet other than Jay Wright who is sufficiently immersed in West African religion, culture, and art (and blessed with poetic talent!) to reach beyond a kind of middling poem that merely quantifies "blackness" through offhand reference to African gods and traditions. What Lorde and Wright share, beyond their abilities to create a fresh, Now World Art out of ancient Old World lore, is a voice or an *idea* of a voice that is essentially African in that it is communal, historiographical, archival, and prophetic *as well as* personal in ways that we commonly associate with the African *griot*, *dyeli*, and tellers of *nganos* and other oral tales. However, while Wright's voice may be said to embody what is masculine in various West African cultures and cosmologies, Lorde's voice is decidedly and magnificently feminine. The goal of *The Black Unicorn* is then to present this fresh and powerful voice, and to explore the modulations within that voice between feminine and feminist timbres. As the volume unfolds, this exploration charts history and geography as well as voice, and with confluence of these patterns the volume takes shape and Lorde's particular envisioning of a black transatlantic tradition is accessible.

R. B. Stepto, "The Phenomenal Woman and the Severed Daughter," *Parnassus: Poetry in Review* 8, No. 1 (Fall–Winter 1979): 315–16

ROSEMARY DANIELL   Throughout ⟨*Zami: A New Spelling of My Name*⟩, ⟨Lorde's⟩ experiences are painted with exquisite imagery. Indeed, her West Indian heritage shows through most clearly in her use of word pictures that are sensual, steamy, at times near-tropical, evoking the colors, smells—repeatedly, the smells—shapes, textures that are her life. Her attention to detail is exacting whether she's describing a supper of hot tamales and cold milk in Mexico City or an evening of bar-hopping in the West Village of two decades ago. Her use of language is often imaginative but uncontrived, as in her description of her first lover, Ginger, as having "hight putchy cheeks" or her reference, in one of the many meals deliciously detailed in the book, to "chopped onions quailed in margarine."

Yet Miss Lorde is at her best when her images become—as they often do—metaphors for states of being: A torn stocking caught in the wind on the side of a tenement building becomes symbolic of her terror when, as a small child, she hangs by one hand from the window of her apartment, only to be saved by her mother's timely return home. Or the day she has begun her first menstrual period: Left alone by her usually ever-present mother in the kitchen, she crushes with mortar and pestle the garlic, onions and celery leaves that will season the meat for dinner; as she pounds—and pounds and pounds—she becomes carried away, the scents from the ground herbs mixing with her own. And her membership at Junter High School in what she calls The Branded, The Lunatic Fringe, is really her wider membership in that part of the population made up of artists, blacks, women, and homosexuals.

Despite her obvious poet's ease with symbol, metaphor, image, her references to herself as poet—a vocation held since childhood—are unemphatic:

". . . sometimes there was food cooked, sometimes there was not. Sometimes there was a poem, and sometimes there was not. And always, on weekends, there were the bars," she writes, describing life with her lover Muriel. And while her downplaying of her commitment to poetry may be partly an attempt to avoid widening the distance between the reader and herself, there is the sense, in *Chosen Poems* as in *Zami*, of a writer who has other, more pressing concerns—such as cooking a meal, making a living, or simply living out the life style that for many homosexuals is an avocation in itself.

Rosemary Daniell, "The Poet Who Found Her Own Way," New York Times Book Review, 19 December 1982, pp. 12, 29

CLAUDIA TATE   C.T.: Would you describe your writing process?

LORDE: I keep a journal and write in it fairly regularly. I get a lot of my poems out of it. It's like the raw material for my poems. Sometimes I'm blessed with a poem that comes in the form of a poem, but other times I've worked for two years on a poem.

For me, there are two very basic and different processes for revising my poetry. One is recognizing that a poem has not yet become itself. In other words, I mean that the feeling, the truth that the poem is anchored in is somehow not clearly clarified inside of me, and as a result it lacks something. Then it has to be re-felt. Then there's the other process which is easier. The poem is itself, but it has rough edges that need to be refined. That kind of revision involves picking the image that is more potent or tailoring it so that it carries the feeling. That's an easier kind of rewriting and re-feeling.

My journal entries focus on things I feel: feelings that sometimes have no place, no beginning, no end; phrases I hear in passing; something that looks good to me; sometimes just observations of the world.

I went through a period once when I felt like I was dying. I wasn't writing any poetry, and I felt that if I couldn't write I would split. I was recording in my journal, but no poems came. I know now that this period was a transition in my life.

The next year, I went back to my journal, and here were these incredible poems that I could almost lift out of it. Many of them are in *The Black Unicorn*. "Harriet" is one of them; "Sequelae" and "The Litany for Survival" are others. These poems came right out of the journal. But I didn't see them as poems then.

"Power" was in the journal too. It is a poem written about Clifford Glover, the ten-year-old black boy shot by a cop who was acquitted by a jury on which a black woman sat. In fact, the day I heard on the radio that O'Shea had been acquitted, I was going across town on 88th Street [New York City] and I had to pull over. A kind of fury rose up in me—the sky turned red. I felt so sick. I felt as if I would drive the car into a wall, into the next person I saw. So I pulled over. I took out my journal just to air some of my fury, to get it out of my fingertips. Those expressed feelings are that poem. That was just how "Power" was written.

C.T.: A transition has to occur before you can make poetry out of your journal entries.

LORDE: There is a gap between the journal and my poetry. I write this stuff in my journal, and sometimes I cannot even read my journals because there is so much pain and rage in them. I'll put it away in a drawer, and six months later, I'll pick up the journal, and there will be the seeds of poems. The journal entries somehow have to be assimilated into my living; only then can I deal with what I have written down.

Art is not living. It is the use of living. The artist has the ability to take the living and use it in a certain way and produce art.

Claudia Tate, "Audre Lorde," *Black Women Writers at Work* (New York: Continuum, 1983), pp. 111–12

BARBARA CHRISTIAN   As a black, lesbian, feminist, poet, mother, Lorde has, in her own life, had to search long and hard for *her* people. In responding to each of these audiences, in which a part of her identity lies, she refuses to give up her differences. In fact she uses them, as woman to man, black to white, lesbian to heterosexual, as a means of conducting creative dialogue. Thus, she asserts that "the results of woman-hating in the Black communities are tragedies which diminish all Black People" and that the black man's use of the label "lesbian" as a threat is an attempt to rule by fear. She reminds white women who fear the anger of black women that "anger between peers births courage, not destruction, and the discomfort and sense of loss it often causes is not fatal but a sign of growth." In "Eye to Eye," she acknowledges the anger that black women direct toward each other, as well as our history of bonding, in a society that tells us we are wrong at every turn. In discussing our condition she reminds black women who attack lesbianism as anti-black of "the sisterhood of work and play and power" that is a part of our African tradition, that we have been taught to see each other as "heartless competitors for the scarce male, the all important prize that could legitimize our existence." This dehumanization of the denial of self, she asserts, "is no less lethal than the dehumanization of racism to which it is so closely allied." And underlying all of Lorde's attempts to have creative dialogue with the many parts of her self is her recognition that the good in this society is tragically defined in terms of profit rather than in terms of the human being.

Lorde's essays are always directed toward the deepening of self, even as she analyzes the ways in which society attempts to dehumanize it. In showing the connections between sexism, racism, ageism, homophobia, classism, even as she insists on the creative differences among those persons they affect, she stresses the need to share the joy and pain of living, through language. In speaking, in breaking the silences about what each of us actually experiences, what we think, in voicing even our disagreements, we bridge the differences between us. Like ⟨June⟩ Jordan and ⟨Alice⟩ Walker's essays, Lorde's collection "broadens the joining," even as it exemplifies another way in which a black woman interprets her experiences.

Barbara Christian, "The Dynamics of Difference: Book Review of Audre Lorde's *Sister Outsider*" (1984), *Black Feminist Criticism: Perspectives on Black Women Writers* (New York: Pergamon Press, 1985), pp. 209–10

JOAN MARTIN   *The Cancer Journals* is an autobiographical work dealing with Audre Lorde's battle with cancer, her horror at discovering that she was being forced to face her own mortality head on, and the lessons she learned as a result of this most painful experience. She talks constantly of fear, anxiety, and strength. And strength is the substance of which she seems made. The opening statement of the Introduction addresses the problem immediately. "Each woman responds to the crisis that breast cancer brings to her life out of a whole pattern, which is the design of who she is and how her life has been lived. The weave of her everyday existence is the training ground for how she handles crisis." She further states, "I am a post-mastectomy woman who believes our feelings need voice in order to be recognized, respected, and of use." And we hear her feelings voiced in a manner both eloquent and disturbingly prophetic. As in her poetry, Lorde states her truths with no holds barred in this short but powerful prose work. Her biggest fear beyond the loss of her breast and the possibility of imminent death is that she should die without having said the things she as a woman and an artist needed to say in order that her pain and subsequent loss might not have occurred in vain. In her own words, she says, "I had known the pain, and survived it. It only remained for me to give it voice, to share it for use, that the pain not be wasted." And like the love she lost as a child and learned to survive without, Lorde has taken the loss imposed on her by death-dealing breast cancer and survived with dignity and new strength. Her adamant refusal to wear a prosthesis after the removal of her breast is an example of that self-esteem we saw developing in the young child. It has emerged complete in Audre Lorde the woman.

Joan Martin, "The Unicorn Is Black: Audre Lorde in Retrospect," *Black Women Writers (1950–1980): A Critical Evaluation*, ed. Mari Evans (New York: Anchor Press/ Doubleday, 1984), pp. 287–88

AMITAI F. AVI-RAM   One of the most powerful of Lorde's later poems, both emotionally and politically, is "Afterimages" (1981). Thematically, the poem is concerned with two painful historical events in Jackson, Mississippi: a flood of the Pearl River, which the speaker must witness through a television interview of a woman victim, and the notorious lynching of Emmett Till in 1955, which the speaker had witnessed through the proliferation of print-media images of his dead and mutilated body. The second and third of four sections are respectively devoted to each of these events. The first section provides a controlling metaphor for the speaker's relation to the violence she must witness and somehow learn and grow from: her eyes are

> rockstrewn caves where dragonfish evolve
> wild for life, relentless and acquisitive
> learning to survive
> where there is no food. . . .

The dragonfish must "learn / to live upon whatever they must eat / fused images beneath my pain." The final section brings all three thematic strands together, and it is this section in particular, along with the close of section

III (on Emmett Till), that avails itself of some interesting uses of *apo koinou* ⟨"in common"⟩.

> A black boy from Chicago
> whistled on the streets of Jackson, Mississippi
> testing what he'd been taught was a manly thing to do
> his teachers
> ripped his eyes out his sex his tongue
> and flung him to the Pearl weighted with stone
> in the name of white womanhood
> they took their aroused honor
> back to Jackson
> and celebrated in a whorehouse
> the double ritual of white manhood
> confirmed.

Here, the phrase "in the name of white womanhood" stands in common as an adverbial modifier both of the lynch mob's horrible acts against Emmett Till (*ripped, flung*) and of the lynchers' exultant trip to the brothel. The sentence thus represents mimetically the position of the White women beneath the Black victim and the White male oppressors, between the agents and the object of violence. At the same time, it associates the men's "protection" of the women (or rather of their *name*) with their sexual exploitation of those same women. This in turn makes possible the comparison between Till and the White women who suffer from a common oppressor, while the women additionally must bear the *name* of the violence against Black men as one of the aspects of their own victimization: "the double ritual."

The irony of the pivotal line, "in the name of white womanhood"—its use of the men's own language to reveal their deceptions and delusions— is signalled by the *name* that is obviously—for us—not the name of the women themselves, their own proper names, but a name placed upon their "womanhood." Thus, to the White men, the women are not so much living beings as a conglomerate abstract symbol; the very sublimation of their bodies into such a symbol is then revealed to be simultaneously also a subordination and an effacement in the White men's trip to the brothel "in [their] name." Indeed, it is that same simultaneous sublimation and effacement that initially encodes the mob's inscription of their power into the body of their victim, as they remove from him specifically all the outward signs of the Black man's ability to receive and to create meaning: "his eyes . . . his sex his tongue." Upon such a deprivation of the Other's body and its meaning, and *only* upon such violence, can the mob rest its own power to create a name, which it then places upon the sex whom they perceive as initially and naturally powerless to speak their own name for themselves.

Amitai F. Avi-ram, "*Apo koinou* in Audre Lorde and the Moderns: Defining the Differences," *Callaloo* 9, No. 1 (Winter 1986): 203–4

GLORIA T. HULL   Lorde's first language was, literally, poetry. When someone asked her "How do you feel?" "What do you think?" or any other direct question, she "would recite a poem, and somewhere in that poem would be the feeling, the vital piece of information. It might be a line. It might be an image. The poem was my response." Since she was hit if she stuttered, "writing was the next best thing." At this point, Audre was well on her way to becoming schizophrenic, living in "a totally separate world of words." She got "stoned on," retreated into poetry when life became too difficult. As miscellaneous poems no longer served to answer questions from herself and others, she began to write her own. These she did not commit to paper, but memorized and kept as a "long fund" in her head. Poems were "a secret way" of expressing feelings she was "still too afraid to deal with." She would know that she "finally had it" when she spoke her work aloud and it struck alive, became real.

Audre's bizarre mode of communication must surely have meant frequently tangential conversations, and certainly placed on her listeners the burden of having to "read" her words in order to connect her second-level discourse with the direct matter at hand. At any rate, her answer to "How do you feel?" or "Do you want to go to the store with me?" could rarely be a simple "fine" or a univocal yes or no.

In high school, she tried not to "think in poems." She saw in amazement how other people thought, "step by step," and "not in bubbles up from chaos that you had to anchor with words"—a kind of "nonverbal communication, beneath language" the value of which she learned intuitively from her mother. After an early, pseudonymously published story, Lorde did not write another piece of prose until her 1977 essay "Poetry Is Not a Luxury." Even though she had begun to speak in full sentences when she was nineteen and had also acquired compositional skills, "communicating deep feeling in linear, solid blocks of print felt arcane, a method beyond me." She "could not focus on a thought long enough to have it from start to finish," but she could "ponder a poem for days." Lorde possessed an admirable, innate resistance to the phallogocentric "white pencil," to being, as she put it, "locked into the mouth of the dragon." She had seen the many errors committed in the name of "thought/thinking," and, furthermore, had formed some precious convictions about her own life that "defied thought." She seems always to have been seeking what she calls, in *Our Dead Behind Us*, "an emotional language / in which to abbreviate time."

> Gloria T. Hull, "Living on the Line: Audre Lorde and *Our Dead Behind Us*," *Changing Our Own Words: Essays on Criticism, Theory, and Writing by Black Women*, ed. Cheryl A. Wall (New Brunswick, NJ: Rutgers University Press, 1989), pp. 170–71

ANN LOUISE KEATING   According to both Chinosole and ⟨Claudine⟩ Raynaud, Lorde's poetic voice has its roots in her mother's "special and secret relationship with words." But by focusing solely on the specialness of the mother's relationship with words—on her euphemisms for unmentionable body parts and the puzzling phrases reminiscent of her island home—it is easy to overlook the effects of her secrecy. Although Lorde does "use the written word to translate the oral poetry of her mother's language," it is the mother's secretiveness, her selective silence, which shapes the daughter's lifelong belief in language's power. In an early section of the novel ⟨*Zami: A New Spelling of My Name*⟩ entitled "How I Became a Poet," Lorde sharply distinguishes her own voice from her mother's by declaring that when her *"strongest words"* remind her of those she heard as a child, she must reevaluate everything she wishes to say. Again, in an interview with Adrienne Rich, Lorde contrasts her own words with those of her mother and explains that while she was growing up she wanted nothing to do with her mother's use of language.

From her mother's silence, Lorde learns the importance of words. As she asserts in "The Transformation of Silence into Language and Action," speech is essential and silence does not really protect. In both this essay and *Zami*, she equates "the tyrannies of silence" with white patriarchal oppression and insists that without language, without the ability to express themselves, women of all colors are powerless to control their own lives. They must "swallow" the words of the father until they "sicken and die . . . still in silence." Forced to accept the language of others, they lack self-definition and are invisible—even to themselves. This inability to reject patriarchal language and speak freely leads to further oppression. As Lorde explains in a 1978 interview, when the dominant ideology is so interiorized that it becomes a part of women's consciousness, they repress both their own speech and that of others, they become the oppressor and the oppressed.

Lorde associates her mother's use of language with this internalized oppression. During childhood, her father and mother spoke as "one unfragmentable unappealable voice." Together, they chose to withhold "vital pieces of information," the realities of racism in everyday life, from their daughter. Perhaps most importantly, Lorde writes that it was "from the white man's tongue" that her mother learned to use language defensively, to ignore or misname those aspects of reality she was unable to change.

Ann Louise Keating, " 'Making Our Shattered Faces Whole': The Black Goddess and Audre Lorde's Revision of Patriarchal Myth," *Frontiers* 13, No. 1 (1992): 22–23

KATIE KING   Gay girls selectively reveal and conceal the paradoxes of race and sex. Lorde wants to remember the connections among women; doing so requires putting together the sexual and psychic attractions to white women with the realities of racism and survival. A little desperately, since the assurance is only partial, but also generously, Lorde offers: 'Lesbians were probably the only Black and white women in New York City in the fifties who were making any real attempt to communicate with each other.' Writing it over at another point, Lorde adds qualifications and alters emphasis—'*So far as I could see*, gay-girls were the only Black and white women who were even talking to each other'—and generalises beyond New York City ('*in this country* in the 1950s') while dismissing the possibilities of other political solidarities: 'outside of the empty rhetoric of patriotism and political movements' (emphasis added). The sacred bond of gayness, always insufficient, is still motivating and hungry. Inside the lesbian bar the meanings of the intersections of race and sex implicitly shift from circumstance to circumstance, and these shifts are reflected in subtle rewritings, partial repetitions, revealing editing, reordered valuations and reordered connections. These shifts destabilise the oppositions black/white, butch/femme, Ky-Ky/role-playing, celebration of women's community/internalisation of homophobia.

One could easily read *Zami*'s depiction of the bar as an indictment of role-playing, even as a 1982 historical reinscription, a response against lesbian s/m with an assimilation of 1950s role-playing into a paradigm of dominance/submission that must be politically rejected. This is surely one lacquered written layer of history in *Zami*. Some of Lorde's judgements and interpretations of the meanings of role-playing are straightforwardly rejecting and certainly spoken from the early 1980s in retrospective analysis:

> For some of us, role-playing reflected all the depreciating attitudes toward women which we loathed in straight society. It was a rejection of these roles that had drawn us to 'the life' in the first place. Instinctively, without particular theory or political position or dialectic, we recognized oppression as oppression, no matter where it came from.

As Lorde writes on here, she offers two simultaneous connections, connections both retrospective and historically separated out. First, she puts role-playing in association with 'the pretend world of dominance/submission'. At the same time, she also depicts its former hegemony in lesbian culture, a hegemony effectively routed now as reflected in the current weight of judgement against it. Lorde continues: 'But those lesbians who had carved some niche in the pretend world of dominance/subordination, rejected what they called our "confused" life style, and they were in the majority.' ⟨. . .⟩

Audre Lorde's biomythography *Zami*, with its focus on the intersection of race and sexuality in the lesbian bar, does not at all reflect the same story as D'Emilio's *Sexual Politics, Sexual Communities*, which is told at the intersection of class and political affiliation. None the less, *Zami*, with its lacquered histories—restricted, salvaged, dreaming of choice and its absence, even at times also 'whitelisting' the gay past—constructs lesbian personal and political identity out of many of the same resources and materials. These resources, materials, and also political investments mark our current productions of gay identities. *Zami* manages too to exemplify what Chicana theorist Chela Sandoval calls 'oppositional consciousness'—in the *rewritings themselves* of the meanings of the bar scene and in the transparent *processes* of rewriting which reveal the locations of the intersections of race, sexuality, language, culture, class, education, age and politics.

The value of this kind of process-bound political specificity I have learned about most clearly from Sandoval and Cherríe Moraga. I believe these two theorists describe especially convincingly the complexities of political identity, as they use creative and intellectual tools made within those overlapping feminist territories, 'the politics of identity' and 'the politics of sexuality'. Lorde belongs with these and other political workers, often women of colour, who are now powerfully reconstructing feminism.

Katie King, "Audre Lorde's Lacquered Layerings: The Lesbian Bar as a Site of Literary Production," *New Lesbian Criticism: Literary and Cultural Readings*, ed. Sally Munt (New York: Harvester Wheatsheaf, 1992), pp. 56–57, 69–70

ANNA WILSON   In the absense of a Black tradition, then, Lorde's biomythography *Zami* initially constructs a lesbian existence that has needs and features in common with the lesbian myth produced by white Anglo-American novelists. Her sexual coming out is described within a series of metaphors for recognition familiar from that tradition: making love is 'like coming home to a joy I was meant for'; the act of lesbian sex is naturalised through being presented as a return to an original knowledge that the protagonist has temporarily forgotten: 'wherever I touched, felt right and completing, as if I had been born to make love to this woman, and was remembering her body rather than learning it deeply for the first time.' This is a country of the body rather than of a people. Audre's community as a young lesbian in New York is defined as sexuality, and it is a community that attempts the utopian separation and newness of lesbian nation: 'We were reinventing the word together'; 'we had no patterns to follow, except our own needs and our own unthought-out dreams'. Yet membership in such a community is purchased at the price of non-recognition of Blackness; Lorde repeatedly describes Audre's 'invisibility' to the white lesbian community as Black; she is admitted only under the assumption of sameness. The lesbian community believes in itself as obliterating difference, 'that as lesbians, we were all outsiders and all equal in our outsiderhood. "We're all niggers," [Muriel, Audre's white lover] used to say.' Yet in Lorde's analysis the lesbian community is not elsewhere but is rather a microcosm of the world outside ⟨. . .⟩ In the white model, the real world recedes before the lesbian community's power to redefine: one reclothed oneself in a new identity and a new way of relating. It is one of Orlando's freedoms in Virginia Woolf's imaginary biography that s/he is able effortlessly to switch between costumes; her sexual fluidity is signalled by this flexibility, and in the same moment it indicates a crucial aspiration: the capacity both to switch between costumes and to cross-dress stands for freedom from gender imprisonment. George Sand said of her experience of cross-dressing, 'My clothes knew no fear.' But for Audre a rigidly stratified dress-code, each item signifying a particular class or role position, expresses not freedom of play but her imprisonment within a system of hierarchised differences. The 'uncharted territory' that she finds in trying to discover new ways of relating in 'a new world of women' is not just uncharted but inaccessible: there is no pathway for the Black lesbian nation. It is from this experience that Lorde constructs the 'house of difference' that she finally articulates as 'our place'; it is a refusal of the aspiration to unity that lesbian nation encodes. The 'house of difference', then, is a movement away from otherworldliness. It accepts the inevitability of a material world where class, race, gender all continue to exist. It is, therefore, a step back towards acknowledging the necessity of reasserting ties of identity with the Black community.

Anna Wilson, "Lorde and the African-American Tradition: When the Family Is Not Enough," New Lesbian Criticism: Literary and Cultural Readings, ed. Sally Munt (New York: Harvester Wheatsheaf, 1992), 81–82

▦ Bibliography

The First Cities. 1968.

Cables to Rage. 1970.

From a Land Where Other People Live. 1973.

New York Head Shop and Museum. 1974.

Between Our Selves. 1976.

Coal. 1976.

The Black Unicorn. 1978.

Use of the Erotic: The Erotic as Power. 1978.

The Cancer Journals. 1980.

A Litany of Survival. 1981.

Chosen Poems, Old and New. 1982, 1992 (as *Undersong: Chosen Poems, Old and New*).

Zami: A New Spelling of My Name. 1982.

Sister Outsider: Essays and Speeches. 1984.

I Am Your Sister: Black Women Organizing across Sexualities. 1985.

Our Dead Behind Us. 1986.

A Burst of Light. 1988.

Apartheid U.S.A. ⟨with *Our Common Enemies, Our Common Cause* by Merle Woo⟩. 1990.

Hell under God's Orders: Hurricane Hugo in St. Croix—Disaster and Survival (with Gloria I. Joseph and Hortense M. Rowe). 1990.

Need: A Chorale for Black Women Voices. 1990.

The Marvelous Arithmetics of Distance: Poems 1987–1992. 1993.

▨ ▨ ▨

Haki R. Madhubuti
b. 1942

HAKI R. MADHUBUTI was born Don L. Lee on February 23, 1942, in Little Rock, Arkansas, the son of Jimmy L. and Maxine (Graves) Lee. Lee's early life was troubled: his father left the family when he was a baby and his mother died when he was sixteen. Forced to work at several jobs (including cleaning a bar) while attending Dunbar Vocational High School in Chicago, Lee served a three-year stint in the U.S. Army (1960–63) before going on to secure an associate's degree at Chicago City College in 1966; he then briefly attended Roosevelt University in Chicago and the University of Illinois at Chicago Circle before dropping out. Since 1963 he had been supporting himself by working as an apprentice curator at the DuSable Museum of African History in Chicago, a job he retained until 1967; he also held positions at Montgomery Ward, the post office, and Spiegel's.

By 1967 Lee was ready to leave business and enter the realms of writing and publishing. In that year he published his first collection of poems, *Think Black*, and several other poetry volumes followed: *Black Pride* (1968), *For Black People (and Negroes Too)* (1968), *Don't Cry, Scream* (1969), and *We Walk the Way of the New World* (1970). These volumes achieved a wide audience because of their accessibility (many of his poems utilize the language of the streets) and their confrontational tone, which harmonized with the Black Pride and Black Power movements of the time. In 1967 Lee also founded the Third World Press and the Organization of Black American Culture (OBAC) Writers Workshop, both of which nurtured and promoted the work of black American writers.

In 1971 Lee published a selection of his best poems, *Directionscore*, as well as a critical study, *Dynamite Voices I: Black Poets of the 1960's*. In 1973 he adopted the Swahili name Haki R. Madhubuti and issued *Book of Life*, the last volume of poetry he would publish for more than a decade. During this period Madhubuti turned his attention to lecturing, essay writing (including such volumes as *From Plan to Planet*, 1973; *The Socio-Politics of Black Exile*, 1976; and *Enemies: The Clash of Races*, 1978), and political activity. He had founded the Institute of Positive Education in 1969, using it as a forum to promote black culture. He also served as writer-in-residence at several universities, including Cornell, the University of Illinois at Chicago, and Howard University (1970–78).

Madhubuti finally published another collection of poetry (with selected essays) in 1984, *Earthquakes and Sun Rise Missions*, followed three years later with another poetry volume, *Killing Memory, Seeking Ancestors*. He secured an M.F.A. from the University of Iowa in 1984. In recent years Madhubuti has again turned to essays and criticism, editing collections of essays on Gwendolyn Brooks (*Say That the River Turns*, 1987) and on the 1992 Los Angeles riots (*Why L.A. Happened*, 1993). He continues to reject assimilationism, vowing that black Americans must cast off white culture entirely and rely on their own culture and values in a racially hostile environment.

Madhubuti is married to Johari Amini; they have two children. Since 1984 he has been a professor of English at Chicago State University. He continues to live and write in Chicago.

▨ *Critical Extracts*

RON WELBURN   *Don't Cry, Scream* is Don L. Lee's third book of black poetry, and to followers of contemporary black literature he needs no lengthy introduction. ⟨. . .⟩

As Miss ⟨Gwendolyn⟩ Brooks points out, Lee is "at the hub of the new wordway." Don L. Lee is a technician, a poet-linguist continuing the development of a new language for black poetics, the language of familiar experience, the same language black readers have grown up speaking.

> Whereas black poets deal in the concrete rather than the abstract (concrete: art for people's sake; black language or Afro-American language in contrast to standard English, &c). Black poetry moves to define and legitimize blackpeople's reality (*that* which is real to us). ⟨. . .⟩

That life in America is already absurd is no secret to Lee; but the absurdity is of the grotesque inhumanity of the "unpeople," not the configuration of their existential limitations. Lee is thematically unpretentious, straight-forward, and sarcastic. He is not burdened by the kind of "ironic vision" that plagues white existentialist poets. These poets carry an apathy across their backs like the weight of dead stone. ⟨. . .⟩ To labor a point cited by Miss Brooks, who indicated that Don L. Lee would never subscribe to what Jascha Kessler mentioned as a "longing for death" which typifies American ("whi-te") poets, it should be further made clear that Lee has a "rendezvous with life," as *Don't Cry, Scream* is his third projection of the sounds of black life—life sounds.

> Ron Welburn, [Review of *Don't Cry, Scream*], *Negro Digest* 19, No. 2 (December 1969): 91–93

PAULA GIDDINGS   Don's ever-increasing awareness ⟨of commu-nity⟩ is not only reflected in his use of the first-person plural but in his ability to create the images which are so important to his poetry. Images which at first were often stark and singular have become profusions of soft but smoldering energy. His images find their being in oral expression—that raps, sings, pounds on old words to form new ones, makes verbs into nouns, nouns into verbs, screams, sings, fills words with color or makes them fall like gentle rain. His language is alive and is not to be doted on for its grace and gentility, like a museum piece. Museums are evidences of dead cultures. In black culture everything possesses the spirit of animation, including black language, which is by nature more metaphoric and poetical, even containing more tenses to express that animation.

Gwendolyn Brooks said of Lee, "Around a black audience he puts warm healing arms," and it is true partly because he uses the language of the black communities. It is the language we spoke when we left the white schools and/or teachers—the language we spoke when we got *home*.

This is very important because it legitimizes black language, which is essential to the poet's goal of legitimizing the black reality, or what should be real for us. He is saying, in effect, that the black verbal expression traditional in the black communities is not an aberration of the "King's English." But what has been "done" to standard English is what the slaves did to the standard church service, or what jazz musicians did to the standard note progression, breathing life into an otherwise prosaic form, making it rich with spontaneity and warm with the reflection and expression of our own culture.

The fact that most of his poetry is meant to be read aloud also recognizes that black people are by tradition an oral people; and that the Baptist minister will always be more effective than a silent reading of the scripture. However, this oral trend does have a distinct disadvantage. Much of Lee's poetry really can't be appreciated unless you hear *him* read it. The trend also demands not only that a poet's poetry be good, but that his delivery be good as well. And black people have never been known for their sympathy or even tolerance for an inadequate delivery. Check out amateur night at the Apollo some time.

The "polyrhythmic, short, uneven and explosive" line of this poetry also conveys a sense of urgency in the recesses of its rhythm. It makes you listen because of the use of that rhythm which serves as a linking force of the diverse elements of the poetry. Rhythm signifies a sense of order, a pulsating foundation from which to internalize the poetry. This can be seen in the verse:

> move
> move to be moved from the un-movable
> into your own, yr/self is own, yrself is own, own yourself.
> go where you/we go, hear the unheard and do,
> do the undone, do it, do it, do it now, Clean
> and tomorrow your sons will
> be alive to praise
> you.

Paula Giddings, "From a Black Perspective: The Poetry of Don L. Lee," *Amistad 2*, ed. John A. Williams and Charles F. Harris (New York: Random House, 1971), pp. 310–12

ANNETTE OLIVER SHANDS   The relevancy of Don L. Lee as a contemporary Black poet revolves around his awareness of a growing apart of the Black and white races in America. The divisiveness that is visible today is somewhat different from the separation that American history books recognize. Blacks, rather than whites, seek to achieve separation today, in answer to America's rejection and dehumanization of a race of people. Don L. Lee, as a contemporary Black poet, makes a strong, definite and direct response to this situation. He offers a viewpoint formulating what Black

Poetry needs to achieve by choosing his audience and by announcing the desired audience response. Perhaps the ultimate degree of his relevancy lies in his chosen language—a language belonging to the under-35 generation of Blacks. The titles of his collected poems—*Black Pride*; *Think Black*; *Don't Cry, Scream*; and *We Walk the Way of the New World*—reflect his chosen language; they coincide with his recognition of the task of a Black poet in that they absorb Blackness rather than negate it, impart a segment of his whole message, summon Black people, his intended audience, invoke the intended response in that they incite action to change practically everything rather than choke with passive acceptance of the way things are.

Lee's response in poetry is revolutionary, as it demands that the Black poet, in a mutual alliance with Black people, interchange, formulate, communicate, possess, and strengthen values *apart from* and completely *unrelated to* the white American society. ⟨. . .⟩

First and foremost, in ascertaining poetics, Lee looks to the people. While William Carlos Williams finds in his own surroundings *the local* and *the variable foot*, Don L. Lee finds the rhythm of a language akin to jazz and *the Black Experience*. His material, or subject matter, relates to the realities facing his audience, namely, Black people; here he secures images and symbols. Of this, he says, "undoubtedly, the true Black Experience, in most cases, is very concrete and is opposed to any unrelated abstractions (concrete: sleeping in subways, being bitten by rats, six people living in a kitchenette)." Furthermore, in considering the duality institutionalized in American society, Lee sees *the Black poet* as distinct from the white poet in the same manner that an apple tree is distinct from a pear tree, as orange juice is distinct from tomato juice, or as Chinese is distinct from English. Next, in discussing the nature of his poetry, Lee gives importance to content, saying:

> The most significant factor about the poems/poetry you will be
> reading is the *idea*. The *idea* is not the manner in which a poem
> is conceived but the conception itself. From the *idea* we move
> toward development & direction (direction: the focusing of yr/
> idea in a positive or negative manner; depending on the poet's
> orientation). Poetic form is synonymous with poetic structure and
> is the guide used in developing yr/ idea. ⟨. . .⟩

Simultaneously as Lee attributes importance to content, he uses a language and form which combine with content for effectiveness. Typical of Lee's language and style are abundant abbreviations and adaptations of Black speech. His various abbreviations are: & instead of *and*; *u*, in place of *you*; *thru* for *through*; *mo*, rather than *more*; *yr*, for *your*; *cd*, as *could*; and *fr* as *from*. These abbreviations serve to promote fluidity of speech and allow rapid movement of the reader's eyes. Moreover, since Lee does not use them consistently, they become the unexpected. In this manner, Lee's technique is comparable to a jazz musician's craft, for a jazz musician plays the unexpected note. Then, in agreement with Black speech, *going to, have to, got to* and *getting* become *gonta, havta, gotta* and *gotten* at times. To further represent Black speech, *bad* may be *baaaaad*, and *homeboy* and *hip* are evident. Other street names are "hog" and "deuce & a quarter," referring to a Cadillac and an Electra 225.

> Annette Oliver Shands, "The Relevancy of Don L. Lee as a Contemporary Black Poet," *Black World* 21, No. 8 (June 1972): 35–37, 39

JASCHA KESSLER   I've not seen poetry in Don L. Lee. Anger, bombast, raw hatred, strident, aggrieved, perhaps charismatically crude religious and political canting, propaganda and racist nonsense, yes; and utterly unoriginal in form and style; humorless; cruel laughter bordering on the insane. There may well be justified insanity, as there is justifiable homicide; in poetry it means the poems cohere neither to things nor to people, not even to themselves. That they arise from reality, misery, and reflect human longings and aspiration to humanity, may be true; but in Lee all is converted to rant. He pays homage to musicians, poets, and novelists, his gratitude for having been shown the way to words and thoughts; but I can't conceive any of the artists he names in his pages recognizing his own influence on Lee. That he has ambition, a fanatic, exalted vision aimed at raising his brothers and sisters out of the burning swamp of the black ghettoes of Newark or Detroit or Chicago, is evident; that he is indignant at the destruction, oppression, evil and sheer helplessness of self-destruction of so many for so long, is laudable; if he can raise black consciousness for a moment, for a millimeter, that will be something achieved—there's also a bonus if he can reveal suffering and disaster to the white mind for its sake too. But poetry? Lee is deluded in thinking he has it. What he has is street language, common enough to most of us; the rest is a farrago of anybody's W. C. Williams and rehashed and rancid LeRoi Jones, mixed with editorials out of *Elijah (Muhammad) Speaks*. Since Lee isn't concerned to address those beyond his claque, he can make up his history, religion, business, politics, anything; but that won't help us much. If he woke up in the nation he calls for, he could appoint himself minister of culture, and might last a while in the job by dint of eliminating everyone else; he's got the gall for that. A real poet couldn't last, though, and never has for long. Lee is outside poetry somewhere, exhorting, hectoring, cursing, making a lot of noise. But you don't have to be black for that, and, if you are, it's hardly an excuse.

Jascha Kessler, "Trial and Error," *Poetry* 121, No. 5 (February 1973): 292–93

EUGENE E. MILLER   Is not Don Lee himself concerned with what black humanness is, how black people shall live? Can I not discern in these poems just what he does consider the supreme good of black life—what value or values he stresses, either directly or by implication, that black human beings possess or should possess, that name the goodness of their lives, their—or his—answer to "how shall we live"?

Or is this approach merely to subsume black life into the colorless blindness of "mankind"? Just another way of saying that, after all, black people are just like white people except for some genetic accidents; just another way of trying to turn black people into white people, because, in the end, white people have all the answers. But is it not possible that the western world's "humanity" is, as someone once said of its God, too small? Is it not possible that Don Lee's poetry, as black poetry, might be able to expand my notions of what it means to be human? Perhaps the very blackness of the poems that I find so difficult to deal with in my usual literary terms constitutes this new element. I do not, maybe cannot, think black because I think only in habitual terms, and cannot recognize what I have not already seen? Maybe there is more creation, more invention in these simple poems than I have been able to realize?

But how can I grasp or come to see what I have never seen before, or to apprehend that for which I have no sense, for which I have never perhaps developed any perceptual organ? Can an eye hear? Can it even see? Is this just another way of expressing that major point made by Don Lee in particular and Blackart in general: that unless one has a black vision, that comes only from being and living black life, one cannot grasp, let alone fully appreciate or evaluate, expressions of that life or experience? Yet there is a ring to these crystal clear, yet baffling, poems of Don Lee's when I flick at them, that tells me, somehow, there is a quality in them. How do I detect that ring, that tone?

Eugene E. Miller, "Some Black Thoughts on Don L. Lee's *Think Black!* Thunk by a Frustrated White Academic Thinker," *College English* 34, No. 8 (May 1973): 1100–1101

HELEN VENDLER   The explosive center of the ⟨Broadside Press's⟩ output is the poetry of Don Lee, now 32, who changed his name last year to a Swahili name, Haki R. Madhubuti. Lee's poems, written in a rapid, jerky, intense speech-rhythm in almost Morse shorthand, have sold over 100,000 copies without any large-scale advertising or mass distribution, a phenomenon which (like the success of Ginsberg's *Howl*) means that something is happening. Lee is not Rod McKuen or Lois Wyse; he does not sell comfortable sentimentality. He sells on nerve, stamina and satire. In him the sardonic and savage turn-of-phrase long present in black speech as a survival tactic finds its best poet ⟨. . .⟩

⟨. . .⟩ The sales of Lee's books will continue as long as his spurts of anger, of derisive force, of bitter warning and of undeniable hope continue to find a mirror in the black readers who wait for each new collection, but it is time for a wider public to hear his voice.

Helen Vendler, "Good Black Poems One by One," *New York Times Book Review*, 29 September 1974, pp. 3, 10

W. EDWARD FARRISON   One of the most prominent contemporary American Negro poets is Don L. Lee. As Dr. ⟨Marlene⟩ Mosher's copious bibliography in her *New Directions from Don L. Lee* ⟨Hicksville, NY: Exposition Press, 1975⟩ shows, Lee has merited her consideration of him as a poet, literary and social critic, and theoretical educational reformer. Lee's reputation as a poet has been established for several years by four booklets of original verse: *Think Black* (1967), *Black Pride* (1968), *Don't Cry, Scream* (1969), and *We Walk the Way of the New World* (1970). In *Directionscore: Selected and New Poems* (1971), Lee collected the introductions and presumably what he considered his most representative poems from the first four booklets and added five new poems. The last-named volume, therefore, may well be viewed as a compendium of what Lee himself considered the best poetry he had written up to the time of the publication of this volume.

In these five works Dr. Mosher found evidence of a shift of Lee's focus from "negative anti-White" in the first two to "positive pro-Black" in the next two and thence in the fifth to an attempt "to give all Blacks a sense of unity, purpose, and direction, so that they may finally 'finish' their 'history' on a successful note." Herein, it appears, is the first half of the new directions from Lee, in which the attempt just mentioned may be properly deemed colossal and idealistic. ⟨. . .⟩

The second half of the new directions from Lee emerges mainly from two of his prose works: *Dynamite Voices, I: Black Poets of the 1960's* (1971) and *From Plan to Planet, Life Studies: The Need for Afrikan Minds and Institutions*(1973). The new directions herein seem to point towards novel if not altogether new or practical stances in which Lee the literary and social critic and Black Nationalist appears as the godfather of a supposedly gestated "Black aesthetic"—whatever that is—and as a revolutionary reformer of "Black education." In considering the latter new directions, Dr. Mosher appeared quite aware of the weaknesses in Lee's criticism and his views concerning Black education and Black Nationalism, but commendably she seemed determined to discuss these as well as the previously noted new directions as sympathetically as possible. She would have done well, however, to correct what is apparently a misconception of Lee's concerning the paucity of Negro literature prior to 1968—that as late as that time there did not exist "an adequate body of work" from which to derive a Black aesthetic. Just what, one is constrained to wonder, is meant here by *adequate*? ⟨. . .⟩

As with a cup brimful of admiration, Dr. Mosher explained at length Lee's elaborate explanation of what Black schools can do "for the Black liberation movement." The explanation is indeed intriguing, but both Lee and Dr. Mosher left one important thing unexplained, namely, how the various procedures suggested can be financed—and all of them would need to be well financed. Once again one is reminded of the old question, not as to whether an Archimedes can lift the world with a lever, but of what can he rest the fulcrum on? As Lee advances in experience and Wisdom, newer and more practicable directions will doubtless emerge from his thinking—directions which, if she continues her interest in Lee's writing, Dr. Mosher should find it progressively easy as well as stimulating to weigh and consider.

W. Edward Farrison, [Review of *New Directions from Don L. Lee* by Marlene Mosher], *CLA Journal* 18, No. 4 (June 1975): 582–84

DARWIN T. TURNER   *Earthquakes and Sun Rise Missions* is Haki
R. Madhubuti's first volume of poetry since *Book of Life* (1973). Although
he has continued to write poetry during this decade, the effort to publish
it has submitted to other priorities—arduous work as the director of the
Institute of Positive Education and of Third World Press, three books of
essays, continuing his work as educator and nation builder, and the responsibilities of a husband and a father. Now the poet has reappeared in a volume
of rich love of Black women, mature, compassionate observation, and cold
contempt of the enemies of Black people. ⟨. . .⟩

⟨. . .⟩ It is as though Madhubuti ⟨in *Earthquakes and Sun Rise Missions*⟩
has chosen to move from the role of virtuoso performer and to assume more
often the role of artistic, prophetic educator. Madhubuti has not abandoned
the earlier style, which he continues to display in such poems as "Negro
Leaderships", "Rainforest", "We Struggle for the People", or "destiny"; but
now he often seeks to fuse poetry and prose, as in "Woman Black" or
"Winterman", for example. He has not forsaken his stern criticism of Blacks
who pursue false values, but he now writes compassionately of the reasons
some do ("Winterman"). There is an increased emphasis on a message of
love for Black women, but there is continuing evidence of love for and
commitment to Black people. As Gwendolyn Brooks wrote in the introduction to *Don't Cry, Scream,* "Around a black audience he puts warm hands."

More than a decade ago, while teachers in schools were complaining
about students' lack of interest in poetry, Madhubuti was proving that people
will listen to and buy poetry that speaks to them, that entertains and educates
them. Now, concerned that some poets have lost their vision and that
other poets' voices have been drowned by the sounds from the ever-present
television sets, he is reaching out poetically once more to urge people to
listen.

> We can do what we work to do.
> measure stillness and quiet
> noise is ever present.
> if we are not careful we will not
> hear the message
> when it
> arrives.

Madhubuti's powerful message will shut off some television sets, redirect
some minds and may invite book burning in some quarters.

Darwin T. Turner, "Afterword," *Earthquakes and Sun Rise Missions: Poetry and Essays of Black Renewal 1973–1983* by Haki R. Madhubuti (Chicago: Third World Press, 1984), pp. 181, 188–89

HAKI R. MADHUBUTI   I have had the privilege to travel far
and deep into other cultures. Any kind of travel to the imaginative mind
is both rewarding and challenging. Travel can also be painful to the culturally
sensitive; for example, it is extremely difficult to enjoy oneself in Haiti and
in certain parts of Afrika. Afrika entered my consciousness in 1960 and
there has not been a day that I have not considered my relationship to that
vast and complex continent.

I first went to Afrika in 1969 to attend the first Pan-Afrikan Festival in
Algeria. After a decade of serious struggle in the United States for black self-
determination, my visit to Afrika was crucial to my cultural development. I
went looking for answers. The past ten years in the U.S. had been an intense
period of struggle and study during which my generation fought to rid itself
of a colonial-slave-centered mindset. My first trip to Afrika was instructive,
but after seven visits to North, East and West Afrika, I am still fighting
with my questions. My searchings have also taken me to the West Indies,
Europe, Asia, and South America. However, as a man of Afrikan foreparents,
the land of the sun has a special meaning for me.

Youth has its own naivety. I long ago lost my innocence in the concrete
of Detroit and the mud of Arkansas. Yet, I was still not prepared for the
land that gave birth to civilization.

My personal journals eat into my poetry. It is in poetry that I have learned
to communicate best. I have become a poet, after fourteen books published
in a twenty-one year period. I now feel comfortable with the description
poet or *writer*. America has a way of forcing even the strongest into denying
reality. Afrika demanded reentry.

In all of my work I've tried to give the readers melodies and songs that
foster growth and questions. I wanted my readers to become a more informed
and better people. I think that my experiences have made me a better
person; I would like to think that I am a good and productive one also.
That is partially what I am working for. Study, work, travel and struggle
have taught me not to take myself too seriously, but to be serious enough
so that others, especially my enemies, do not mistake love and caring for
weakness.

Haki R. Madhubuti, "Prologue: Getting to This Place," *Killing Memory, Seeking
Ancestors* (Detroit: Lotus Press, 1987), pp. ix–x

JULIUS E. THOMPSON   Madhubuti's work has been able to touch the core of the black experience for the black masses. He has had an especially tremendous impact on younger blacks. He seems to have a special grasp of the urban predicament of black people in America on the one hand, and an ability to speak to them of hope for the future, on the other. In his early work he spoke of giving "positive direction" to black people and serving as ". . . a positive example for the Black community, not another contradictor." Thus, Madhubuti's poetry was able to connect with the Black Revolution of the 1950s through the 1970s. It directly encouraged black responsibility for black life, a new definition of black leadership, the need for black control of community images and the strengthening of black consciousness. His talents were especially applauded by black students from the elementary grades to the senior high, college level and beyond. Students bought tens of thousands of his books. Like Alex Haley's *The Autobiography of Malcolm X* and Frantz Fanon's *The Wretched of the Earth*, his early books were avidly read in college dormitories, and for study group discussions.

What then do the masses of black people see in Madhubuti's work? The author's first five books of poetry (*Think Black, Black Pride, Don't Cry, Scream, We Walk the Way of the New World* and *Directionscore*) are the foundations on which his fame and major contributions to black letters rest. This body of work offers the community insight into ten major concerns of black people: 1) nationalism and the international meaning of Pan-Africanism; 2) black identity—group, male and female; 3) the search, as poet Margaret Walker puts it, for "something" for our lives; 4) the Africanness of black people everywhere (note his status as the Marcus Garvey among contemporary black American poets of the 1960s); 5) the essence of the urban core of modern black life, from the perspective of the black male in the Midwest; 6) black music as a freedom song; 7) alienation and the search for black consciousness to replace alienation in our lives; 8) a writing style that can get to the heart of the black condition in few words—blackness with an open mind for black people; 9) a strong sense of history and politics and an appeal to the black masses (Madhubuti offers the public an excellent oral interpretation of his own poetry and has given readings and lectures at more than one thousand institutions, cultural centers and conferences in the United States and abroad); and 10) a literary product suitable for wide distribution at low cost, which has encouraged blacks to buy and read his works.

Madhubuti's last three collections of poetry, *Book of Life* (1973), *Earthquakes and Sun Rise Missions* (1984), and *Killing Memory, Seeking Ancestors* (1987), are somewhat less effective, in tone and mood, when compared to his earlier achievements. Indeed, the author has experienced a period of lesser influence as a poetic voice in the late 1970s and 1980s. His last three books of poetry indicate this problem. His last major book of poetry published by Broadside Press was *Book of Life*; then followed his name change in 1973. The later work showed a new focus on repeated questioning; a shift from black culture to philosophy and everyday politics; more preachment—more argumentativeness, less humor and irony, more pain—in short, less poetry; and a greater focus on ideology. In general, since the mid-1970s Madhubuti has shown a greater interest in writing essays than poetry, and this process is reflected in the lesser quality of the poetry he has produced.

Nonetheless, in spite of Madhubuti's decline as one of the leading African-American poets of contemporary times, he remains a major voice and continues to read his poetry and lecture widely. One must also note that twenty years is a very long time to maintain a dominant position in the creation of first-rate poetry.

Julius E. Thompson, "The Public Response to Haki R. Madhubuti, 1968–1988," Literary Griot 4, Nos. 1–2 (Spring–Fall 1992): 19–21

◈ Bibliography

Think Black. 1967.

Back Again, Home (Confessions of an Ex-Executive). 1967.

Black Pride. 1968.

Assassination. 1968.

For Black People (and Negroes Too): A Poetic Statement on Black Existence in America with a View of Tomorrow. 1968.

Don't Cry, Scream. 1969.

One Sided Shoot-out. 1969.

We Walk the Way of the New World. 1970.

Directionscore: Selected and New Poems. 1971.

Dynamite Voices I: Black Poets of the 1960's. 1971.

To Gwen with Love: An Anthology Dedicated to Gwendolyn Brooks (editor; with Patricia L. Brown and Francis Ward). 1971.

Kwanzaa: An African-American Holiday That Is Progressive and Uplifting. 1972.

The Need for an Afrikan Education. c. 1972.

From Plan to Planet: Life-Studies: The Need for Afrikan Minds and Institutions. 1973.

Book of Life. 1973.

Black People and the Coming Depression (with Jawanza Kunjufu). 1975.

A Capsule Course in Black Poetry Writing (with Gwendolyn Brooks, Keorapetse Kgositsile, and Dudley Randall). 1975.

The Socio-Politics of Black Exile. 1976.

Enemies: The Clash of Races. 1978.

Earthquakes and Sun Rise Missions: Poetry and Essays of Black Renewal 1973– 1983. 1984.

Say That the River Turns: The Impact of Gwendolyn Brooks (editor). 1987.

Killing Memory, Seeking Ancestors. 1987.

Black Man: Obsolete, Single, Dangerous? Afrikan American Families in Transition: Essays in Discovery, Solution, and Hope. 1990.

Confusion by Any Other Name: Essays Exploring the Negative Impact of The Blackman's Guide to Understanding the Blackwoman (editor). 1991.

Why L.A. Happened: Implications of the '92 Los Angeles Rebellion (editor). 1993.

⟐ ⟐ ⟐

Clarence Major
b. 1936

CLARENCE MAJOR was born in Atlanta, Georgia, on December 31, 1936. After his parents' divorce he moved to Chicago with his mother, although retaining connections with the South by frequent visits with his father and other relatives. Major began writing at the age of twelve, and continued to experiment in both fiction and poetry throughout high school while reading voraciously in American, English, and foreign literature. He developed a passion for the visual arts and in 1953 studied briefly at the Art Institute of Chicago, but he felt he lacked technical skill and abandoned his art studies. At this time he published a small pamphlet of poetry, *The Fires That Burn in Heaven* (1954).

In 1955 Major joined the air force, concurrently studying at the Armed Forces Institute. After his discharge in 1957 he worked in a steel factory in Omaha. During this same period he also began editing and publishing the *Coercion Review*, launching his fruitful literary career. In 1966, after issuing two mimeographed volumes of poetry, he moved to New York and became associated with the Harlem Education Program at the New Lincoln School. Major has subsequently been a lecturer at Sarah Lawrence College (1972–75) and a professor of English at Howard University (1974–76) and, since 1977, the University of Colorado at Boulder.

Although he has continued to write poetry, Major is best known for his seven novels. The first, *All-Night Visitors* (1969), was published by the Olympia Press and was extensively edited so as to emphasize the sex scenes and downplay the portrayal of character. Major's next novel, *NO* (1973), is the first to introduce his characteristic postmodernist or "experimental" techniques, including rapid shifts of point of view, authorial interruptions of the narrative, and unusual typographical devices. These techniques are particularly evident in *Reflex and Bone Structure* (1975), which won wide acclaim from critics and reviewers, and *Emergency Exit* (1979). Major's more recent novels are *My Amputations* (1986; winner of the Western States Book Award for fiction), *Such Was the Season* (1987), and *Painted Turtle:*

Woman with Guitar (1988). A collection of short stories, *Fun & Games*, was issued in 1989.

Major was a columnist for the *American Poetry Review*, has been a reviewer for *Essence* and *Library Journal*, and has edited several anthologies of black literature. He is also an accomplished lexicographer, responsible for *The Dictionary of Afro-American Slang* (1970). His earlier essays have been collected in *The Dark and Feeling: Black American Writers and Their Work* (1974) and features many of his provocative opinions on black literature and culture. He has been the recipient of many awards and grants and has been a guest lecturer at universities around the world.

Major has been married three times and lives with his current wife, Pamela, in Boulder, Colorado.

❂ *Critical Extracts*

FRANK MacSHANE   Clarence Major appears to have an ambition ⟨. . .⟩ to explore a new range of experience. There is no indication in *Swallow the Lake* of the order in which the poems were written, but from internal evidence they seem to be reprinted in reverse chronology. Those at the end of the book are well made anecdotal poems that are skillful but not remarkable. Major himself seems to have been dissatisfied with this limited achievement, for in a poem with a higher emotional pitch, called "The Revered Black Woman," he writes:

> Teach me my emotional shallowness.
> Teach me my message, only you know.
> From your black breasts. Melodies of hurt.
> Tender ache, afro-blue, afro you.

What Major wants is to be able to write poems that relate his talents as a writer to his condition as a black citizen of the United States. So much of his experience seems irrelevant, and the rest is hard to express: "feelings I could not / put into words into themselves into people." Later in the same poem he speaks of "ideas I could not break nor form." Major's poems often betray the struggle he is going through and document his attempt to make a resonant statement. He does not want to be just another Black protest poet, a role unworthy of his talent. And so he experiments; and as often as not he fails. The lines of his verse are disjointed; he plays with shapes and punctuation: at this point his work is tentative. But it should be understood that this struggle is being carried on at an advanced level, and that it is brought on by a dissatisfaction with simple formulae. That is what makes *Swallow the Lake* an interesting book.

> Frank MacShane, "A Range of Six," *Poetry* 118, No. 5 (August 1971): 297–98

UNSIGNED   The job of making beautiful things out of cultural scraps, of building a compassionate language from the crackling voices of urban America, has occupied many of those poets who have come of age since World War II. Clarence Major ⟨in *Swallow the Lake*⟩ attacks the problem with a kind of tense, fearful honesty, and comes out of it . . . well enough. The "Lake" of the title is (at least in one poem) Lake Michigan, and "I couldn't swallow it," the poet says. But in a sense the book itself does manage to swallow the Lake—with the broken civilization it reflects— and to rearrange the components of its failure as an expression of the loves and the nightmares of a sensitive man. It is a way of salvation that requires poetry, and Major, although not always successful, brings some splendid poems from it.

> Unsigned, [Review of *Swallow the Lake*], *Virginia Quarterly Review* 47, No. 1 (Winter 1971): xx

---

JOHN O'BRIEN   *Interviewer:* You and I have talked before about the relationship between your poetry and fiction. What do you see as the relationship between the two?

Major: Much of my poetry is purely fictional. I sincerely believe good poetry should be fictional. I work hard to make all my poems work as fiction. My newest book of poems which hasn't been published yet, *The Syncopated Cakewalk,* is pure fiction. I think that it was Carson McCullers who said that poetry should be more like fiction and that fiction should be more like poetry. I am working very deliberately to break down what I think are the false distinctions between poetry and fiction.

Interviewer: Is there an essential difference, though, that still exists? Does it have to do with the use of language or with the fact that fiction is still narrative in nature?

Major: No, I don't see the difference. But I am really in a state of transition with all of this. It is rather difficult for me to abstract theories about what this means and where I'm going with it.

Interviewer: I know that you attended the Art Institute in Chicago for a while. Has painting affected your writing in any way?

Major: The Art Institute experience has often been misunderstood. It didn't involve any academic classes. I was there on a fellowship to sketch and paint. I learned a lot in those days, but mainly on my own, upstairs in the gallery and in the library. I was very serious about painting. I almost painted my mother out of house and home actually. We nearly ran out of space, but my mother always encouraged me to paint. She wanted me to become a painter. I think my experience with painting, the way that I learned to see the physical world of lines, color, and composition, definitely influenced my writing.

Interviewer: Can you describe you work habits?

Major: They change all the time because they depend on the thing I'm doing. If I'm writing a group of short stories, I might work exclusively on one each day. If I'm writing a series of poems I might do one or two a day.

Interviewer: How much revision do you do?

Major: I revise endlessly. Even after publication. I am not one of those writers who sees publication as a cut-off point.

Interviewer: Eli in *All-Night Visitors* says something very interesting and I wonder whether or not it describes your reasons for writing: "the universe is not *ordered,* therefore I am simply pricking the shape of a particular construct, a form, in it."

Major: I don't know. I suppose writing comes from the need to shape one's experience and ideas. Maybe it assures us a future and a past. We try to drive away our fears and uncertainties and explain the mystery of life and the world.

John O'Brien, "Clarence Major," *Interviews with Black Writers* (New York: Liveright, 1973), pp. 137–39

KOFI AWOONOR   I first met Clarence Major on one of those dismal rainy and wintry and painfully nontropical nights of a Long Island winter. His evening's reading was a varied poetic and anguished political journey into the Black experiences of Haiti, and of his native America. There was rage and fire crackling within the passionate delineation of the poor and the wretched of our earth, Black earth. The rage was born in the marvelous anger that is Chicago, nursed on the mean alleyways of racial despair. But it is rage that was held firmly in control, modulated in a Cesairean anguish of the understatement, enclosed in the maturing teardrop, not of futility but of infinite passionate hope.

It is an easy assumption (fashionably believed by white critics) that all Black writers have only one theme—race and the color line. This naive assumption yet again harbors built-in images of the racial stereotypes. That Black poets are first and foremost human beings will come as a great surprise to most non-Black readers. And that their poetic careers are not all drawn in the frenetic racial epithets and white-baiting insults and exaggerated proclamations of so-called racial pride (newly discovered in the Sixties, and worn as a badge of redemption, buttressed by colorful costumes and large Afro coiffures). That Clarence Major's poetry is concerned with liberation and freedom is virtually a cliché. But that it is concerned with the resilience, ebony unyielding fibers in spite of the pain and the hurt, constituting a wonderful tribute to man, is the ultimate truth that emerges in these poems. Of all contemporary younger black poets of America, Major is perhaps the most composed, and yet the most articulate voice that has emerged. He shares with the best of his age the three distinct qualities of all "aboriginal" (meaning coming from the earth, of the primeval essence, divine) poetries, namely a firm and incontrovertible and almost intuitive power and control over language—the word that informs the chant and the mystical moment of all Creation, and inclusive of all its bludgeoning irony, the rhetorical humor, the cumulative outburst at trance point, and the ultimately distinct fact of having something to say. In short, this poetry shares a common subsoil with the first poetries of the world—complex, and infinite, they are prayers, incantations, invocations, curses, shamanistic cure hymns, and, ultimately, they carry and explode the religious moment of the dance.

> Kofi Awoonor, "*The Syncopated Cakewalk:* An Introduction" (1974), *Black American Literature Forum* 13, No. 2 (Summer 1979): 73–74

HAROLD WRIGHT   In 1927, Duke Ellington's band opened at Harlem's famed Cotton Club. One wonders if Clarence Major's book ⟨*The*

Theatre" / 1928 Blues). Then there is a tapestry-of-a-poem (one of the best in the book: "Madman of the Uncharmed Debris of the South Side") in which Major employs obscure references, a suggestion of the supernatural, tidbits of history, and other erudite meanderings.

Harold Wright, "Five Black Poets: History, Consciousness, Love, & Harshness," *Parnassus: Poetry in Review* 3, No. 2 (Spring–Summer 1975): 161–63

FANNY HOWE   Major's early work, by a leap of the imagination, can be seen geometrically as a star, or asterisk. The center is hot, the edges are myriad and take off into many directions. In the more recent work, the geometrical vision is that of a cross—vertical and horizontal and austere. He views other people as a series of details (horizontal); their history, or the cakewalk, is horizontal too. But all these figures must pass through a central point, himself, the poet; and so a moral viewpoint which is vertical emerges. The presence of the writer is here, as witness. Morality is one symptom of sanity. The narrator, as witness, serves justice by seeing all sides of a matter.

Major's language, achieved by long struggle, is original and should be useful to anyone honestly concerned with modern poetic diction. He has created a kind of code. What is not stated is what the poem is about. But that's a secret. It is said that a poem should not seem, but be. The modern poem does not so much "be" as imply, by the use of sound and tone. Major's poetry has tone. And tone is what you hear when someone speaks to you, far more closely than the sense of the words. Tone, in poetry, is achieved by line length, spacing, commas, periods, etc., rather than by a choice of words.

In the main, Major's poetry is never free of the tone of pain. Never sentimental, nor empty of humor, the poetry is still singed, burning. Those moments of pure delight encountered and transcribed by ⟨Robert⟩ Creeley or ⟨William Carlos⟩ Williams are not found in Major's work. And it is way down there, at that level of tone and mood, that the individual poet's voice remains linked to his history. While it is true that good art bests class, race, and economics, the effects of those three are still the tools used in the construction of good art. The absence of a historical memory is what accounts for the vacuity of much contemporary work. Without historical memory, questions of good and evil, guilt, and responsibility are meaningless.

Cotton Club) does not warrrant a brief introduction to this significant period in Black history. A biographical note says Major's writings have appeared in over 125 publications; he is also an editor (*The New Black Poetry*), a critic ("Open Letters," regular columns in *The American Poetry Review*), a novelist (*NO, All Night Visitors*), and a recognized pathfinder in the New Black Literature. In *Interviews with Black Writers* he recants statements made about Black writers in "a Black Criterion" (*The Journal of Black Poetry*, 1967). In that article (reprinted in *Black Voices* 1968, and *Nommo*, 1972), Major outlined a rather monolithic position for Black writers. He now believes Black writers should select any subject matter of technique that is amenable to them. His current stand indicates important growth.

Major himself has been in the forefront of experimental poetry and prose. In prose he fits "loosely" into a category with William Melvin Kelley and Ishmael Reed. But his influences and antecedents in poetry are not so easy to identify. He is usually very competent as a writer, and he has written better poetry than *The Cotton Club* (see *Swallow the Lake* and *Symptoms and Madness*), which is economic almost to the point of emaciation. His subject matter is "vital," as Gwendolyn Brooks might put it. Few Black poets today, excepting Robert Hayden and Jay Wright, are working well with history. Of the attempts being made, too many are laden with forced "integration." Major, however, is aware of the need to preserve and present a Black past. In the title poem he tells us to

> . . . honor
> the institutions, the
> idea of duke. tho a person,
> human through his own
> nights. sleeping late,
> being slow at home. knew
> & remember jungle nights.
> recorded harlem on
> the open wings of a
> bluebird.

Major conducts narrative tours of Harlem and urban Black America primarily during the first two or three decades of the Twentieth Century. He looks at Lenox Avenue ("In the Crowd on Lenox Ave. & 135th Street"), Black participation in World War I ("1919"), white inhibitions at the dawn of the Freudian Age ("Ladies Day: 1902"), the Great Depression ("1930: Hardtimes"), and the joys and agonies of Black entertainers ("Black

Major, with his facility for poetic language, and his personal history, could have exploited both by fusing them into a slick and popular expression. What is honorable about his work is the unusual task it assumes, of welding a complex modern diction to a constant historical consciousness. There are not many writers, black or white, engaged in this struggle, and it must be lonely.

Fanny Howe, "Clarence Major: Poet & Language Man," *Black American Literature Forum* 13, No. 2 (Summer 1979): 69

NATHANIEL MACKEY   Major's poetry, I'm saying, exhibits a certain refractoriness, as though it wants to surround itself with "No Trespassing" signs. This quality seems to have to do with a nostalgic, even narcissistic desire for something like the uncompromised naiveté of childhood. He writes of Richard Wright, for example:

> I try to imagine the type of work Richard Wright would have
> done had he developed into another type of person. As a child he
> wrote a story that was of "pure feeling." In his later work there
> was always some ideology behind everything. I like to play with
> the idea that original innocence might have saved him from many
> hallucinations had he been able to save *it*. ⟨*The Dark and the Feeling*⟩

The desire for a "gut" level of "pure feeling" and "original innocence" strikes me as a futile one, doomed to frustration if one is to work within language at all. What is language, after all, if not a social pact (an ideology), the basis, in fact, of all other social pacts? Even the deconstructive assault on language is finally a testimony to its importance and power—is, quite simply, a *linguistic* assault on language. Baraka once wrote:

> A compromise
> would be silence. To shut up, even such risk
> as the proper placement
> of verbs and nouns. . . .

But we aren't much given to silence. A certain use of language which, in short-circuiting predication, approximates silence is as close as we get. The futility of its fight against language, against the omnivorousness of ideation, leads me to say of Major's poetry what he tells us John A. Williams said of

All-Night Visitors. It too "gives off a kind of gentle helplessness and anger with no place to go."

Nathaniel Mackey, "To Define an Ultimate Dimness: Deconstruction in Clarence Major's Poems," *Black American Literature Forum* 13, No. 2 (Summer 1979): 67–68

RICHARD PERRY   Mr. Major has said that one of his objectives in writing is to "attempt to break down the artificial distinctions between poetry and fiction." *My Amputations* is distinguished by a rich and imaginative prose poetry of evocative power. Sometimes the effect is spectacular, like the eruption of fireworks against a dark, featureless sky: "In that terrain [I] sweated my way along the floor (ground, desert) of an orgy of heavy laughter, dry tongues; voiceless friction, dry areas, yellow eyes, red skin, sharp fingernails; breasts uneven and staccato teethprints in shoulders and necks." At other times the language is a distraction that calls attention to itself and delays the unfolding of a story I want very much to continue reading.

One of the most provocative aspects of *My Amputations* is Mr. Major's third-person narrator. Street-smart, versed in the blues, jazz, literature, art, European classical music and philosophy, this narrator is familiar with the cultural signposts of Western civilization. Not only is he hip and learned, he is brash, often injecting himself into the novel by commenting on the action or blurring what small distinctions exist between reality and dream. He strikes me as a voice who knows who he is, an ironic and sometimes disconcerting counterpoint to the tale of a man whose thirst for identity literally threatens his life.

The narrator doesn't reveal the source of his identity, at least not directly, and for good reason. Were we able to isolate him outside the novel, he would probably smile and say that the question of identity is extremely personal and not easily deciphered. Perhaps, sometimes, it is not decipherable at all. But Mr. Major has demonstrated in *My Amputations* that the attempt to do so can prove the stuff of an imaginative and compelling tale. As to whether Mason Ellis finds out who he is, I'm not telling.

Richard Perry, "Hunting the Thief of Identity," *New York Times Book Review*, 28 September 1986, p. 30

REGINALD MARTIN   Th⟨e⟩ belief in the metaphysical nature of blackness also comes up in Clarence Major's 'A Black Criteria', originally published in 1967 in *The Journal of Black Poetry*. This brief polemic is really the highest literary mark of the black aesthetic in the 1960s; it also serves as the link between the original black aesthetic and the new black aesthetic, as it contains already settled phases, and adds new parts more refined and up-to-date. From this work, later black aestheticians were able to expand into areas suggested by the long, organic line of notions of the black aesthetic which were so well-encapsulated and so well-expressed in Major's list of 'criteria'. Speaking of the ability and the necessity of blackness drawing in everyone, Major writes:

> We must shake up not only our own black brothers but the
> superficial and shoddy people stumbling in the brainlessness of the
> western decline. We must use our black poetic energy to
> overthrow the western ritual and passion, the curse, the dark ages
> of this death, the original sin's impact on a people and their
> unjust projection of it upon us black people; we must lead
> ourselves out of this madness and if our journey brings out
> others—perhaps even white people—then it will be good for us
> all. We must use our magic, as brother Leroi ⟨Jones⟩ says.

Major suggests that because of their ceaseless oppression, black leaders (read 'poets', as in traditional African community governance, every individual is a leader and every leader a poet) would always remember what it meant to be despised, and, thus, always do what is intrinsically 'right' for people. This assumption becomes bound inextricably into the black aesthetic. It welcomes all, but always insists that everyone remember what blackness is to ensure that he/she does not forget how to be empathetic, compassionate, human. Major writes, 'If we black poets see ourselves and our relationships with the deeper elements of life and with all mankind perhaps we can break thru the tangled ugly white energy of western fear and crime.'

Finally, Major ends with a point which had always been obvious in the beliefs of the original shapers of the black aesthetic, but which had not before been so precisely stated; that is, that art exists both for its own sake *and* for the sake of the people. It hopes to entertain, illuminate, or help. It is not purely the art of the state, directed by state notions on what art should do or be; nor is it merely fluff, what Ishmael Reed calls 'landlord art' when speaking of the ballet. It should serve some useful, human-edifying function as well as entertain or earn money for its creator. Major writes:

> The nightmare of this western white sadism must be fought with a superior energy and black poetic spirit is a powerful weapon.
>
> With the poem, we must erect a spiritual black nation we can all be proud of. And at the same time we must try to do the impossible—always the impossible—by bringing the poem back into the network of man's social and political life.
>
> Total life is what we want.

And with that statement, 'Total life is what we want', Major solidifies once and for all the black aesthetic on the side of a different and better way of life, heretofore not known, as yet undefined, and encompassing everyone.

Reginald Martin, *Ishmael Reed and the New Black Aesthetic Critics* (London: Macmillan Press, 1988), pp. 19–20

CLARENCE MAJOR   If there were disadvantages in being out of step, there were just as many advantages. I was beginning to engage myself passionately in painting and writing, and this passion would carry me through a lot of difficulties and disappointments—simply because I *had* it. I saw many people with no passionate interest in *anything*. Too many of them perished for lack of a passionate dream long before I thought possible.

At fourteen, this passionate need to create (and apparently the need to *share* it, too) caused me to try to go public—despite the fact that I knew I was doing something eccentric. One of my uncles ran a printing shop. I gathered enough confidence in my poetry to pay him ten dollars to print fifty copies of a little booklet of my own poetry. The poems reflect the influence of Rimbaud, van Gogh, and Impressionism generally—I *even* used French words I didn't understand.

Once I had the books in hand, I realized that I didn't know more than *three* people who might be interested in seeing a copy. I gave one to one of my English teachers. I gave my mother three copies. I gave my best poet friend a copy. I may have also given my art teacher, Mr. Fouche, a copy. And the rest of the edition was stored in a closet. They stayed there till, by chance, a year or two later, I discovered how bad the poems were and destroyed the remaining copies.

Clarence Major, "Necessary Distance: Afterthoughts on Becoming a Writer," *Black American Literature Forum* 23, No. 2 (Summer 1989): 205

▨ *Bibliography*

The Fires That Burn in Heaven. 1954.

#2. 1959.

Love Poems of a Black Man. 1965.

Human Juices. 1966.

Writers Workshop Anthology (editor). 1967.

Man Is Like a Child: An Anthology of Creative Writing by Students (editor). 1968.

The New Black Poetry (editor). 1969.

All-Night Visitors. 1969.

Dictionary of Afro-American Slang (editor). 1970, 1994 (as *Juba to Jive: A Dictionary of African-American Slang*).

Swallow the Lake. 1970.

Symptoms & Madness. 1971.

Private Line. 1971.

The Cotton Club: New Poems. 1972.

NO. 1973.

The Dark and Feeling: Black American Writers and Their Work. 1974.

The Syncopated Cakewalk. 1974.

Reflex and Bone Structure. 1975.

Emergency Exit. 1979.

Inside Diameter: The France Poems. 1985.

My Amputations. 1986.

Such Was the Season. 1987.

Surfaces and Masks. 1988.

Painted Turtle: Woman with Guitar. 1988.

Fun & Games. 1989.

Some Observations of a Stranger at Zuñi in the Latter Part of the Century. 1989.

Parking Lots. 1992.

Calling the Wind: Twentieth Century African-American Short Stories (editor). 1993.

Thylias Moss
b. 1954

THYLIAS MOSS was born Thylias Rebecca Brasier on February 27, 1954, in Cleveland, Ohio, the only child of Calvin Theodore and Florida Missouri Gaiter Brasier. Both of Thylias's parents came from the South: her father originated from Cowan, Tennessee, and worked for the Cardinal Tire Company, while her mother was the daughter of a farmer from Valhermosa Springs, Alabama. Thylias grew up in a loving and stable environment, with her parents encouraging her youthful attempts at literature: she wrote a short story at the age of six and a poem at seven.

After graduating from Alexander Hamilton Junior High School and John Adams High School, Thylias entered Syracuse University. She remained there for two years (1971–73) but found the racial tensions at the college difficult to endure and withdrew. Shortly afterward, in July 1973, she married John Lewis Moss, a man she had met at the New Bethlehem Baptist Church in Cleveland when she was sixteen.

Moss eventually returned to college, this time attending Oberlin and receiving a B.A. in creative writing in 1981. Two years later she earned an M.A. from the University of New Hampshire. In that same year, 1983, she published her first book of poetry, *Hosiery Seams on a Bowlegged Woman*. Moss had won the Academy of American Poets College Prize in 1982 for the poem "Coming of Age in Sanduski" and was encouraged by the Cleveland State University Poetry Center to compile a volume of her poetry. *Hosiery Seams* attracted relatively little attention but was representative of many of the themes found in Moss's work: deep concern about the role of both minorities and women in society, a religious sensibility that is nonetheless highly critical of the social and intellectual repressiveness of conventional religion, and a probing of her own mental and emotional states as she encounters the varied phenomena of life.

Moss has received many awards and grants to continue her work, including grants from the Kenan Charitable Trust and the National Endowment for the Arts and a fellowship from the Artists' Foundation of Massachusetts.

Since the mid-1980s she has been teaching at Phillips Andover Academy in Massachusetts.

Moss subsequently published three books of poetry in three years: *Pyramid of Bone* (1989), *At Redbones* (1990), and *Rainbow Remnants in Rock Bottom Ghetto Sky* (1991). The first, solicited by Charles Rowell of the University Press of Virginia, was first runner-up for the National Book Critics Circle Award. Moss attained celebrity with *Rainbow Remnants*, which won the Wytter Bynner Award. She has won other awards as well, including the Pushcart Prize and the Whiting Writer Award.

In 1993 Moss published a children's book, *I Want to Be*, and *Small Congregations*, a volume containing selections from her earlier work along with new poems. She is at work on a collection of short stories and another volume of poetry.

❖ *Critical Extracts*

UNSIGNED   This ⟨*Hosiery Seams on a Bowlegged Woman*⟩ is a fitting title for Thylias Moss's first book of poems because in it she reveals how women-related subjects such as marriage, motherhood, rape, abortion, and the complicated emotions between fathers and daughters all contribute to the slight bending of a sensitive individual's poetic vision. She builds many of her images and metaphors on passages from the Bible and rituals in the Baptist church. ⟨. . .⟩ In several poems, she explores her own ethnic roots as an American with Cherokee, Choctaw, and African ancestry; however, Moss is not calling for bold, public, political action as do some of the black women poets in Erlene Stetson's *Black Sister* or Amiri and Amina Baraka's anthology *Confirmation*. Instead, Moss is at her best as an artist when she is engaged in the autobiographical mode—the act of self-discovery through writing one's personal history.

Unsigned, [Review of *Hosiery Seams on a Bowlegged Woman*], *Choice* 21, No. 6 (February 1984): 823

UNSIGNED   If Thylias Moss's résumé is sedate (attended Oberlin, teaches at Phillips Academy, has earned an artist's fellowship), her poety is anything but. These poems ⟨*Pyramid of Bone*⟩ are raw, violent, full of anger, self-loathing, and defiance. And there is humor, albeit perverse, as in "The Undertaker's Daughter Feels Neglect"; like her father, whose wife "played dead" at the conception, she is "attracted / to things that can't run away from me." Moss's imagination is fantastical and mythical—she reads the minds both of a seamstress and of God.

> Unsigned, [Review of *Pyramid of Bone*], *Virginia Quarterly Review* 65, No. 3 (Summer 1989): 100

SUE STANDING   If *At Redbones* were a lightbulb, it would be 300 watt; if it were whiskey, it would be 200 proof; if it were a mule, it would have an awfully big kick. The poems in Thylias Moss's third collection ⟨. . .⟩ crackle with wit and wild surmise. In Moss's poems, wild women might get the blues, but the meek don't inherit the earth. Apothegms follow one another like a series of karate blows: "Absence of prejudice is a white lie"; "Birds of prey aren't holy"; "Monastic silences govern many marriages." ⟨. . .⟩

Sometimes Moss takes a one-shot idea and rides it a little too hard, as in "Faith in a Glass" (the speaker keeps faith instead of dentures in a glass by the bed) or "Provolone Baby" (variations on the cliché of throwing the baby out with the bathwater). But while a few of the poems are slight, they are never predictable. And when she's on target, as she is most of the time, Moss's verbal energy and righteous anger fuse into a cocktail as potent as one you might get at Redbones, the bar to which the book title refers and in which several poems in the book are set: "You go to Redbones after / you've been everywhere else"; "Free love had / been Redbones since black unemployment / and credit saturation."

In *At Redbones*, the neo-surrealism of Moss's earlier work has been transformed into a powerful blend of riveting imagery and dead-on social commentary. The communion wafers, grits, and sugar of these poems are "put on the table for surgery, not feast."

> Sue Standing, [Review of *At Redbones*], *Boston Review* 16, No. 1 (February 1991): 28

GLORIA T. HULL   ⟨Moss⟩ possesses absolutely stunning poetic skill and wields a kind of deceptively prose-like line and narrative sensibility that are still loaded with brilliant images, word play, and pregnant ellipses. This skill she unites with one of the bleakest, most sardonic visions I have ever encountered in an African American woman writer (for a comparison, think of Adrienne Kennedy, although Moss is the more assured and palatable of the two). With Moss, we have to give up cultural shibboleths about family, religion, nurturing, strength, and survival and be confronted with a lack of hope/hopefulness, which I admit was somehow disturbing to me. Here is the imprint of a casualty who not only walks among us, but speaks with eloquent savagery about the lost battles and doomed, ongoing war. As careful as I am about autobiographical criticism, I would nevertheless like to know more about the person who set this world in motion. ⟨. . .⟩

⟨. . .⟩ The entire book ⟨At Redbones⟩ is filled with ⟨. . .⟩ bloody Eucharistic imagery, Biblical lore, sacrilegious bitterness, and existential reliance on the ravaged self within a malevolently regimented universe—all juxtaposed with quotidian matter from our daily (white and black) lives. The only redemption here is the seeing, not the vision.

Gloria T. Hull, "Covering Ground," *Belles Lettres* 6, No. 3 (Spring 1991): 3–4

MARILYN NELSON WANIEK   Last week when two of my graduate students looked up for breath from a discussion about who owns the signifiers in *Invisible Man*, I thought, "Say what?" But I said, "That's very interesting" and wondered silently whether we could take our break a few minutes earlier than usual. So I feel I must define my use of the word "interesting" when I write here that Thylias Moss's third collection, *At Redbones*, is a very interesting book. What I mean is that although there are individual passages which seem private or weak to me, I recognize that a fine rage is at play in these pages. Moss's rage is distinctly Black, but more than that; it is the rage of faith. From an apparently Catholic upbringing and equipped with a sound theological background, Moss asks wide ranging questions about contemporary society and world history, confessing her doubt while offering an authentically Christian response. ⟨. . .⟩

Moss's quarrel is not with Christ, but with the distant silence of God, who, in "The Adversary," is

> . . . a man, subject to
> the quirks of maleness, among them that need
> for adversary, for worthy opponent, for just short
> of equal. And that's Satan, the runner up . . .

In "Spilled Sugar" she tells us that "we have to redefine God; he is not love at all. He is longing." God's silence allows the reading of Christianity which turns it into an instrument of oppression, not of liberation. For the ghetto-bound people who crowd the pages of her book, Christianity teaches utter submission. ⟨. . .⟩

Yet Moss rejects neither God nor Christ. She understands the ironic liberation of Christian love. In "A Catcher for an Atomic Bouquet," a poem which begins with a reference to the PBS series about the Civil Rights Movement, "Eyes on the Prize," she describes a life filled with the family responsibilities we recognize as characteristic of many Black women's lives: "a / baby from a teen-ager's body, a daughter from / a sister-in-law declared unfit." Where is the vaunted prize, she asks;

> When the baby tugs at me he is no prize; a prize
> just doesn't force its acceptance. You could
> easily look at him thinking how you didn't bring
> him into the world, he isn't really your
> responsibility. You just signed your name on
> a sheaf of paper that could have been one of the
> usual bad checks. You know, however, who's doing
> all the insisting that the baby stay in the world.
> Who's loving the insistence. Insistence is the prize.

In the suffering love of the people—most of them Black women—who crowd the pages of this collection, Moss finds an image of sainthood. Love becomes a powerful liberating force, a Eucharist of human community ⟨. . .⟩

At Redbones is a powerful and a painful book, a book which takes many risks. It's very interesting. I admire it greatly.

Marilyn Nelson Waniek, "A Multitude of Dreams," *Kenyon Review* 13, No. 4 (Fall 1991): 220–23

SUZANNE GARDINIER   Thylias Moss's poetic re-vision of history ⟨in *Rainbow Remnants in Rock Bottom Ghetto Sky*⟩ comes through a polished magnifying glass, in an intensely focused beam with the power to expose and to burn. ⟨. . .⟩

This poet has published three books in three years ⟨. . .⟩ and the work is similar enough to be taken as a whole, divided by chance into three parts. ⟨. . .⟩

Pyramid of Bone is dedicated to "my mother who made it to the dean's list of preferred housekeepers; she is a maid of honor." In the three books there are several poems that center on her; but the most revealing glimpses come in the middle of discussions of other things ⟨. . .⟩

In *Rainbow Remnants*, the poet's mother appears most fully in "Poem for My Mothers and Other Makes of Asafetida"; asafetida is a folk medicine, one the poet calls "my church in a bottle": "nasty asafetida, tastes like the bootleg, jackleg / medicine it is / curing me as only generations can . . ." In this poem Moss's sharp humor is evident, but doesn't require understatement; the praise words roll on and on, incantatory, invoking the unlikely character of what heals, searching it out of its hiding places:

> . . . there are
> no eyes except the ones I look into and fall in love, right
> into Mama's pupils, the past dark with dense ancestry, all
> who came before having to fit into the available space of
> history which is existence's memory and year after year
> the overcrowding worsens . . .
> . . . asafetida still on the shelf, oil in the puddle
> still ghetto stained glass, still rainbow remnants in rock
> bottom ghetto sky like a promise of no more tears, asafetida
> bottle floating there, some kind of Moses, some kind of
> deliverer . . .

You don't have to walk far from here to find the deep, nourishing current that is this poet's preoccupation with God. These books chart the stages of her private re-creation; in a note to "The Warmth of Hot Chocolate" in *The Best American Poetry 1989*, she writes that she will have none of "that voyeur God I met in Sunday school before old enough to start kindergarten, not the one who created weak flesh then condemned, *damned* for that very weakness; not him." The path to reconciliation is not simple for this poet of sass and backtalk, who describes a buffalo stampede as "footsteps whose sound / is my heart souped up / doctored, ninety pounds / running off a semi's invisible engine." ("The Rapture of Dry Ice Burning Off Skin as the Moment of the Soul's Apotheosis"—what a maker of titles she is!) Her nearest saint is Thomas, "jugging his hands into / wounds" ("Eucharistic Options"); her verse theology pivots on the argumentative distinctions and qualifications of a Talmudic scholar, laced with "Not even," "Yet also," "But" and "Besides," and with credos of unbelief. "Now the cyclone spirals above my house," she writes in the last poem of *Pyramid of Bone*; "I vow not to go to heaven / if that's the only ladder."

Suzanne Gardinier, "Bootleg, Jackleg Medicine: Curing as Only Generations Can," *Parnassus: Poetry in Review* 17, No. 1 (1992): 66–69, 71–72

ALVIN AUBERT   There is a bountiful tension in Thylias Moss's poetry between her Afro- and Euro-American cultural and literary lineages. Her inventive amalgamation of material from these two sources generates a strikingly witty and allusive style. The result is surrealistic, binary poems in which the *real* is never overwhelmed, as it might easily be, by its dream opposite. The poems are shielded from that hazard, principally, by the concreteness and humor with which they emphasize important issues.

⟨. . .⟩ From her first publications, *Hosiery Seams on a Bowlegged Woman* (1983) and *Pyramid of Bone* (1989), Moss establishes a "province" in which imaginatively conceived speculation lays claim to bona fide cognition. Through a unique, extraordinarily complex, surrealistic combination of the real and the fantastic, Moss claims magic realism as a place for sociopolitical discourse—even a singularly appropriate territory for that purpose, in its radical unsettling of the senses and concurrent limbering of the imagination for heightened perceptions and keener perspectives on things. ⟨. . .⟩

Moss's poems reflect not only a deep emotional capacity on the part of their personae but a profound intellectual commitment as well, in that balancing of emotion and thought many still acknowledge as essential to the creation of fine poetry. Her eyes seek everywhere for apt juxtapositions, and they are marvelously comprehending. Her ear is finely tuned to the right intonation and pitch, and her precise, at times metaphysical wit never fails to spark life into the experiences she renders with unfailing fidelity throughout her work.

Moss's poetry sensitively and unapologetically melds materials from the poet's African- and European-American cultural and literary traditions, while it affirms universal human values. The poems are richly complex and not always immediately accessible, but that is part of their aesthetic value; they impel re-reading as—to borrow an expression from ex-slave Frederick Douglass's *Narrative of the Life*—the light breaks upon us by degrees.

Alvin Aubert, "Bountiful Tension," *American Book Review* 13, No. 6 (February—March 1992): 29

ALDON L. NIELSEN   If the poems of Thylias Moss have always employed an imagery more insistently surreal than ⟨Lucille⟩ Clifton's, they worry some of the same blue notes. Often that imagery adds just the needed grace note, as in the closing of the poem "Lunchcounter Freedom": "When knocked from the stool / my body takes its shape from what / it falls into. The white man cradles / his tar baby. Each magus in turn. / He fathered it, it looks just like him / the spitting image. He can't let go of / his future. The menu offers tuna fish, / grits, beef in a sauce like desire. / He is free to choose from available / choices. An asterisk marks the special." Few among us can bring such particulars of new comprehension to such well-known events.

> Aldon L. Nielsen, [Review of *At Redbones*], *MultiCultural Review* 1, No. 2 (April 1992): 73–74

MARK JARMAN   There is a handful of successful poems in Thylias Moss's fourth book ⟨*Rainbow Remnants in Rock Bottom Ghetto Sky*⟩. One of them, "Poem for My Mothers and Other Makers of Asafetida," which contains the phrase that is the book's title, is first rate. These poems succeed for many of the same reasons that the others fail. Moss constructs an elaborate syntax, often discursive, yet seeking always to make distant connections and to illuminate them by the flame of her insight and imagination. When she succeeds, the results are breathtaking ⟨. . .⟩ But often Moss does not find her way. Though every poem contains something brought to radiance, many poems begin nebulously and grope their way to an almost crystallized argument-in-an-image; or, after a clear start, the poem ends in murk. Sometimes the murk is opaque syntax; sometimes it is changing subject in midstream. ⟨. . .⟩

Moss's large and expansive poems many times seem like exercises in association. She gives us everything she has thought of without pruning. I am ambivalent about the necessity of all the verbiage in her poems, but recognize that she is trying to manipulate a narrative syntax that poets like Norman Dubie and Roger Weingarten have often worked with. The difference between these poets and Moss is that she is not narrative at all. Charles Simic, who chose her book for the National Poetry Series, calls her a "visionary storyteller," but she tells no stories. She pirouettes in place, flinging sparks and cinders. The book is quite a performance. Curiously one of the best poems is "Interpretation of a Poem by Frost." It deserves a place in future anthologies and ends movingly with an echo of Frost's most famous poem:

> She has promises to keep . . .
> And miles to go, more than the distance from Africa to
>   Andover
> more than the distance from black to white . . .

I wish I liked all the poems better than I do, but while I admire her ambition, I find that Moss shows a kind of complacence in assuming that putting one thing on one side of an equals sign and one on another is imagination. Consider her image of a bible in "Congregations."

> His bible warms his hands, never
> leaves them, a dialysis, transfusion that keeps him alive . . .

A dialysis is not a transfusion. In "Time for Praise," extending a metaphor of a car as a whale that has swallowed Jonah and his family, she is led to call a Toyota "a whale with a door." Finally, this is the first poet I have encountered who, in the poem "News," actually has used the word *hopefully* as it is currently employed, which is to say incorrectly. Moss's errors appear to be the result of hurried composition. Often they are part of her poetry's dazzling improvisatory effects, but just as often they are not.

Mark Jarman, "The Curse of Discursiveness," *Hudson Review* 45, No. 1 (Spring 1992): 163–65

RITA SIGNORELLI-PAPPAS   I wish that I could ⟨. . .⟩ recommend the work of Thylias Moss for its graceful staying power, but I cannot. ⟨. . .⟩ While the poems in her fourth collection, *Rainbow Remnants in Rock Bottom Ghetto Sky*, are attractive in their verbal energy, most fail to cohere.

No less a poet than Charles Simic praises Moss's "wildness," but what he sees as a virtue strikes me as a central deficit of her work. That is, she keeps the surfaces of her poems so active that meaning seldom has a chance to clear. In poem after poem, images are introduced but not expanded to allow reader involvement, and questions raised go unresolved.

Moss's problem with writing accessible work becomes apparent in the book's very first poem, "Renewal at the Pediatric Hospice." The title suggests that the speaker has gained something from seeing children under the duress of imminent death, but the tone of the poem that follows is oddly breezy and disaffected. The focus on the children's brave suffering never successfully condenses; exactly how and why they provided inspiration is not apparent as the maker watches them:

> fill the whites of their eyes with snow, sculpt
> the iris into the pupil's plow that clears
> the field of vision for spring in which the white
> becomes shells and the irises, emerging chicks.

In this passage the random movement from snow-playing, to sculpting, to plowing, and, finally, to the first stirrings of spring in the short space of four lines distracts and confuses; there is no recovery time for the reader to make the transition from one disparate action to the next. ⟨. . .⟩

Still, Moss's work is rich in inventiveness. If in time she achieves a greater artistic discipline, we can look forward to a poet of considerable power.

Rita Signorelli-Pappas, "Poets Practiced and Premiering," *Belles Lettres* 7, No. 4 (Summer 1992): 63

UNSIGNED   A much-lauded poet brings her gifts for stretching language and patterning images to the perennial, pedestrian query, "What do you want to be?" An African American girl ⟨in *I Want to Be*⟩ ponders this question as she meanders home, and her thoughts seem to take as many detours as she does on her journey. She begins playfully—"I made a grass mustache, a dandelion beard, and bird nest toupee"—and grows ever more abstract: "I double-dutched with strands of rainbow. Then I fastened the strands to my hair and my toes and became a fiddle that sunbeams played. Then I sang with the oxygen choir." When she reaches home, the girl voices a string of aspirations: "I want to be quiet but not so quiet that nobody can hear me. I also want to be sound, a whole orchestra with two bassoons and an army of cellos. Sometimes I want to be just the triangle, a tinkle that sounds like an itch." Some readers may need to be guided through the kaleidoscope of metaphors that tumble across the pages; considering each image individually may elicit the greatest response.

Unsigned, [Review of *I Want to Be*], *Publishers Weekly*, 5 July 1993, p. 71

▦ *Bibliography*

Hosiery Seams on a Bowlegged Woman. 1983.

Pyramid of Bone. 1989.

At Redbones. 1990.

Rainbow Remnants in Rock Bottom Ghetto Sky. 1991.

I Want to Be. 1993.

Small Congregations: New and Selected Poems. 1993.

Ishmael Reed
b. 1938

ISHMAEL REED was born on February 22, 1938, in Chattanooga, Tennessee, the son of Henry Lenoir, a fundraiser for the YMCA, and Thelma Coleman; he took his name from his stepfather, Bennie Stephen Reed, an autoworker. The family moved to Buffalo in 1942, where Reed spent a few years at Buffalo Technical High School before graduating from East High School in 1956. He then attended the State University of New York at Buffalo, but had to withdraw in 1960 for lack of funds. At this time he married Priscilla Rose, with whom he would have two children before separating in 1963; they divorced in 1970.

Reed began working at the Talbert Mall Project, a black housing project in Buffalo. This experience led to a period of social activism, which included work on a newspaper, the *Empire Star Weekly*, and a controversial radio station, WVFO. In 1962 Reed moved to New York City, where he edited an underground magazine, the *Advance*, in Newark, New Jersey; he also participated in the Umbra Workshop, a black writers' group, and, in 1965, organized the American Festival of Negro Art.

Reed had begun writing satirical sketches in college. In 1967, the year he moved to Berkeley, California, his first novel, *The Free-Lance Pallbearers*, was published. This wide-ranging satire set the tone for Reed's other novels, whose only unifying themes are outrageousness and a refusal to toe a party line: *Yellow Back Radio Broke-Down* (1969), a vicious attack on Christianity; *Mumbo Jumbo* (1972) and *The Last Days of Louisiana Red* (1974), parodies of the detective novel in which a black detective uses HooDoo to probe African-American cultural history; *Flight to Canada* (1976), an ironic imitation of the slave narrative; *The Terrible Twos* (1982) and its sequel, *The Terrible Threes* (1989), satires on conservative politics and religion; *Reckless Eyeballing* (1986), a send-up of black feminism; and *Japanese by Spring* (1993), an attack on academic life.

Reed has also distinguished himself as a poet. His first volume of poetry was *catechism of d neoamerican hoodoo church* (1970), and it was followed by

Conjure: Selected Poems 1963–1970 (1972; nominated for the National Book Award and the Pulitzer Prize in poetry), *Chattanooga* (1973), *A Secretary to the Spirits* (1978), and *New and Collected Poems* (1988).

In 1970 Reed married Carla Blank, a dancer, with whom he had one child. The next year, with Steve Cannon and Al Young, he founded the Yardbird Publishing Company, which published an annual *Yardbird Reader* from 1972 to 1976; Reed has also won acclaim for his anthologies, *19 Necromancers from Now* (1970) and *Calafia: The California Poetry* (1979). In 1976 he formed the Before Columbus Foundation to promote the work of ethnic writers.

As an essayist Reed is as outspoken as he is as a novelist and poet. Four collections of his essays have appeared: *Shrovetide in Old New Orleans* (1978), *God Made Alaska for the Indians* (1982), *Writin' Is Fightin'* (1988), and *Airing Dirty Laundry* (1993). In much of his work, especially his novels and essays, Reed has faced accusations of misogyny and of being more successful at attacking his perceived enemies than advocating his own beliefs. But Reed was a pioneer of multiculturalism as opposed to the "monoculturalism" that he sees as still dominant in the United States.

In spite of his hostility to the academy, Reed has been a guest lecturer at many universities, including Yale, Harvard, Columbia, and Dartmouth. He has been the recipient of many awards, including a Guggenheim Award for fiction, an American Civil Liberties Award, and a Pushcart Prize.

Critical Extracts

ISHMAEL REED   I wrote my second poem at the age of 14 (1952) while serving time at Buffalo Technical High School, Buffalo, New York. (The principal was a six-foot math teacher with broad shoulders.) A rhyme, its subject was Christmas. Earlier my mother and her co-sales women at Statler's Department Store, on Fillmore Avenue, in Buffalo, commissioned me to write a poem celebrating a fellow employee's birthday. I rose to the occasion with another rhyme.

I didn't write another poem until dropping out of college in 1960. Swept away by the "wide gap between the social classes," I moved into Buffalo's notorious Talbert Mall Project (a horrible experience, the only friendly event being the birth of my daughter, Tim). A period of political activism was followed by one of cynicism. I took part in a political campaign, writing publicity, registering voters, and knocking on doors, in the snow; on behalf of a black councilman. (It turned out that he had secretly thrown the election for a bigger job.)

All of my early attempts at poetry were lost in an old car abandoned on the freeway while I was enroute to New York (1962).

"The Ghost of Birmingham" (1963) shows the influence of people I studied in college: Yeats, Pound and the prosey typography is similar to that found in Blake's "The Marriage of Heaven and Hell." (Excuse me. I know that it's white culture. I was a dupe, I confess.) ⟨. . .⟩

"The feral pioneers" was written while my wife and I were starving in Berkeley, California (1967); unsophisticated nATiOnaLIStS denied me a teaching job when I refused to end my lectures with Sieg Heil!! Perceptive people will notice that certain images are derived from the Donner Pass episode; Marcia Herskovitz will notice more than that.

"Badman of the guest professor" was written while I taught in Seattle, Washington (Winter 1969). Although the "straight" "square" "upright" Americans gave me every consideration and courtesy, radical/liberals were as evil as they could be. They didn't like me because I couldn't, like John Carlos, run around the track a few times or didn't have a rapist's past history; behaving like something romping about the rooftops, looking crazy, in "The Murders in the Rue Morgue." One of them, because I wasn't teaching his kind of reading list, mischievously placed a copy of the *MLA Style Sheet* among my student's textbooks at the bookstore. (I found its discussion of the semicolon to be quite weak.) Unlike Jackie Robinson, who, when a similar incident occurred, petted the black cat tossed onto the field, next to where he was seated on the bench; I boiled the black cat in a poem until it was down to its simmering mojo. The result was "Badman. . . ."

Ishmael Reed, "Foreword," *Conjure: Selected Poems 1963–1970* (Amherst: University of Massachusetts Press, 1972), pp. vii–viii

---

GEORGE LAMMING   Ishmael Reed is a prolific writer who also works in more than one medium. His novels (*Free-Lance Pall Bearers, Yellow Back Radio Broke-Down, Mumbo Jumbo*) have already consolidated his reputation as one of those black writers who refuse to be categorized according to the revelance of his theme. He asks no favors of any orthodoxy, but lets his imagination make its bid for the creation of new forms. Yet one cannot fail to notice the craft and discipline with which he controls the natural swing and bounce of his verse.

In his latest collection, *Conjure*, Reed offers us a sharp and provocative contrast in style. If ⟨Derek⟩ Walcott's echoes are those of the classical humanist, grave and formal, Reed's tone and rhythm derive from the militant tradition of the black underground. But his is an unusual brand of militancy; it is much concerned with the politics of language. He argues for a clean, free struggle between the liberating anarchism of the black tongue and the frozen esthetic of a conventional White Power. "May the best church win/ shake hands now and come out conjuring." His verse is distinguished by a fine critical intelligence, and his stance before the wide variety of American life is supremely confident. He can evoke with poetic realism the savagery which shaped the pioneering spirit as well as crystallize the fraudulence at the heart of the "civilizing" mission.

> George Lamming, [Review of *Conjure*], *New York Times Book Review*, 6 May 1973, p. 37

WILLIAM HEYEN   Ishmael Reed's poems jump out after me. *Conjure* is a book of wonders. The poems are bullets. I don't think I've ever been hit by anything as funny and wicked as Reed's rolling, insistent, goofy, austere, absurd, slippity-bop. These lines are from "Badman of the Guest Professor":

> its not my fault dat yr tradition
> was knocked off wop style & left in
> d alley w/pricks in its mouth. i
> read abt it in d papers but it was no
>   skin off my nose
> wasnt me who opened d gates & allowed
> d rustlers to slip thru unnoticed. u
> ought to do something abt yr security or
>   mend yr fences partner
> dont look at me if all dese niggers
> are ripping it up like deadwood dick;
> doing art d way its never been done.

Ishmael is a black cowboy outcast bum whose soul goes back to Osiris who invented popcorn and would "rather dance than rule" ("why i often allude to osiris"). "The Jackal-Headed Cowboy," "The Gangster's Death" (a powerful and prophetic anti-war poem, maybe the best we've had out of the Viet Nam horror), "I am a cowboy in the boat of Ra," "The Black Cock," "Catechism of neoamerican hoodoo church"—all are nasty, and major poems. Reed also gives us an essay, "Neo-Hoodoo Manifesto," which defines his non-western-civ. head and where it came from (not Eliot Pound von Goebbels, but the Fiestas, Ma Rainey, Marie Laveau who conducted HooDoo rites in the 1880's; not Moses Nixon but Little Richard Black Hawk). *Conjure* is an outpouring of spirit, an exorcism. I envy the way Reed has gone out to what tells him what he is. He's scary, and we "can't keep a good church down," and maybe it's his turn now, and maybe we can't keep him in the fields after he's seen Berkeley, and maybe we can't bank on his lazy no-good unprofitable ilk any longer. But he's a real poet.

William Heyen, "Four Realities," *Poetry* 122, No. 4 (July 1973): 239

PETER MEINKE   I don't think there is any one poem in *Chattanooga* as lively as "I Am a Cowboy in the Boat of Ra" from his first book, *Conjure* (1972), but some of them have the same engaging mixture of mythology, history (particularly black history), folklore, literary references and hip street argot. Like William Carlos Williams and Ferlinghetti, whom he sometimes resembles, Reed is not really as experimental or "free" as he at first seems, as in these lines from his fine ballad, "Railroad Bill, a Conjure Man":

> Now Hollywood they's doing old
> Bill they hired a teacher from
> Yale. To treat and script and
> Strip old Bill, this classics
> Professor from Yale.

That is he frequently takes something like a "natural" quatrain and breaks it up into five or six lines to give it a looser feeling. In his novels like *The Free-Lance Pall Bearers* (1967), Reed comes across like a sort of black Nathanael West, but his poetry is often gentler, more subtle, as in "Jack Notes" which begins "Being like a colored poet / is like going over / Niagara

Falls in a Barrel" and ends "But what really hurts is / you're bigger than the / Barrel."

I suppose *Chattanooga* can be called black poetry, but it's a far cry from, say, that of Don Lee or Bob Kaufman. Reed has his own "neo-American Hoodoo" esthetic, a voice that is recognizable as his own:

> I'm going to strut all over your
> Point like Old Sam Grant did
> My belly full of good Tennessee
> Whiskey, puffing on
> A .05 cigar
> The campaign for Chattanooga
> Behind me
> breathing a spell
> Ponying up for
> Appomattox!

Peter Meinke, "Peter Meinke on Five Poets," *New Republic*, 24 November 1973, p. 26

ISHMAEL REED   Q. What is your opinion of recent black poetry?
     A. Much of it is successful. One of the glaring problems, however, is that there isn't as much variety among the critical approaches as there is in the writing the critics are examining. Of course some of the critics only examine the writing of a particular school of black poetry and play like that's the whole thing, like other schools and individuals don't exist. I mean, how could somebody look at the black poetry of the last twenty years (I'm reluctant to call it black since some of the most inflated of the reputations—inflated by a magazine that has been pushing skin lighteners for twenty years—were people who are by my observation very "fair-skinned" and some of these people come on the "blackest"; I hate to bring this up but we're supposed to be "scientists" aren't we) and say that black poetry is directed to the end of "Freedom and Liberation" and based upon "black speech and music" when an examination would show that the majority of language material is American or English and that the poets and novelists have been influenced by not only music but graphics, painting, film, sculpture—all disciplines and all art forms—and write about all subjects.
     They say music because they are social realists and music is the most popular art form of the masses. You can be influenced by music while you're

asleep but reading is hard work. Of course listening to Cecil Taylor, Bill Dixon, and others is hard work, too, but when these critics talk about "music" they don't mean those musicians; they want to make it easy for them and a lot of nonsense that goes down stems from this desire. They are basically social workers and not critics.

Now, if these social realist critics were so interested in "Freedom and Liberation" why would they jive around with the recent cultural history of a people they're supposed to be championing—depriving them of the knowledge of how rich and varied their culture is and was? Why, if they were so hot about "black poetry" would they omit any reference to major figures who were responsible for its developments: Calvin Hernton, Lorenzo Thomas, Joe Johnson, Albert Haynes, Charles and William Patterson? Why do they hardly mention the *Umbra* poets, who were writing black poetry in the early sixties? Why would they leave out some of the excellent poets who've been writing since then in favor of promoting one particular school that originates from the screaming wing of the New York School of poets, "personalism," and borrows so much from the examples of the Black Mountain poets that you can't pick up an anthology without someone like Richard Ellmann saying black poets would be nowhere if it were not for Olson, Williams, Ginsberg, et al., which is just about as mischievous as someone saying black female poets are superior to black male poets, as Kenneth Rexroth wrote in *American Poetry in the Twentieth Century*, published by Herder and Herder, p. 158.

Anyway, truth will out and already people are beginning to see that the 1960s was a richer period in Afro-American writing than most thought and that the tricksters' school of Afro Lit did a cover-up, put up a cultural Watergate on people. ⟨. . .⟩

Anyway, the field nigger got all the play in the sixties. This field nigger romanticism came out of places like Howard University, which is apparently a hotbed of lumpen, field nigger, proletariat, professional street nigger chic. Maybe it's about time people started paying attention to other types of slaves and free blacks from the past. Maybe this generation should listen to shoemakers, masons, bakers, brick and tile makers, inventors, butchers, scientists, cabinetmakers and upholsterers, carpenters and joiners, printers, dentists, barbers, physicians, teachers, musicians, architects, and others. They were there, too, and maybe they have a lesson to teach the present.

Ishmael Reed, "Self-Interview" (1974), *Shrovetide in Old New Orleans* (Garden City, NY: Doubleday, 1978), pp. 140–43

DARWIN TURNER   Who or what is the poet Ishmael? An intellectual anti-intellectual. A religious opponent of religion. A duelling pacifist.
A black antagonist champion of blacks. A poet influenced by Yeats, Pound,
Blake, and the Umbra poets. A Black Arts poet who attacks Black Arts
critics and poets. A satirical creator of myths. An ideologue who derides
ideologies. A poet who ranges in allusion from Nixon to Wotan and Osiris.
A poet of the topical and the ancient. A poet ignored in Stephen Henderson's
trenchant analysis of the blackness of contemporary black poetry (*Understanding the New Black Poetry*, 1973), but whose poetry offers a point-by-
point illustration of Henderson's analysis. Stir these contradictions together
slowly in a vat of satire; whirl yourself wildly until dizzy; then pour slowly.
The brew is the poetry of Ishmael Reed, to be sipped as delicately as one
might sip a poison of 2 parts bourbon, 1 part vodka, and a dash of coke. There
is no guarantee that every drinker will like the concoction. Occasionally, the
sip is flat. Most often, however, it is quickly intoxicating. ⟨. . .⟩

Reed vitriolically attacks the corrupt values and venal slogans slavishly
venerated by "proper" Americans: pep pills (competitive drive), the artifi-
cially induced fetish for cleanliness and unblemished pale skin, antiseptic
sexuality, etiquette, and other superficial paraphernalia of an "elegant"
culture. His two-line insert of polite phrases is a mocking transition and
prologue to the conversion of these values into a food that can be eaten
only by indestructible people: an explosive stew "topped with kegs . . . of
whipped dynamite and cheery smithereens." Evoking the images of blacks
and black culture that whites have used pejoratively, the African-American
god-narrator prophesies that blacks will pass through the baptism of fire
and dance with the sun.

Reed's showmanship and conjuring can be spellbinding. Like T. S. Eliot,
he demands that his readers comprehend his allusions; but unlike Eliot, he
presumes that many who approach with child-like innocence will understand, or be fascinated by the sounds.

Darwin Turner, "A Spectrum of Blackness," *Parnassus: Poetry in Review* 4, No. 2
(Spring–Summer 1976): 209–10, 217–18

NATHANIEL MACKEY   Reed's work invests in and validates
black culture in a way not terribly out of line with the pronouncements of
the Black Aesthetic theorists. Like them, he argues the affinities or kinship

ties between African cultures and New World African or Neo-African cultures. While shying away from the political aspect of Pan-Africanism, he does insist upon a common cultural matrix which makes, say a Senegalese griot, a Mississippi Delta bluesman and a Trinidadian calypsonian relevant to one another. His work also celebrates ancient Egypt, a characteristic gesture of the black cultural nationalism of the sixties, the nationalist impulse of which the Black Aesthetic movement was a part. One also finds Reed making use of black folklore and the black oral tradition throughout his work, one of the things the Black Aesthetic theorists say the black artist should do. Reference to HooDoo beliefs and practices, to dances like the Calinda, the Charleston, and the Funky Chicken, and allusions to blues and "jazz" musicians abound. A poem such as "Railroad Bill, A Conjure Man" (*Chattanooga*) continues the literary appropriation of oral/folk forms and themes (in this case the epitome of the black folk-hero, the "bad nigguh") begun by earlier poets like Sterling Brown and Margaret Walker. In addition to the essentially rural folk culture, Reed also celebrates urban folk or "street" culture, the words of a poster advertising a dance at Esther's Orbit Room in Oakland, or in his tendency to "signify" in poems like "Columbia," "Dragon's Blood," "Badman of the Guest Professor," "The Atlantic Monthly, December 1970," and "Al Capone in Alaska." In fact, the satirical thrust of all of Reed's writing ⟨. . .⟩ is very much in the tradition of "the dozens." ⟨. . .⟩

The point at which Reed and the Black Aesthetic spokesmen part company is the issue of artistic freedom. While Reed's work does many of the things the Black Aesthetic says that black writing should, he objects to the idea of himself or any other writer being *ordered* to do these things. If a black painter out of a genuine inspiration or desire to do so paints a picture of oranges nourishing black guerrillas, fine. But if he does so only in deference to Ron Karenga or some other arbiter of the Black Aesthetic, something's wrong. The central tenet of Neo-HooDooism is artistic freedom, a belief in the indispensability of individual inventiveness and intuition: "Neo-HooDoo believes that every man is an artist and every artist a priest. You can bring your own creative ideas to Neo-HooDoo" (*Conjure*).

Nathaniel Mackey, "Ishmael Reed and the Black Aesthetic," *CLA Journal* 21, No. 3 (March 1978): 357–59

ROBERT MURRAY DAVIS   Ishmael Reed's political and esthetic intransigence might well be responsible for his relative neglect by all critical schools, for in all of his work he has gone out of his way to reject, among others, the New York literary establishment; Jewish critics of Black literature; other Black writers and critics of differing political, esthetic, and even physical hue; and the whole idea of English departments, which, he argues with a logic even more irritating than his ad hominem attacks, should be made part of ethnic studies programs. Certainly it would be easier to ignore Reed than to argue with him, but academic critics are masochistic enough to overlook everything except the lack of viable critical approach to Reed's work, especially to his novels. While it is possible that all of us should seek training in voodoo mythology and ritual, though even this might annoy Reed, perhaps it would be more immediately useful to look at some conventional approaches to his fiction: comparative myth and genre, defined in terms both of literary theory and popular cultural. And while none of Reed's six novels can be regarded as typical, *Yellow Back Radio Broke-Down* illustrates most spectacularly Reed's "main job": "to humble Judeo-Christian culture."

As everyone familiar with Eliot, Joyce, and other modernists will see at once, the fact that Reed uses mythologies from various times and cultures offers nothing new in itself. There are, however, at least four major differences between the use of myth by the modernists and by Reed: shape; sources; cultural authority; and formal authority. Of course, he does all of these things in the context of specific works, not in a programmatic fashion, and in any case one should not subject him to a rigid format. ⟨. . .⟩

In his movement towards kinetic art as well as other aspects of his theory, Reed has departed as far from the spirit and method of the Modernists as he can. Whether or not in practice it is possible to use myth at all and not be in some sense bound by and to it, theoretically it is possible, and obviously it is possible to loosen the bonds and play with them, even to do rope tricks like Loop or Reed in *Radio*. Whether or not the method works, and it is difficult to make any method work in or out of literature, depends upon its embodiment in the individual work. Just as some Charlie Parker solos are better than others, depending in part on the complementary interaction between underlying received structure and the soloist's melodic inventiveness, so Reed can be more or less successful. I believe that he works best where he has firm structure against which to play his variations, and a structure, like the Western or the mystery, which is part of his lived experience rather than, like the Antigone and St. Nicholas stories, the product of research. In either case, there is no virtue per se in the method Reed has adopted, and he seems to be in danger of repeating method if not mythologies. On the other hand, the method is none the worse for being repeated if it is being refined and perfected. Since Reed will be only forty-five when this essay is published (no great age for a novelist or satirist), he and his audience should have plenty of time to discover whether "a way of thinking that's considered 'way-out' or even 'crazy' " will come to seem commonplace or ho-hum.

> Robert Murray Davis, "Scatting the Myths: Ishmael Reed," *Arizona Quarterly* 39, No. 4 (Winter 1983): 406–7, 420

JEROME KLINKOWITZ ' Those dour guardians of official culture Ishmael Reed calls "high-ass Anglo critics" have always had trouble with his work, especially when they try to segregate facts from fiction. Even his partisans have rough going from time to time as they try to pigeonhole this writer who's built much of his career on the flamboyant eclipse of stereotypes. Take a friend who's been wondering if he should zap poor Ishmael for being a "grant-hoarder" (the term is Reed's and he isn't one). This investigator's crowning argument is that among the contributors' notes to *Yardbird Lives!* (coedited with Al Young for Grove Press in 1978), Reed simply lists himself as "a businessman," as if admitting he's in league with the folks who run America's acronymic corporations and grants establishments.

"Hey wait," I beg my friend and cite Reed's disclaimer from the first page of his funniest novel, *The Last Days of Louisiana Red* (Random House, 1974), a note which warns that "in order to avoid detection by powerful enemies and industrial spies, nineteenth-century HooDoo people referred to their Work as 'The Business.' " The inspired grant-getting hustle my friend rightly condemns is hardly The Business our novelist describes, for if you read into *Louisiana Red* you'll find the HooDoo Businessmen have their own name for such shenanigans every decent person would deplore: Moochism, as in Cab Calloway's "Minnie the Moocher." But for the victims of a monocultural education, artists like Calloway don't exist. ⟨. . .⟩

Syncretism is one of the few formally abstract words in Reed's critical vocabulary, and he feels it is the key to a true national American literature reflecting the uniquely multicultural art which has evolved here. "Anglo" culture, as he calls it, then becomes one element among many, and the only loss is that of a dominant intellectual academy sworn to upholding the beliefs of a long-dead order. Gabriel Garcia Marquez says much the same about his own multicultural, coastal Caribbean background where, as opposed to the rigidly colonial Spanish culture of the highlands capital in Bogota, history and fiction were allowed to blend, making truth "one more illusion, just one more version of many possible vantage points" where "people change their reality by changing their perception of it." Within this aesthetic, fact and imagination become one. And as our present age has been shaped by this union, so Reed creates a common method for writing novels and essays by using the best of it while warning of its dangers when abused.

Jerome Klinkowitz, "Ismael Reed's Multicultural Aesthetic," *Literary Subversions* (Carbondale: Southern Illinois University Press, 1985), pp. 18–19, 21

MICHAEL BOCCIA   The most obvious critical question to ask about *Cab Calloway Stands In for the Moon* is if the work is poetry or prose. It is neither, yet it is both. It is, as its subtitle explains, "D Hexorcism of Noxon D Awful (D Man Who Was Spelled Backwards)," that is a hex, a spell, a conjure. One foot in poetry, one foot in prose, this piece is in the netherword of genre. Reed's creations are usually curses against convention, spells upon spelling, sins against syntax, libels on language. This work is no different. In this "hexorcism," Papa La Bas uses his spectral powers, his moho, to drive off an enemy of the people, the evil Noxon, who pollutes the planet and destroys democracy.

Reed is most innovative through the imitation and synthesis of diverse art forms into writing. He fractures forms as we know them, and then fuses new shapes from the wreckage. Reed parodies form as much as he parodies ideologies by distorting familiar and traditional art forms to his own ends. *Cab Calloway Stands In for the Moon* is surrealistic, made of history and poetry, lists and musings, nightmares and dramas, all rolled into a crystal ball wherein Reed sees the foibles of Western culture.

Reed is the Jazzman of poetry, the Collage Artiste of fiction, the Shaman of Soul, and as such he transforms language as well as form. Language is hoodooed into submission: Reed transmutes "The" into "D," capital letters are forced to bow down, and quotation marks vanish. Even Reed's symbols, which include but transcend traditional interpretations, reflect the eclectic nature of his art. Symbols from ancient Egypt blend with lyrics of popular songs, astrology with baseball. The New York Yankees and Ammon Ra, Cab Calloway and the Moon, Minnie the Moocher and Richard Nixon, all share the stage.

Michael Boccia, [Review of *Cab Calloway Stands In for the Moon*], *Review of Contemporary Fiction* Vol. 7, No. 3 (Fall 1987): 250–51

REGINALD MARTIN   What is the position of Ishmael Reed within and external to the new black aesthetic? It is my assertion that Reed's work fails to meet the demanded criteria from the major aestheticians such as Addison Gayle, Houston Baker, and Amiri Baraka on these points:

(1) Reed uses humour, especially satire (in all his works, but especially *Mumbo Jumbo*) in dealing with subjects only entertained with seriousness before. Humour was an early insertion in the tenets of the original black aesthetic, but the tenor of the times in the 1960s, when the new black aesthetic was solidifying, demanded a direct confronting of social issues, and this was most often done in serious prose. For example, critics still have a difficult time handling Reed's *The Freelance Pallbearers* (1967), which was extreme satire containing negative black characterizations. Some critics have seen Reed's use of humour as a shirking of responsibility on his part; that is, he should be responsible (read serious) toward the serious problems which face black Americans.

(2) On the surface, Reed's protagonists are good role models only in that they are extremely intelligent and witty. Unlike the often totally serious and unflippant characters of other writers, Reed's main characters use wit and humour when faced with an oppressive society, as in *The Freelance Pallbearers* and *Yellow Back Radio Broke-Down* (1969), and not weapons, steadfastness, or religious dedication. Though his characters must be examined closely to see the positiveness they really convey, critics such as Baker and Baraka have denigrated Reed's humorous characterizations with the labels 'spurious' and 'unfocused'.

(3) Reed's work is often surreal. He opposes hate with humour, often synchronically presented, as in *Yellow Back Radio Broke-Down* and *The Terrible Twos* (1982), to achieve a textual structure that is not easily identifiable on the 'plain surface'. Critics have said that this is an attempt to escape discussing critical social issues.

(4) Reed's microcosms, being surreal, do not easily lend themselves to an identifiable social macrocosm; it is sometimes difficult for the reader to find a common experience to which to relate. Thus, that part of the new black aesthetic which insists on its own version of 'universality' is disappointed and repelled by Reed.

(5) Reed refuses to accommodate the demands of the adherents and leading aestheticians of the new black aesthetic, and confronts them, by name, in print; further, he refuses to accommodate the tastes of the general public, black or white, which has limited expectations and boundaries for the American writer who is black, as in *The Last Days of Louisiana Red* (1974) and *Flight to Canada* (1976).

Reed's battle with the new black aesthetic critics began early in his career. From the very start, he has disliked being categorized and seems to find it impossible to play the literary game by the rules of others.

> Reginald Martin, *Ishmael Reed and the New Black Aesthetic Critics* (New York: St. Martin's Press, 1988), pp. 41–43

DARRYL PINCKNEY   Reed came of age in the 1960s, "the decade that screamed." His family roots are in Chattanooga, Tennessee. He was born in 1938, grew up in Buffalo, New York, dropped out of the university there in 1960, worked for a local militant newspaper where he defended black prostitutes against the brutality of the police, wrote a play, and in 1962 took his belongings in a plastic bag to downtown Manhattan. The black movement was beginning to heat up; avant-garde black magazines appeared on the scene. LeRoi Jones, Reed's contemporary, had been to Cuba and had ceased to be a Beat poet. Reed joined the Umbra Workshop, a forerunner of Jones's Black Arts Repertory School. In 1965, the year Jones established his school in Harlem and turned away from interracial politics, Reed headed a black newspaper in Newark. (He was later to be associated with the magazine *Yardbird* and to run his own small press.) In 1968, he moved to Berkeley where he has been teaching ever since; and in 1979 he settled into the kind of neighborhood in Oakland that, he says, his stepfather and mother "spent about a third of their lives trying to escape."

Many black intellectuals in the 1960s sought to rehabilitate their identity through Islam, Black Power, or the principles of Ron Karenga, who held that black art must show up the enemy, praise the people, and support the revolution. Words were seen as weapons and whites were accused of "the intellectual rape of a race of people," but Reed was too quirky to become merely a black separatist. At his most rhetorical he claims to have a multinational, multi-ethnic view of the United States. He concocted his personal brand of chauvinism, one designed to dispense with the black writer's burden of interpreting the black experience.

> Darryl Pinckney, "Trickster Tales," *New York Review of Books*, 12 October 1989, p. 20

◈ *Bibliography*

The Free-Lance Pallbearers. 1967.

Yellow Back Radio Broke-Down. 1969.

19 Necromancers from Now (editor). 1970.

catechism of d neoamerican hoodoo church. 1970.

Yardbird Reader (editor; with Al Young). 1972–76. 5 vols.

Mumbo Jumbo. 1972.

Conjure: Selected Poems 1963–1970. 1972.

Chattanooga. 1973.

The Last Days of Louisiana Red. 1974.

Flight to Canada. 1976.

Poetry Makes Rhythm in Philosophy. 1976.

Shrovetide in Old New Orleans. 1978.

Yardbird Lives! (editor; with Al Young). 1978.

A Secretary to the Spirits. 1978.

Calafia: The California Poetry (editor). 1979.

The Terrible Twos. 1982.

God Made Alaska for the Indians: Selected Essays. 1982.

Reckless Eyeballing. 1986.

Cab Calloway Stands In for the Moon. 1986.

New and Collected Poems. 1988.

Writin' Is Fightin': Thirty-seven Years of Boxing on Paper. 1988.

The Terrible Threes. 1989.

The Before Columbus Foundation Fiction Anthology: Selections from the American Book Awards 1980–1990 (editor; with Kathryn Trueblood and Shawn Wong). 1992.

Airing Dirty Laundry. 1993.

Ishmael Reed: An Interview (with Cameron Northouse). 1993.

Japanese by Spring. 1993.

Carolyn M. Rodgers
b. 1945

CAROLYN MARIE RODGERS was born on December 14, 1945, in Chicago, the daughter of Clarence and Bazella (Colding) Rodgers. After attending public schools in Chicago, she entered the University of Illinois in 1960 but left the next year; she then enrolled at Roosevelt University in Chicago, where she received a B.A. in 1965.

During college and after graduation, Rodgers held various jobs to support herself, mostly in community service. She also became a political activist in the 1960s, fighting for the rights of blacks in a white society and the rights of women in a male society. Rodgers met various black writers in Chicago and joined the Organization of Black American Culture Writers Workshop and Gwendolyn Brooks's Writers Workshop, where she worked on her poetry.

Rodgers's first collection, *Paper Soul,* was published in 1968; it won the Conrad Kent Rivers Memorial Fund Award. The poems in this volume reveal Rodgers's revolutionary ideology and are written in dialect, often with experimental grammar and syntax. *Songs of a Black Bird* and *2 Love Raps* appeared the next year. In 1975 Rodgers published *how i got ovah: New and Selected Poems*, which brought her much celebrity and critical acclaim (it was nominated for a National Book Award). Revolutionary politics still appear in the collection, but overall it is highly autobiographical, with the focus shifting from the communal to the personal. In the process of fashioning her own rhythms and examining more personal topics, Rodgers has perhaps written more original and distinctive poems in *how i got ovah* than in her previous collections. Her next volume, *The Heart as Ever Green* (1978), also reveals a noticeable maturity of theme and refinement of technique.

After spending five years as a social worker, Rodgers began a teaching career in 1968 at Columbia College in Chicago. She has subsequently taught at the University of Washington, Albany State College, Malcolm X College, and Indiana University. In 1983 she received an M.A. from the University of Chicago. Her poetic output has been slim in the last decade or so, although she has published two more collections, *Translation* (1980) and *Finite Forms* (1985), and a novel, *A Little Lower Than Angels* (1984). She has also written short stories and has served as a book reviewer for the *Chicago Daily News* and a columnist for the *Milwaukee Courier*.

▩ *Critical Extracts*

SARAH WEBSTER FABIO   "Great!" was my first reaction to *Paper Soul*. "Why great?" was "something else." Carolyn Rodgers seems to know what she is about in each poem, and she does whatever it is she sets out to do with utmost precision. I think that this mastery of material is very important.

Hoyt Fuller's description of this writer in the introduction is very appropriate, and his comments on her poetry intimate the integration of artist and artistry so evident in her work. She is "boldly eloquent, brandishing words like steel knuckles . . . sometimes cold . . . young and vulnerable and open to life . . . But she is real . . ." And of her work:

> Her poems are bridges on which the heart and will may pass from
> the world her disgust would level, to the world her love would
> build. Her prose is spare and angular, geared to essence, but hard
> only when she wills it; and always it is stamped with an elegance
> so effortless and deep that it seems inborn: it is like her own
> frame, slim and straight, and as subtly feminine as a virgin's blush.

"Eulogy" and "Now Ain't That Love" are fine poems: the first is filled with pathos and rhetoric of concern and the latter with the stutter of fluttering pulse, knocking knees, drooled words marking a bad case of puppy love. Sometimes, in a poem such as "Soliloquy," the aim is to project a human voice and the special quality of that voice—the rhythm, force, persuasion in the direction, in this case 13 words. The title and the description of the setting, ironically, use twice as much language as does the actual capsule drama; this economy of words is a very black thing, I think, almost as black as the young fellow's cool stance toward an affair and the excess of feeling involved by it which threatens to "sweat up! / mah / do . . ."

Sarah Webster Fabio, [Review of *Paper Soul*], *Negro Digest* 17, No. 11 (September 1968): 51

DUDLEY RANDALL   She has satiric and witty poems also. "The Last M. F.," where she renounces the word *muthafucka* but uses it no less than 11 times, is clever. "Year, i is uh shootin off at the mouth" uses surprises effectively. "Greek Crazeology," I think, fails. The poet doesn't keep her cool enough to generate wit or humor. The victim should be impaled on a jest, but there is no jest here. It's interesting to note how in amorphous free verse there is a striving toward shape, toward form, like water shaping itself into raindrops as it falls from clouds. Often it takes the form of repetition or parallelism. In this poem the words *ducks, weeds, dogs, tics* and *worms* are repeated like the studied repetitions of some satiric poem. It cuts like a knife. It has brevity, surprise, and point.

There are other poems of delicate lyricism, intense feelings: "What Color Is Lonely," "6:30," "Breakthrough," "Me, In Kulu Se & Karma," with fine lines like "the sweet changes we are as Blacks;" "hours that / trickle befo me like unfreezin water;" "spread my fingers / in hair coarse thickets;" "and wish us me to sleep."

In her second book, Carolyn Rodgers shows herself as a sensitive and gifted poet, with variety and richness. The flaws and fripperies are minor, and could have been eliminated by careful revision, scrupulous editing (but again the poet has to heed the editor), or frank comment from a friend (but again the poet has to heed the friend; some poets jump bad at criticism).

Dudley Randall, [Review of *Songs of a Black Bird*], *Black World* 19, No. 10 (August 1970): 52

DON L. LEE   Carolyn Rodgers reveals obvious elements of her personality in her poetry. In her first book, *Paper Soul*, there are glimpses of greatness. ⟨. . .⟩ The poems are controlled and heavy. For a first book, she definitely cuts the smell of newness. In her latest book, *Songs of a Black Bird*, she continues to break rules and suggest the real, but doesn't carry the power or the creativeness of *Paper Soul*. There is feeling in the new book, but nothing to match "Now Ain't That Love" or "For Some Black Men" from her first volume.

The first "pome" in the new book is not a poem. It is not even a prose poem and belongs more in the category of a short story or prose sketch. "Jesus was crucified or It Must Be Deep" is a good piece of work but does not stand up as poetry. The only part that approaches poetry in style, line arrangement and images is the first page, but beyond that we have pure and good prose. In the poem "Greek Crazeology," she fails by using too many words. ⟨. . .⟩

Yet to sense the weaknesses of Sister Rodgers in a few poems only makes us more aware of her strengths in others. She works well in poems like "Breakthrough," "Me, in Kula Se & Karma" and "for h. w. fuller." It is difficult to believe that the care, time and effort that produced these poems went into the book as a whole. If she had been as careful with many of the poems in this second volume as she is in "for h. w. fuller," the book would have been a success.

> Don L. Lee, *Dynamite Voices I: Black Poets of the 1960's* (Detroit: Broadside Press, 1971), pp. 54, 57, 59

JOSEPH McLELLAN   These short lyrics ⟨*how i got ovah*⟩ were written over a period of years and deal with a variety of subjects: revolution, generation conflict, people known and loved and lost, growing up in Chicago where "just living was guerrilla warfare," and a slow discovery of the enduring values in a black religious heritage that was once scorned. Read together, they blend finally into one eloquent poem which is the story of a life.

> Joseph McLellan, [Review of *how i got ovah*], *Washington Post Book World*, 18 May 1975, p. 4

UNSIGNED   This collection of new and selected poems ⟨*how i got ovah*⟩ gives a representative view of the sensitivity and integrity Miss Rodgers brings to the act of writing black poetry. Her forte is the personal narrative poem, the impact of which is strongest in oral performance. Thus a number of the poems here, unfortunately, suggest the poet is more interested in pure experience than in rendering experience as poetry. Nevertheless, the poet treats spiritual aspects of black life, the getting over, with a tenderness that is rare in the new black poetry.

> Unsigned, [Review of *how i got ovah*], *Virginia Quarterly Review* 52, No. 1 (Winter 1976): 21, 24

HILDA NJOKI McELROY   It is interesting to note that most of
the poems in *How I Got Ovah* are written in the lyric mode from a first-
person perspective. The *persona* in each poem is so well established and
developed that one feels well acquainted and involved with this speaker in
a very personal manner. Though some poems are deeply personal at times,
the reader/audience is never excluded from these experiences. Probably
because Carolyn Rodgers' works cover such a wide range of human experiences her sermons/songs/tales seem to often be addressed to us though we
know the poet is female and the poems reveal a female *persona*, I have noticed
that male students in my Interpretation of Black Poetry class frequently find
Rodgers' works to be equally valid for male or female.

Skillfully utilizing rhythmic devices from our Afrikan oral tradition in
the title poem, "how i got ovah," the *persona* seems to be speaking directly
to those of us in the Black diaspora who share the sufferings of a displaced
people:

> i can tell you
> about them
> i have shaken rivers
> out of my eyes
> i have waded eyelash deep
> have crossed rivers
> have shaken the water weed out
> of my lungs
> have swam for strength
> pulled by strength
> through waterfalls with electric beats
> i have bore the shocks
> of water deep deep
> waterlogs are my bones
> i have shaken the water free of my hair
> have kneeled on the banks
> and kissed my ancestors of the dirt
> whose rich dark root fingers rose up reached out
> grabbed and pulled me rocked me cupped me
> gentle strong and firm
> carried me
> made me swim for strength
> cross rivers
> though i shivered
> was wet was cold
> and wanted to sink down

> and float as water, yea—
> i can tell you.
> i have shaken rivers
> out of my eyes. ⟨. . .⟩

In "The Children of Their Sin," Rodgers is like the old Afrikan folk-
teller—entertaining and instructing us about our weakness, contradictions
and inner conflicts. Combining many devices from the African folk tale,
Rodgers deals basically with self-hatred. In order to re-inforce this theme,
Rodgers, in a fantastic display of craftpersonship, utilizes present/mythic
time, cosmic sounds/rhythms, and vivid imagery. In the present time in part
one, the *persona* establishes the irony and contradictions by explaining how
she left her job one evening of poet-teaching Black people how to love one
another and on the way home she refused to sit next to a Black brother
because he looked "mean and hungry, poor and damply cold." Rather, she
chose to sit next to a white man because he "was neatly new yorkish
antiseptically executive."

> Hilda Njoki McElroy, [Review of *how I got ovah*], *Black World* 25, No. 4 (February
> 1976): 51–52

GEORGE E. KENT   Carolyn M. Rodgers' *how i got ovah* contains
new and selected poems from the body of her work. Such older favorites
as "Jesus Was Crucified, or It Must Be Deep," "It Is Deep," "Somebody
Call," "c. c. rider," "U Name This One," "to Gwen," and "For H. W.
Fuller," are included.

Newer poems often involve a revaluation of older values. The simplicities
about the black church and religion are re-studied ⟨. . .⟩ The church gets
praise for its communal work and for steady building, in contrast to the
unproductiveness of the militant rhetoric which criticized it and tried to
give instruction. Other successful religious poems include "how i got ovah,"
"how i got ovah II," and "Living Water." ⟨. . .⟩

The religious poems are occasionally threatened by the attempt to mix
religious and hip diction, as the term "shimmy" would illustrate. The poem
"Jesus must of been some kind of dude" seems also to suffer from this mixture
of diction. In addition to new poems devoted to religion, there are also

simply new poems which reveal sharp craftsmanship, and an interesting poem of introduction by Angela Jackson.

George E. Kent, "The 1975 Black Literary Scene: Significant Developments," *Phylon* 37, No. 1 (March 1976): 112–13

WALTER SUBLETTE   Carolyn Rodgers' poetry has received more than mild critical interest for some time. It was considered special well before 1976, when her collection, *How I Got Ovah*, was a National Book Award nominee. Yet since that time, Rodgers' reputation has spread considerably. Her poetry is tightly crafted free verse that unpretentiously combines the black American vernacular and the straightforward American style. It is absent of fashionably extreme attitudes, and achieves a distinct presence by cementing private poetic vision with grim but poignant understanding. In *The Heart as Ever Green*, this fusion of poetic vision and spiritual compassion is extremely pronounced, producing a kind of contemporary black American poetry that is warmly honest, immediately direct, and clearly accessible.

Rodgers makes strong use of the word "heart" in the title. As supported in the poems, the heart is meant to be a reservoir of containment. In it the patiently waiting expectations of all black people are protectively housed. It is a place of necessity from which the black race observes life, the observation itself made tolerable through the realization of inevitable social change. That change will one day bring freedom as well as personal and collective growth. It seems important to realize that the image of the heart is not used to express pessimistic hope, but realized certainty. It is a place of warm solidity, of relative security, whose sustaining power is the awareness of past and present suffering. It is a place of pride and dignity, of indestructible strength and enormous love. And since the heart is suspended in time as an impregnable constant, it is appropriately affixed with the color green in anticipation of the time it may realize its full fruition.

The Heart as Ever Green is a poetic statement on the condition, attitude, and determination of black people. Carolyn Rodgers has given us a strong, dignified, and beautiful book of poems. At the core of this work is a sensibility that is framed in the notion that black suffering will be alleviated in time.

That may be an accurate, perceptive, and honorable belief, but is nonetheless one that not all black contemporary poets would agree with.

Walter Sublette, "Poetic Voices of Hope and Rage," *Chicago Tribune Book World*, 19 November 1978, p. 10

ESTELLA M. SALES   The expression "how I got ovah" slips fluently from black colloquialism into a black gospel song and on into the black slang vernacular with unobstructed ease. Presently it is the title of Carolyn Rodgers' latest volume of poetry, *How I Got Ovah*.

The meaning of the recurring expression is generally defined by its contextual usage and can be appropriately connotative of how one has triumphed spiritually; how one has overcome worldly hardships; how one has outwitted his adversary; or merely how one has swindled his loved ones. In Carolyn Rodgers' book, many of these connotations emerge; however, another unique connotation is given shape by the thematic structuring of the book. The poet writes on the seemingly disjointed and ostensibly contradictory aspects of black life. She is not afraid of the contradictions; she consciously seeks them out, then reconciles their differences by poetically presenting their interrelatedness. The poet 'gets ovah' the waters of confusion that flow between the contradictions by crossing certain metaphorically symbolic bridges. These bridges she comes to recognize are her own inner voice, her ancestral rootedness, her Christian faith, and her parental support. Other supportive structures in the bridges are her church community and her extended black community. So the unique connotation of 'getting ovah' in Carolyn Rodgers' book would be bridging the separating waters, reconciling the contradictions or piecing together the seemingly dichotomous entities of black life.

The major dichotomies that are patterned throughout the book are (1) black revolutionary tactics as opposed to Christian ethics, (2) the black past as opposed to the present, (3) the black younger generation as opposed to the older generation, (4) idealistic dreams as opposed to dead-end awakenings, and (5) the individual poetic voice as opposed to the conscious, collective poetic voice. Often, more than one dichotomous pattern is being dealt with simultaneously in the same poem. ⟨. . .⟩

In her untitled poem (p. 6), the poetic statement is consummated. The persona realizes, after being caught up in a whirlwind of voices, that she is confused and "cannot remember / where to listen." Once away from the screaming voices, silence reflows and the poet returns "cradling creation in the silences." The poet has listened to the (ideological) voices till deafened by them and only after that point does she realize that through creative silence, or listening to her own inner voice, she is able to create. Listening to her own inner voice is her poetic bridge of "getting ovah."

> Estella M. Sales, "Contradictions in Black Life: Recognized and Reconciled in *How I Got Ovah*," *CLA Journal* 25, No. 1 (September 1981): 74–75, 81

ANGELENE JAMISON   Rodgers treats a wide range of topics in her poetry, including revolution, love, Black male-female relationships, religion, and the complexities of Black womanhood. Not only does she bring a Black perspective to these subjects, but through keen insight, intuition, and expert craftsmanship she brings the unique vision and perception of the Black woman. Through a skillfully uncluttered use of several literary devices, she convincingly reinterprets the love, pain, longings, struggles, victories, the day-to-day routines of Black people from the point of view of the Black woman. Gracefully courageous enough to explore long-hidden truths, about Black women particularly, her poetry shows honesty, warmth, and love for Black people. Rodgers is a "straight-up" poet, a "singer of sass and blues" with a "sanctified soul." Forcing one to recognize the complexities of being, she "make u testify to truth." Her language "remind u of the people on the corner / her words be leaning on the building there." Eloquently employing various Black linguistic forms, she speaks in the idiom of those whose sentiments she reflects. ". . . country and street and proper too," as Angela Jackson points out, Carolyn Rodgers is "a choir in herself."

Most striking about her poetry was her ability to describe so realistically the emotional dilemmas of the Black female artist in a poem entitled "Breakthrough." Originally published in *Songs of a Black Bird*, "Breakthrough" describes the poet's "tangled feelings . . . about ev'rything. . . ." What is perhaps the most outstanding quality of the poem is the poet's use of rhythmic Black speech and imagery to describe the inner turmoil of the Black woman as artist, and her coming to grips with the confusion.

"Breakthrough" sent me searching for other works by and about this woman who had put in poetic form such feelings and emotions, those with which so many Black women struggle. I discovered there is very little criticism, but there is poetry, poetry which particularly reflects not only an incredible honesty and perception about Black women but an ability to articulate "what Black women mean." With depth and insight, she reveals the fears, insecurities, needs, yearnings, etc., with a poetic "I know, I've been there, I *am* there" realness.

> Angelene Jamison, "Imagery in the Women Poems: The Art of Carolyn Rodgers," *Black Women Writers (1950–1980): A Critical Evaluation*, ed. Mari Evans (New York: Anchor Press/Doubleday, 1984), p. 378

BETTYE J. PARKER-SMITH   It can be fairly accurately claimed that Carolyn Rodgers' artistic achievements have undergone two distinct and clear baptisms. The first can be viewed as being rough-hewn, folk-spirited, and held 'down at the river' amid water moccasins in the face of a glaring midday sun; the climax of a 'swing-lo-sweet-chariot' revival. These were her OBAC (Organization of Black African Culture) years. This organization, a Petri dish for young Black writers of the sixties, was guided principally by the late Hoyt W. Fuller, Jr., then editor of *Black World*, and served, if only temporarily, to arrest the psychological frailty of Carolyn Rodgers, who was "slim and straight, and as subtly feminine as a virgin's blush." Fuller recalled that when he first met her at an OBAC social function, she was "skinny and scared," verbalized an interest in writing, and telegraphed a need to be stroked. Being the unhealthy flower she was, Carolyn Rodgers responded naturally to his quiet mood and healing voice. ⟨. . .⟩ The format of the OBAC workshops helped cushion Rodgers' insecurities; its members provided a strong support system for each other. It was as a member of this literary coterie, this small in-group of novice writers and intellectuals, that she made her initial impact. In introducing her first volume of poetry, *Paper Soul*, Fuller prepared us for what was to come: "Carolyn Rodgers will be heard. She has the artist's gift and the artist's beautiful country." This first period of her writing includes her first three volumes, *Paper Soul, 2 Love Raps*, and *Song of a Black Bird*. It is characterized by a potpourri of themes and demonstrates her impudence, through the use of her wit, obscenities, the argumentation in her love and revolution poems, and the pain and presence of her mother. She questions the relevance of the Vietnam War, declares war on the cities, laments Malcolm X, and criticizes the contradictory life-style of Blacks. And she glances at God. These are the years that she whipped with the lean switch, often bringing down her wrath with stinging, sharp, and sometimes excruciating pain. She is very exact about her focus:

> I will write about things that are universal So that hundreds, maybe even thousands of years from now, White critics and readers will say of me, Here is a good Black writer, who wrote about truth and universal topics. . . . I will write about Black people repossessing this earth, a-men.

To be sure, she was clairvoyant and uncompromising. Her poetry was colored by a young woman's contempt for injustice and a young rebel's sensitivity to the cost of freedom in a corrupt world where race takes precedence over everything else.

On the other hand, the second baptism takes place just before Carolyn Rodgers is able to shake herself dry from the first river. This one can perhaps be classified as a sprinkling and is protected by the blessings of a very fine headcloth. It is more sophisticated. It is cooler; lacks the fire and brimstone of the first period. But it is nonetheless penetrating. The two volumes that characterize this phase are *How I Got Ovah* and *The Heart as Ever Green*. At this point, Rodgers moved away from Third World Press, the publisher that accommodated most of the OBAC writers and which published her first three volumes, to a larger commercial publishing house. She also broke, it seems, abrasively with OBAC. She moved back inside her once lone and timid world. With OBAC she had demonstrated signs of strength and assertiveness. These characteristics are not visible in this stage and she returned to her old form of insecurity. In fact, her frailty seemed to have returned doublefold, wrapped itself around her physical and psychological self. This was the moment when she received recognition from a larger and more diverse reading audience. However, her celebrity was short-lived. The poetry that represents this period is rather specific. She cross-examines the revolution, its contradictions, and her relationship to it. She listens to her mother's whispers. And she embraces God.

Bettye J. Parker-Smith, "Running Wild in Her Soul: The Poetry of Carolyn Rodgers," *Black Women Writers (1950–1980): A Critical Evaluation*, ed. Mari Evans (New York: Anchor Press/Doubleday, 1984), pp. 395–97

◈ *Bibliography*

Paper Soul. 1968.
Songs of a Black Bird. 1969.

2 Love Raps. 1969.

For Love of Our Brothers (editor). 1970.

Now Ain't That Love? 1970.

For H. W. Fuller. 1971.

A Long Rap: Commonly Known as a Poetic Essay. 1971.

Roots (editor). 1973.

how i got ovah: New and Selected Poems. 1975.

The Heart as Ever Green. 1978.

Translation. 1980.

A Little Lower Than Angels. 1984.

Finite Forms. 1985.

Sonia Sanchez

b. 1934

SONIA SANCHEZ was born Wilsonia Driver on September 9, 1934, in Birmingham, Alabama, to Lena and Wilson L. Driver. Sonia's mother died when she was one, and she and her sister Pat spent several years with various relatives before being taken by their father to New York City. There Sanchez attended public schools and then Hunter College, where she received a B.A. in 1955. After graduating, she entered a graduate program at New York University but withdrew after a year.

Sanchez became swept up in the revolutionary social movements of the 1960s. Her first two collections of poetry, *Home Coming* (1969) and *We a BaddDDD People* (1970), reflect her militant, antiwhite stance, inspired in part by the example of Malcolm X. She incorporates dialect and profanity into her pithy, biting poems, and the tone is usually combative. Sanchez unleashed some of her rage at America's Anglocentric educational system. Her criticisms, however, were followed by suggestions, and she has become a powerful advocate of black studies programs.

Sanchez herself began a long teaching career in 1965 at the Downtown Community School in New York. After stints at several universities, including San Francisco State College, the University of Pittsburgh, Rutgers, Amherst, and the University of Pennsylvania, she joined the staff of Temple University in Philadelphia in 1977, where she is currently a professor in the departments of English and women's studies. Her anthology, *Three Hundred and Sixty Degrees of Blackness Comin at You* (1972), collects poetry written by her students in a creative writing class in Harlem.

In 1968 Sanchez married activist Etheridge Knight, with whom she had three children. The marriage, however, was troubled, and Sanchez and Knight later divorced. This experience may perhaps have helped to make her aware of the increasing tensions between black men and black women, which she has addressed both in poems and in the play *Uh Huh: But How Do It Free Us?* (1975). Sanchez has written several other plays, including

Sister Son/ji (1969), *The Bronx Is Next* (1970), and *I'm Black When I'm Singing, I'm Blue When I Ain't* (1982).

Sanchez's later poetry volumes—including *A Blues Book for Blue Black Magical Women* (1974), *I've Been a Woman* (1978), and *Generations* (1986)—are more specifically feminist in orientation, treating Sanchez's personal growth while celebrating women in general. One of her most celebrated volumes is *homegirls & handgrenades* (1984), a collection of autobiographical prose poems. The volume received an American Book Award from the Before Columbus Foundation.

Sanchez has also done considerable writing for children. *It's a New Day* (1971) is a poetry collection for "young brothas and sistuhs," while *The Adventures of Fathead, Smallhead, and Squarehead* (1973) is a juvenile short story. Sanchez has also compiled a collection of short stories for young readers, *A Sound Investment* (1980).

Sanchez continues to teach and write in Philadelphia.

◈ *Critical Extracts*

DON L. LEE   Sonia Sanchez has moments of personal loneliness that are not akin to some philosophical abstraction, but come because of the absence of someone, her man, who is real. She is intense, able to do many things simultaneously, as in "Short Poem," from her first book *Homecoming*:

> My old man
> tells me i'm
> so full of sweet
> pussy he can
> smell me coming.
> maybe
>   i
>
>   shd
>   bottle
>   it   and
>   sell it
>   when he goes.

It screams the fertile sense of being a woman desired. Irony suggests an attitude toward sex life that's natural. It can't be sold. She reveals a self-blues and an obscenity that's funny and easy for Black people to relate to.

Sonia Sanchez understands that the mind of the negro works at a very conscious level; his skin tonality maintains this consciousness. Sonia enables us to move under her conscious tonality into blackerfields. Truedarkness. She pushes. Her one word lines are like well worked sentences and her metaphors and images are those we go to sleep/wake up with for days. We identify, double. The poems in the first book are not those of a first book poet. The poet is skilled/confident to the point of oversay. Saying more than it be's. Her poems/poetry will not fail to impress the stagnant mind and will open little holes in the blk/brain with poisonlines as indicated in "Homecoming."

> this is for real.
>   black.
>   niggers.
>   my beauty.
>   baby.
>   i have learned it
>   ain't like they say
>   in the newspapers.

For the negro, reality is real (reality: whatever controls yr/thought process, controls yr/pure & unpure actions). Blackpeople's reality is controlled by alien forces. This is why Sonia Sanchez is so beautiful & needed; this is also why she is dangerous. The Black artist is dangerous. Blk/art moves to control the negro's reality, moves to negate the influences of the alien forces. Sonia's word usage is positive. Her direction is aimed/armed to do damage to the nigger's control center. His mind. Poeple will be looking/ hoping/trying to shoot her down. Back shooting, they will not face her. We know that "fuck u muthafuckas" will turn a lot of evil minds around. The true/pure people will read on. they will confess, to themselves. That's important—her poetry helps you face yr/self. Then, actually, u will be able to move thru/out the world an face otherpeople as true Blackperson.

Don L. Lee, *Dynamite Voices 1: Black Poets of the 1960s* (Detroit: Broadside Press, 1971), pp. 48–49.

SEBASTIAN CLARKE   The ordering of the role the Black woman can play as designated by Sonia corresponds to the philosophy of the Bantu in relation to the three phases of evolution as Man, as complete Man. First, she accepts that she is a woman, the feminine dimension, which is an acceptance of the first principle—man, Monad, revealed in his masculinity; the second principle in man's evolution to becoming *humanized*, towards becoming a person, is revealed in Woman, Dyad, fecundity; Man is now responsible to each other, but is not freedom, and is incomplete without Triad, child, i.e., without becoming mother. The complete cycle—Man-Woman-Child. These priciples as designated by the Bantu, as unconsciously designated by Sonia, reveal the extent and degree to which the depth of an African sensibility still pervades her consciousness despite the severance from native Africa for over 400 years. This philosophy is essentially the key towards achieving harmony and unity within the Black family.

In terms of the stylistic quality of her writing it is incontestable that she is one of the forerunners of the New Breed. The language and rhythm of her poetry reflect the language and speech-rhythm of Black people—revealing her most pristine desire as that of maximum communication to her audience in a language that they are not foreign to. One white critic said that the "young" Black writers are fakes because they use "word-acrobatics" in their writing. But the vibrations of Black people would have manifested itself adversely if the "fakery" of these poets was a reality, since the Black poets function within and for the Black community. Black people are a vibratory, emotional and all-feeling people, they are moved very much by their feeling-being. So that the rhetoric of that white critic has no foundation or relevance to the feelings of the Black poets' audience. In fact, the style, the writing style, of these Black poets is not unique or original—it is a very old form that has its tradition in white writers like William Carlos Williams and Lawrence Ferlinghetti. The *innovative difference* is that the style is transformed, is given creative life, by the uniqueness of the content of these poets' creations.

In terms of the negativism or positivism of Sonia's work, there is one thing that is certain—that nowhere in her poetry is there a question of "identity" posed in any form. Sonia Sanchez has transcended that, and so have most of the other writers and poets of this generation; it has never been a question or a theme in her poetry. Hers is more significant and profound—like the releasing of the *id*, the demon of the new Black Magic. It is a poetry of destiny, a declaration of self-determination, Black people as intrinsically being separated, in their philosophy and essentially in their sensibility as a nation, from the murderous, masochistic and decadent society that is called white America.

Sebastian Clarke, "Sonia Sanchez and Her Work," Black World 20, No. 8 (June 1971): 98

BARBARA WALKER   In a time when society breeds groups like the Women's Liberation Movement, blacks have begun to reflect on their roles as women. The theatre continuously utilizes the stage as an exclusive device to portray the innermost feelings of the people in their society. One of the controversial figures of the theatre today, who has made a unique attempt in her writing to present us with a realistic look at the "woman thing," is Sonia Sanchez.

There is more than just being witty and 'heavy on the cap,' because Sonia's writing is not the result of a meticulously developed writing style colored with "it's hip to be black" now syndrome. Her writing is her lifestyle colored with a natural warmth and honest outlook on people and herself.

Most of us identify best with her poetry. Only recently, people have become aware of her ability as a playwright.

"It's sort of a different kind of writing," she said. "I've always written poetry since I was a little girl. In terms of plays, sometimes you can't always say things in poems. You can't always say what you want to say. People don't always listen.

"I moved into plays in the 60's specifically because of my dialogue and poems," she explained. "Imamu was doing *Black Fire*. He asked me to do a play and I did *The Bronx Is Next*. It got there too late, so only my poems were in it. The next time, Ed Bullins was doing the Tulane Drama Review. So I did *The Bronx Is Next* for that. I constructed a play where Black revolutionaries decide to burn out Harlem. My vision at the time was that the buildings in Harlem were full of rats and roaches. The only way to get them out was by burning them. In the play is a character called the 'black bitch.' A woman who is all of us. I took women who I had seen, heard, talked about in the community. What's interesting is that she has this white lover, a policeman, this kind of gets her into difficulties with the band of black revolutionists.

"Not long after Ed Bullins called me long distance when I was in California organizing a Black studies program. He was doing *Plays from the Black Theatre*.

'I want you to do a play for me.' Then I had twins and was feeling sorry for myself, tired and beat up because twins will do that to you. He called. I knew I hadn't got the plays out. So I said 'I just had twins.' He said, 'Don't tell me your problems. I don't tell you to have twins.' I needed that kind of thing because it just made me pop up and I wrote *Sister Sonji*. I worked from 10:30 p.m. to 5 a.m. in the morning."

> Barbara Walker, "Sonia Sanchez Creates Poetry for the Stage," *Black Creation* 5, No. 1 (Fall 1973): 12

GEORGE E. KENT   Sonia Sanchez's latest book, *A Blues Book for Blue Black Magical Women,* possesses an extraordinary culmination of spiritual and poetic powers. It is in part an exhortation to move the rhythms of black life to a high peak through deep and deeper self-possession; in part an address to all, with specific emphasis upon women; in part, a spiritual autobiography. Actually, one gets trapped in rhetoric; the separate strands entwine themselves together and are pervasive, for the most part. The book consists of five parts: Part I, urging women to move out of false paths created by racism into the queenly existence of self-possession, purpose, direction; Part II, describing autobiographically Sonia's own psychological and spiritual evolution in the past; Part III, focusing on the present and giving her transition and rebirth into the Muslim vision; Part IV, a brief celebration of rebirth; and Part V, ringing with visions and celebrations. Although the spiritual journey finds its vitalizing point in a movement toward the Muslims, the spiritual and poetic power has nourishment even for the unready. In the book's conception of woman and her role, there seems to be both the influence of the Baraka group and that of the Muslims.

A *Blues Book* is a mountain-top type poem. That is, it is the poetic rhythms of one who has climbed from the valleys and is now calling others up from the low, the misted flats. A number of radical writers have attempted to create the mountain-top type, without sufficient awareness of the traps to be evaded. At the very least, it seems to require that one dislodge the ego from the center of one's concerns. If one has not dealt with the ego, if one is not really at the top or at one of the peaks, the ego whips out patronizing gestures and tones to the multitude.

It seems to me that the author has escaped such traps. I feel in the poems a genuine humbleness, love, and thankfulness, brightly leavening the exhortations. The voice is that of a struggler mindful of the journey and further humanized by it, an achievement emphasized by the confessional and testifying parts of the book.

George E. Kent, "Notes on the 1974 Black Literary Scene," *Phylon* 36, No. 2 (June 1975): 197–98

CLAUDIA TATE   C.T.: How does being black, female, and a one-time member of the Nation of Islam constitute a particular perspective in your work?

SANCHEZ: I wrote as a child. When I first started to write, I stuttered. Always at the core of my being was the realization that I was black, not that I knew I was oppressed, but that I knew I was black. I might have said "Negro" years ago. I knew something was wrong, but I didn't know the terminology to explain it or what to do about it. I was in Alabama then. There were simple things, like going to a house where my grandmother worked, and we were in the kitchen and heard the way she was talked to. But I could not verbalize my feelings. When we went into elevators in stores, white people always wanted to touch us and say, "Aren't they some nice little children." I would always draw back because I knew something was wrong, but my stepmother allowed this to happen, and I was always very angry about that. Because I knew they had no business touching me. I somehow knew that because she was black, she let that happen. I remember asking my stepmother four times why she couldn't try on a hat she wanted to buy, and each time I didn't get an answer. That I remember. ⟨. . .⟩

Although I was a very shy child, a very introspective child, one who stuttered, one who was not very self-confident, there were some things that I was sure of. One of the things which has propelled me all my life is when a principle is violated. America has violated many principles as far as black people are concerned and that's why I do battle with her. I do battle not because I think it's cute or militant but because America has violated a race of people. This means that my whole life has been dedicated toward the eradication of those violations.

I went into the Nation of Islam in 1972. I had been in New York for a couple of years, and had watched a lot of people who were "in the Nation." When I joined I didn't change my basic lifestyle, my writing. I had children, and I thought it was important for them to be around people who had a sense of nationhood, a sense of righteousness and morality. I wanted them to be exposed to this behavior. You cannot talk about progress for people unless you also talk about morality. The Nation was the one organization that was trying to deal with the concepts of nationhood, morality, small business, schools. . . . And these things were very important to me.

> Claudia Tate, "Sonia Sanchez," *Black Women Writers at Work* (New York: Continuum, 1983), pp. 138–39

D. H. MELHEM   In both poetry and drama, Sanchez maintains she is trying to reach all kinds of audiences. She sees no real change in Black life since the sixties, and says, "I couldn't write *Homecoming* and *We a BaddDDD People* now." While the point of Black Pride has been made, it is time to progress from there toward concrete gains, by organizing well and powerfully through—and here she differs radically from Madhubuti— interracial coalitions. "Organize in terms of particular issues?" I ask her. "Always, always, always," she replied.

Sanchez offers this advice to beginning writers:

> Read and read and read and read everything you can get your
> hands on. One of the things Louise Bogan told me was,
> "Whatever you write, read aloud. Your ear will be the best friend
> you will ever have." And join a workshop at some point when
> you really feel you want to work more and/or apprentice yourself
> to a poet or writer and study with her or him. ⟨. . .⟩

In a recent telephone conversation, I discussed with the poet her latest book, *homegirls & handgrenades* ⟨. . .⟩ Lyricism, the gift of her love poetry, moves the first two sections, "The Power of Love" and "Blues Is Bullets"; animates the humanitarian poems of "Beyond the Fallout"; and splashes the public poems of "Grenades Are Not Free."

In stories like "Just Don't Never Give Up on Love," relating an encounter with an old woman on a park bench, and "Bluebirdbluebirdthrumywindow," about a chance encounter with a homeless Black woman ("This beached black whale.") in a Pennsylvania Station restroom; "Bubba" and "Norma," bright friends from her childhood and school, who stayed behind in Harlem among the rubble of their thwarted dreams, Sanchez reveals the compassionate immediacy with which she relates to the lost ones of earth, and her felt responsibility as an artist to voice their inarticulate despair.

Richness of that voice culminates in public poems of the last section. As she writes to Ezekiel Mphahlele, the exile returning to South Africa after twenty years; addresses Dr. Martin Luther King, Margaret Walker, Jesse Jackson; reflects on the June 12, 1983 March for Disarmament; and exhorts Third World working-class people in "MIA's (missing in action and other atlantas)"; visionary hopefulness transforms her anger and pain into a call for action. "MIA's," the concluding poem, interspersed with Spanish and Zulu, explodes its real and surreal images to light a landscape of suffering from Atlanta to Johannesburg, South Africa.

D. H. Melhem, "Sonia Sanchez: Will and Spirit," *MELUS* 12, No. 3 (Fall 1985): 95–97

JAMES ROBERT SAUNDERS   It is appropriate when analyzing a work such as *Homegirls and Handgrenades* (1984) to wonder about what might have been the motivation for its subject matter and form. It might be declared by some that this is just another long line of Sonia Sanchez's books of poems. Her very first volume, *Homecoming* (1969), was an impressive display of staggered-lined poems with word-splitting diagonals. *We a BadddDDD People* (1970) and *It's a New Day* (1971) contained even more of the same stylistic devices. Part of Sanchez's early effort was to experiment with words in verse to create a new perspective on how blacks should perceive themselves within the context of a nation struggling to admit them into the fold of social equality. Although the task remains incomplete, one can nevertheless sense a development on the part of the poet as she advances her work to include the mystical *A Blues Book for Blue Black Magical Women* (1973) as well as *Love Poems* (1973) where there can be seen an attempt to reconcile all the various aspects of black culture for the benefit of progress. *I've Been a Woman* (1978) and *Under a Soprano Sky* (1987) are further examples of how the author has examined, in particular, the plight of black women as they strive toward freedom in a world not always conducive to that undertaking.

Nonetheless, it is in *Homegirls* where Sanchez delivers what Henry Louis Gates has characterized as "the revising text . . . written in the language of the tradition, employing its tropes, its rhetorical strategies, and its ostensible subject matter, the so-called Black Experience." Gates further explains how many black writers have either consciously or subconsciously "signified" on previous authors' works so as to explore their own impressions while yet remaining faithful to certain literary strategies used by their predecessors. The former slave, Olaudah Equiane, wrote his narrative based to a large extent on what a previous slave narrator, James Gronniosaw, did. Ralph Ellison's *Invisible Man* (1952) is largely a response to the literary work of Richard Wright. And recently, Alice Walker has drawn on the basic themes and dialect style of Zora Neale Hurston to render her prize-winning novel, *The Color Purple* (1982). This tradition of signifying on what other writers have done is a deep-rooted feature of black writing that has as its origin the culture of blacks as a whole. It is, interestingly enough, the mark of black culture in its most creative posture, that of being able to play upon what is available, in terms of form and substance, and convert it into something new and unique.

Such is the achievement of Sanchez who, in *Homegirls*, has rendered a marvelous collage of thirty-two short stories, poems, letters, and sketches that often ring loudly with the truth of an autobiographical fervor.

James Robert Saunders, "Sonia Sanchez's *Homegirls and Handgrenades*: Recalling Toomer's *Cane*," *MELUS* 15, No. 1 (Spring 1988): 73–74

HOUSTON A. BAKER, JR.   The riddle for the critic who would deal with the *sound* of Sonia Sanchez—the renaissancism of *her* transmission and passage of the word through a community of sharers—is how did an Alabama black child who turned away from the world surrounding her and found introspective refuge and psychological defense in stuttering move in her maturing years to achieve her own resonant articulation? When asked how she ceased stuttering, Ms. Sanchez tells of an act of will in which she simply decided to cure herself. When asked how she moved from introspection and moderate Americanism to active, nationalist cadences, she points to a moment on a Sunday evening in the sixties when she put aside a resolution to avoid Malcolm X's speeches and refused to be bound by an agreement among fellow workers in New York CORE that Malcolm was a racist to be shunned at all costs.

> Malcolm sent the word out that you could not have any kind of demonstration in Harlem unless he was a part of it. And so I remember saying to some people in the [CORE] office: "God, this man, he's nothing but a racist anyway. What is he gonna do?"

> Everytime he'd come to speak at demonstrations we were having,
> we'd walk back over to the office and go in there until he was
> finished and then come back for our part. But one day, a rainy
> day . . . I listened to Malcolm as the rain was drizzling . . . And I
> stood there with the rain hitting me and I kept looking and I
> kept listening . . . The danger of Malcolm and probably of
> Farakann, is that they . . . pull middle class people toward them
> . . . Our poems were almost direct results of how [Malcolm]
> presented things . . . always that strong line at the end—the kick
> at the end that people would repeat, repeat, and repeat, always a
> finely tuned phrase or line that people could remember.

Malcolm's speech, with its penetrating logic and obvious commitment, converted Sanchez forever. The vision that she seized on a rainy New York afternoon comes powerfully home in a characterization found in elegiac stanzas that she wrote for the brilliant Muslim leader:

> he was the sun that tagged
> the western sky and
> melted tiger-scholars
> while they searched for stripes.
> he said, "fuck you white
> man. we have been
> curled too long. nothing
> is sacred now. not your
> white faces nor any
> land that separates
> until some voices
> squat with spasms."

Houston A. Baker, Jr., "Our Lady: Sonia Sanchez and the Writing of a Black Renaissance," *Reading Black, Reading Feminist: A Critical Anthology*, ed. Henry Louis Gates, Jr. (New York: Meridian, 1990), pp. 327–28

JOANNE VEAL GABBIN   *Homecoming* (1969), Sanchez's first book of poems, is her pledge of allegiance to blackness, to black love, to black heroes, and to her own realization as a woman, an artist, and a revolutionary. The language and the typography are experimental; they are aberrations of standard middle-class Americanese and traditional Western literary forms. As such, they reflect her view of American society, which perceives blacks as aberrations and exploits them through commercialism, drugs, brutality, and institutionalized racism. In this book and the poetry that follows, the vernacular and the forms are clear indications of her fierce determination to redefine her art and rail against Western aesthetics. *Homecoming* also introduces us to a poet who is saturated with the sound and sense of black speech and black music, learned at the knees of Birmingham women discovering themselves full voiced and full spirited. The rhythm and color of black speech—the rapping, reeling, explosive syllables— are her domain, for she is steeped in the tradition of linguistic virtuosity that Stephen Henderson talks about in *Understanding the New Black Poetry*. Black music, especially the jazz sounds of John Coltrane, Ornette Coleman, and Pharoah Sanders, pulse, riff, and slide through her poetry.

In her second volume, *We a BaddDDD People* (1970), Sanchez is wielding a survival sword that rips away the enemy's disguise and shears through the facade of black ignorance and reactionism. Arranged in three groups, "Survival Poems," "Love/Songs/Chants," and "TCB/EN Poems," the poems extend the attack begun in *Homecoming* and tell black people how to survive in a country of death traps (drugs, suicide, sexual exploitation, psychological slaughter via the mass media) and televised assassination. Her message, however, is not one of unrelieved gloom, for it is rooted in optimism and faith: "know and love yourself." Like Sterling A. Brown's "Strong Men" and Margaret Walker's "For My People," "We a BaddDDD People," the title poem of the volume, is a praise song that celebrates black love, talent, courage, and continuity. The poems appear rooted in a courage learned early from aunts who spit in the face of Southern racism and sisters who refused to be abused by white men or black men. In this volume, Sanchez reveals her unmistakable signature, the singing/chanting voice. Inflections, idiom, intonations—skillfully represented by slashes, capitalization (or the lack of it), and radical and rhythmic spelling—emphasize her link with the community and her role as ritual singer.

Joanne Veal Gabbin, "The Southern Imagination of Sonia Sanchez," *Southern Women Writers: The New Generation*, ed. Tonette Bond Inge (Tuscaloosa: University of Alabama Press, 1990), pp. 181–82

FRENZELLA ELAINE DE LANCEY   One of the few titled haiku written by Sonia Sanchez, "Walking in the rain in Guyana" is an excellent example of both the poet's artistic vision and artistry:

> watusi like trees
> holding the day like green um/
> brella catching rain.

Elements consistent with definitions of classical Japanese haiku as a lyric verse form in three unrhymed lines, with a 5-7-5 syllable count are evident, so, too, is the requisite emphasis on external nature. The clarifying title tells us that this haiku derives from a walk in the rain in Guyana and announces the poet's intention to "localize" the haiku in a particular manner. Sanchez uses Afrocentric motifs to textualize the haiku, making it not some universal statement about rain and tree but a particular experience, filtered through the poet's consciousness. Though Guyana is located in South America, African people are among its inhabitants; the watusi trees evoke images of the Burundi Watusi, again, images associated with Africa. Sanchez localizes this image by inserting "like" in the first line, forcing it into service as she forges an adjective-phrase, "watusi-like" to describe the trees. Such techniques signal the reader: this is haiku with a difference. ⟨. . .⟩

Sanchez's transformation of the form is more radical than mere structural alteration, although she sometimes changes the structure of the haiku by using simile, conjunction, and metaphor. Her use of these structural markers can always be identified as functional; they are used to make the haiku speak her words, reveal her vision. In fact, Sanchez's use of the form is a revolutionary textualization of both structure and form. Sometimes working within the structural strictures of classical Japanese haiku form, other times altering the form to fit her needs, and always textualizing it, Sanchez forces the form to accommodate her vision. By imbuing the haiku form with Afrocentric motifs, Sanchez textualizes the form in a specific manner, and in the instances where she must abrogate universally observed strictures, she does so to force the haiku to conform to her needs and her vision. In her haiku, then, the effect is a movement through the uneven strictures imposed by dicta reintroduced for the English haiku. Referring specifically to her book I'VE BEEN A WOMAN, Sanchez discusses her use of haiku and tanka, and her conscious use of African themes. In I'VE BEEN A WOMAN, she points out, "I have haiku, tankas, and again, the movement towards what I call 'African' ideas and feelings and also the movement toward a black ethic and a feminine one too."

Frenzella Elaine De Lancey, "Refusing to Be Boxed In: Sonia Sanchez's Transformation of the Haiku Form," *Language and Literature in the African American Imagination*, ed. Carol Aisha Blackshire-Belay (Westport, CT: Greenwood Press, 1992), pp. 21–23

REGINA B. JENNINGS   It is obvious that revolutionary fervor characterized some of Sanchez's work, but it is essential for understanding her poetics, as well as the neo-aesthetic of the sixties, to recognize that anarchy was not the goal. These poets considered themselves to be word soldiers for black people, defending their right to have equality, honor, and glory. In each of Sanchez's volumes of poetry, for example, one finds the artist handling themes that include love, harmony, race unification, myth, and history. Her poetic personas are diverse, incorporating themes from China, to Nicaragua, to Africa. Yet, there is a pattern in her figurative language that blends an African connection. In this article, I shall examine the Afrocentric tropes that embody Sanchez's poetics. To use Afrocentricity in this regard is to examine aspects of traditional African culture not limited by geography in Sanchez's work. A body of theory that argues such an African commonality is in Kariamu Welsh's *The Concept of Nzuri: Towards Defining an Afrocentric Aesthetic*. Using her model will enable this kind of topological investigation.

Houston A. Baker, Jr. presents a different aesthetic in *Blues, Ideology, and Afro-American Literature*. This book is a point of departure from Africa, concentrating solely on discussions of African American art from a black American perspective. On the back cover of *Under a Soprano Sky*, Baker maintains that blue/black motif appears in selected works by Sanchez. Baker's definition of the blues constitutes a transitory motion found precisely in this motif. The blues manifests itself in Sanchez's prosody in varying degrees and in differing forms. It determines shape and category, directs the vernacular, and informs the work. To demonstrate this specific vitality in Sanchez's poetry, Baker's construct of a blues matrix is an apt qualifier.

One can identify the blues as matrix and Afrocentric tropology in Sanchez's literary vision when one understands the significance of her axiology. Her ethics informs not only her creativity but her essays and articles as well. Her focus is to inscribe the humanity of blacks to challenge the Eurocentric perspective of black inferiority. Her particular axiology emerged during the greatest period of social unrest between white and blacks. In the sixties, African American artists deliberately fused politics and art to direct social change. That Sanchez's axiology influenced her ethics has to be considered in order to understand why her poetry inverts the tropology of "white" and "black." The artists of the black Arts Movement were at war with America. Their tone and perspective encouraged black people to rethink their collective position and to seize control to direct their destiny.

> Regina B. Jennings, "The Blue/Black Poetics of Sonia Sanchez," *Language and Literature in the African American Imagination*, ed. Carol Aisha Blackshire-Belay (Westport, CT: Greenwood Press, 1992), pp. 119–20

◉ *Bibliography*

Home Coming. 1969.

Liberation Poem. 1970.

We a BaddDDD People. 1970.

It's a New Day: Poems for Young Brothas and Sistuhs. 1971.

Ima Talken bout the Nation of Islam. 1972.

Three Hundred and Sixty Degrees of Blackness Comin at You (editor). 1972.

We Be Word Sorcerers: 25 Stories by Black Americans (editor). 1973.

The Adventures of Fathead, Smallhead, and Squarehead. 1973.

Love Poems. 1973.

A Blues Book for Blue Black Magical Women. 1974.

I've Been a Woman: New and Selected Poems. 1978.

A Sound Investment: Short Stories for Young Readers. 1980.

Crisis in Culture: Two Speeches ⟨"The Poet as a Creator of Social Values"; "The Crisis of the Black Community"⟩. 1983.

homegirls & handgrenades. 1984.

Generations: Poetry 1969–1985. 1986.

Under a Soprano Sky. 1987.

Autumn Blues: New Poems. n.d.

Behind the Bamboo Curtain. n.d.

Continuous Fire: A Collection of Poetry. n.d.

Ntozake Shange
b. 1948

NTOZAKE SHANGE was born Paulette Williams on October 18, 1948, in Trenton, New Jersey, the oldest child of a surgeon and a social worker. With her two younger brothers and sister she grew up in Trenton, at an air force base in upstate New York, and in St. Louis, Missouri. Her father painted and played percussion in addition to his duties as a physician, and she met many leading black figures in sports and the arts. She read widely as a child, and in her teens began to rebel against her privileged life. A turning point occurred when she was bussed to an all-white school for the gifted in St. Louis; she was, she says, unprepared for the hostility and harassment of white students.

Paulette Williams went on the Barnard College, where she majored in American studies, specializing in black American music and poetry. At Barnard she became active in the civil rights movement. After graduation in 1970 she went to the University of Southern California, teaching while earning a master's degree in American studies; the following year she changed her name, after consulting friends from the Xhosa tribe, who baptized her in the Pacific Ocean with her new African name. *Ntozake* means "she who comes with her own things"; *Shange* means "who walks like a lion."

Shange went on to teach in the women's studies program at Sonoma State College and began writing poetry intensively. Soon she was reading it at women's bars, accompanied by friends who were musicians and dancers. Out of these performances grew her first theatrical production, or "choreopoem," *For Colored Girls Who Have Considered Suicide/When the Rainbow Is Enuf*, a celebration of the survival and triumph of black women. Shange and her friend, choreographer Paula Moss, moved to New York City in the mid-1970s and first performed *For Colored Girls* in a jazz loft in SoHo in July 1975. The show evolved through a series of highly successful Off-Broadway productions, then opened uptown at the Booth Theatre in the fall of 1976; it was published in book form the next year. Shange, who had been in the show's cast since its first performance, remained in the Broadway production for one month. *For Colored Girls* played on Broadway for two years, then was taken by touring companies to Canada, the Caribbean, and other cities in the United States.

Shange's second major work to be staged in New York was *A Photograph: A Study of Cruelty*, termed a "poemplay" by its author. The production, which explores the relationship between a black woman dancer and her talented but unsuccessful photographer lover, ran at the Public Theatre during the 1977–78 season but received mixed reviews; it was published in a revised version as *A Photograph: Lovers in Motion* (1981). Shange did not appear in this play, having formed a three-woman ensemble called the Satin Sisters, who read their poetry against a background of jazz at the Public Theatre Cabaret.

Shange has written and performed in several theatrical pieces in New York in recent years, including *From Okra to Greens* (1978; published 1985). Her adaptation of Bertolt Brecht's play *Mother Courage and Her Children* was presented at the Public Theatre in 1980. Of her other plays, only *Spell #7* (1981) has been published. Her published books of verse include *Nappy Edges* (1978), *A Daughter's Geography* (1983), *Ridin' the Moon in Texas* (1987), and *The Love Space Demands* (1991). Shange has issued the novels *Sassafrass, Cypress & Indigo* (1982) and *Betsey Brown* (1985) as well as a volume of essays, *See No Evil* (1984).

✦ *Critical Extracts*

HAROLD CLURMAN   In a number of respects this work ⟨*For Colored Girls Who Have Considered Suicide/When the Rainbow Is Enuf*⟩ is unique. Its stress is on the experience of black women—their passionate outcry, as women, within the black community. There is no badmouthing the whites: feelings on that score are summed up in the humorously scornful lines addressed to a black man which begin: "ever since I realized there was someone callt a colored girl, a evil woman, a bitch or a nag, I been tryin' not to be that and leave bitterness in somebody elses cup. . . . I finally bein real no longer symmetrical and inervious to pain . . . so why don't we be white then and make everythin' dry and abstract wid no rhythm and no feelin' for sheer sensual pleasure. . . ." The woman who utters these words, like all the others, speaks not so much in apology or explanation of her black condition but in essential human protest against her black lover whose connection with her is the ordinary (white or black) callousness toward women. Thus she asserts "I've lost it / touch with reality / I know who's doin' it. . . . I should be unsure, if I'm still alive. . . . I survive on intimacy and to-morrow. . . . But bein' alive and bein' a woman and bein' colored is a metaphysical dilemma."

This gives only a pitifully partial notion of the pain and power, as well as the acrid wit—"so redundant in the modern world"—which much of the writing communicates. The thematic emphasis is constantly directed at the stupid crudity and downright brutality of their own men, which, whatever the causes, wound and very nearly destroy their women. These women have been driven to the very limits of their endurance (or "rainbow") and are desperately tired of hearing their men snivel that they're "sorry." Part of the joy in the performance lay in the ecstatic response of the women in the audience!

Harold Clurman, "Theatre," Nation, 1 May 1976, p. 542

JANET BROWN   Although *For Colored Girls* has many protagonists rather than one, its pattern of symbolic action is clearly a search for autonomy opposed by an unjust socio-sexual hierarchy. The search for autonomy in *For Colored Girls* succeeds, however, more thoroughly than in any of the other plays studied. Thus, it is the most idealistic of the plays examined as well.

The successful resolution to the search for autonomy is attributable first to the communal nature of the struggle. *For Colored Girls* has many agents who share in the same struggle, but just as significantly, none of these agents is able to transcend the unjust hierarchy alone. Rather the play's pattern of symbolic action shows a progression of sympathetic sharing and support among women culminating in the communal recitation and singing that ends the play.

Secondly, the play's optimistic resolution results from the agents' affirmations of self building through the play. The colored girl who at the beginning of the play "doesn't know the sound of her own voice: her infinite beauty," affirms by the end of the play that she has found God in herself. These two elements in the achievement of autonomy, sisterhood and self-realization, are symbolically united in the final song which affirms the holiness of self and which is sung by the whole community of women on stage.

Finally, the achievement of autonomy in *For Colored Girls* is not only socio-sexual or psychological but spiritual as well. The spirituality of the play's resolution, reflected in images of blessing hands, the spirits of women of the past haunting present-day women and the female god women find in themselves suggests the spiritual transcendence of sexism described by Mary Daly in *Beyond God the Father*. Such a transcendence, Daly says, will be "an ontological, spiritual revolution, pointing beyond the idolatries of sexist society and sparking creative action in and toward transcendence."

Just as Daly describes, the agents in *For Colored Girls* confront their own "non-being" in the fact of their "non-existence" as persons in the unjust hierarchy. Sechita has learned to disbelieve the grotesque distortion which is society's reflected image of her. The lady in sequins and feathers understands that without her costume she is nothing to the men who court her. The woman who lives in Harlem knows that she has no right to live and move freely in the world. ⟨. . .⟩

Thus, *For Colored Girls* is among the most idealistic of the plays studied, reflecting the feminist philosophy outlined by Daly more fully than any of the other plays studied. As Daly does, the play goes beyond denunciation of the unjust *status quo* to evoke an alternative, non-hierarchical order based on sororal community and a recognition of the worth of each individual. In *For Colored Girls* the agents' affirmation of individuality and community transcends the socio-sexual hierarchy, making the play an idealistic statement of the feminist impulse.

> Janet Brown, *Feminist Drama: Definition and Critical Analysis* (Metuchen, NJ: Scarecrow Press, 1979), pp. 129–31

SANDRA HOLLIN FLOWERS ⟨. . .⟩ there is definitely a crisis.

Individually we have known this for some time, and lately black women as well as black men are showing growing concern about the steady deterioration of their relationships. Black literature, however, has lagged somewhat behind. The works which usually comprise Afro-American literature curricula and become part of general reading materials, for instance, show the position of the black man in America; but generally we see the black woman only peripherally as the protagonist's lover, wife, mother, or in some other supporting (or detracting) role. Certainly black women can identify with the predicament of black men. Black women can identify, for example, with the problems articulated in Ellison's *Invisible Man* because they share the same predicaments. But for black women the predicament of the black male protagonist is compounded by concerns which affect them on yet another level. This, then, is what makes *Colored Girls* an important work which ranks with Ellison's *Invisible Man*, Wright's *Native Son,* and the handful of other black classics—it is an artistically successful female perspective on a long-standing issue among black people. If, however, black men fail to acknowledge the significance of *Colored Girls*, if they resent it or insist that it does not speak to their concerns or is not important because it deals with "women's issues," then the crisis is more severe than any thought it to be.

Colored Girls is certainly woman's art but is also black art, or Third World art, as Shange probably would prefer to have it designated. Its language and dialect, its geography, its music, and the numerous allusions to Third World personalities make it an intensely cultural work. Many of these characteristics, however, are peculiar to Shange's upbringing, education, and experiences, with the result that the piece loses universality at points, as in the poem "Now I Love Somebody More Than." But even here, black audiences are sure to know which lady loved gardenias; they will know the Flamingoes and Archie Shepp and Imamu. Then there is the poem "Sechita" in which the dancer is linked to Nefertiti, hence to Africa and Olduvai Gorge, the "cradle of civilization"—all of which puts into perspective the cheapening of Sechita by the carnival audience. While "Sechita" speaks to the degradation of black womanhood, "Toussaint" speaks, with subtle irony, of the black woman's awakening to the black man.

Sandra Hollin Flowers, "*Colored Girls:* Textbook for the Eighties," *Black American Literature Forum* 15, No. 2 (Summer 1981): 51–52

SANDRA L. RICHARDS   Although the epistemology of experience within an African world view is inseparably cognitive *and* intuitive, Shange's protagonists, who are African people raised within the Western perspective, tend to feel that they must opt for one mode of knowledge over the other. Their Western heritage teaches them to see experience as fragmented rather than holistic and to value rational over emotional systems—hence, the dialectic of combat breath vs. will to divinity.

In *Spell #7*, subtitled a "quick magic trance manual for technologically stressed third world people," Shange tackles the iconography of "the nigger." Underneath a huge blackface minstrel mask, a master of ceremonies promises to perform a different kind of magic designed to reveal aspects of Black life authentically. The minstrel performers move through the pain of dance steps and memories associated with Black entertainment for white America on to the release of more private, improvisational party styles. In doing so, they banish the hideous mask along with their stage personae, thereby creating a safe space in which to expose secret hopes, fears, or dreams. 〈. . .〉

Shange draws upon two distinct traditions in contemporary Western theatre. In her commitment to combat breath, she achieves some of the effects described in Bertolt Brecht's dramatic theories. Chief among the German dramatist's tenets is the view that theatre must be an analytical forum which exposes bourgeois illusions and stimulates audiences to think objectively about the causes of social and personal ills. By constructing most of her plays as a series of poetic monologues, occasionally interrupted by conventional dialogue, she takes advantage of the telegraphic, elusive quality of poetry to encourage audiences to listen with close, critical attention; the resultant episodic structure diminishes the audiences' empathetic tendencies by denying them the opportunity to gain a more rounded sense of character. Additionally, the women's contrariness can function like Brecht's *Verfremdung* effect as an alienation device which keeps observers at a more objective, thinking distance from the characters. But because this contrariness also emotionally engages spectators, after a performance they are apt to demand answers to questions like, "Why are these women so strange; what does it mean? Is Shange describing reality accurately? How do I feel about what she describes?" Most importantly, in debating their responses to Shange's views, they can initiate a process of change in the world outside the theatre.

Sandra L. Richards, "Conflicting Impulses in the Plays of Ntozake Shange," *Black American Literature Forum* 17, No. 2 (Summer 1983): 74–75

CLAUDIA TATE   C.T.: When did you first know you were a writer?

SHANGE: I wrote when I was a child. I wrote stories. Then it became very difficult for me to get through school because somebody told me that "Negroes"—we weren't "black" then—didn't write. Some racial incident blocked my writing, and I just stopped. I can't remember exactly when it was. I started writing again in high school. I wrote some poetry, and it was published in a high-school magazine. That same year I'd been writing a lot of essays in English class, and I would always write about black people. Then I was told that I was beating a dead horse, so I stopped writing again. I started back at it when I was nineteen.

C.T.: Do you intend to include white people in your work?

SHANGE: I would never have a white person in a story I wrote with the possibile exception of "the white girl" [*Spell #7*] piece. I have no reason to do it. I was writing this real funny thing last night in my head. It was about my putting a story in a time capsule so that people in the year 20,000 could find it. It was a conversation with a white director: "Yes, I think it's wonderful that you think it's so good that you think it should be all white. Yes, I think it's fine that you think, even though the character is black, a white actress could do it so much better because you know black people really can't talk, although I remember that when my mother was speaking to me in my house, I never heard her talk like the white girl you're going to hire is going to talk like a black person. Then again, I'm only black, so how would I know how best to do it? Yes, I think it's wonderful that you think that because it's a black character you absolutely have to have this white actress play her because she's so good. And where in the world could you find a black person who could play her? I mean, after all it is a black character, and you know a black actress isn't perfectly trained to do this. So, yes, I think you should take my name off it and give me my money. Yes, it's perfectly all right if you use the story as is, but remember nobody in the world will believe that these people were really white. I mean, after all, they sweat."

This business is very sick. The theater is very sick. I feel really badly about it, though I'm compelled to keep working in this medium. What keeps me in the theater has nothing to do with an audience. It has to do with the adventure that's available in that little, three-dimensional stage. I can see a character who exists for me in one way become a real human body. That's a great adventure for me. I don't care. Theater gives my stuff what I cannot give it. Actors spend as many years learning how to act as I've spent learning how to write. Actors spend many years trying to give me something that I don't have. They make the piece come alive in a new way. For example, writers think they know how their characters sit. But if you give a piece to Avery Brooks or Laurie Carlos or Judy Brown or Mary Alice, how they sit can change everything. The timbre of their voices, how they walk, what they do, become available as a communal experience. You cannot read a book with somebody. Whereas, when you have a character there in front of you, that's somebody you know and anybody else sitting there with you would know also. Theater helps me, as a writer, known where I didn't give a character enough stuff, or where I told a lie. It's just a glorious thing to see actors make my characters come alive. But I don't like it when my artist-self has to be confined so that other people can understand. In the theater you have to do this; otherwise, they call your work "performance pieces," which means that you should be a white person and live downtown. Obviously, I can't do that.

> Claudia Tate, "Ntozake Shange," *Black Women Writers at Work* (New York: Continuum, 1983), pp. 171–73.

MAUREEN HONEY   Ntozake Shange dedicates her latest book of poems ⟨A Daughter's Geography⟩ to her family, most especially to her daughter; and it opens with an epigraph consisting of a poem written by a woman in revolutionary Cuba. Both the dedication and the epigraph anticipate the major theme of the book, which is that Third-World peoples are united by a long history and current oppression: that all of them are members of the same family with a common enemy. This theme is rendered by a voice more fierce than angry, more determined than defiant. It is a revolutionary volume, informed by a sensibility of struggle and hope. ⟨. . .⟩

This volume delights, inspires, and enlightens. Shange's political astuteness, ear for the street, and earthiness are a rare combination and one to be savored.

> Maureen Honey, "A Sensibility of Struggle and Hope," *Prairie Schooner* 58, No. 4 (Winter 1984): 111–12.

ELIZABETH BROWN-GUILLORY   Shange's theater pieces, beyond the commercially successful *For Colored Girls Who Have Considered Suicide/When the Rainbow Is Enuf*, have gone virtually unnoticed in critical studies. One case in point is Shange's *A Photograph: Lovers in Motion*, a drama that "comes closest to play form in that there is a logical progression of action and dialogue, with some detectable growth in at least one of the five characters." Though the stages of growth are not as readily detected as in plays by ⟨Alice⟩ Childress and ⟨Lorraine⟩ Hansberry, Michael in *A Photograph: Lovers in Motion* does embark on a journey that results in her wholeness. Shange's integrity as a dramatist who seeks to "transcend or bypass through music and dance the limitations of social and human existence" is not compromised in this theater piece, but rather is enhanced by the depth of these characters. Not only is *A Photograph: Lovers in Motion* an exploration of lives, but it is a drama that answers some of the whys of human behavior as the heroine grows and becomes a catalyst for the growth of her lover. ⟨...⟩

Blacks have traditionally turned to singing and dancing as coping strategies because those areas were open to blacks in white America. Shange's dramatic structure is exciting and innovative and, in at least one play, *A Photograph: Lovers in Motion*, the poet/playwright merges traditional dramatic structure with identifiable African American self-expression.

> Elizabeth Brown-Guillory, *Their Place on the Stage: Black Women Playwrights in America* (Westport, CT: Greenwood Press, 1988), pp. 97, 100

MARY K. DeSHAZER   *Spell #7* ⟨...⟩ focuses partly on sexist oppression but mainly on issues of color and class. The grotesque minstrel-show parody that begins the play jolts the audience with that familiar, insidious brand of racism once labeled comedy; and the magician's opening speech reveals the impact of internalized oppression on Black children who wanted desperately to be made white. "What cd any self-respectin colored american magician / do wit such an outlandish request," lou wonders as he recounts this story, besides put away his magic tools altogether, for "colored chirren believin in magic / waz becomin politically dangerous for the race." But now lou is back with his magic, he tells us, and "it's very colored / very now you see it / now you / dont mess wit me." The play quickly becomes an angry reclamation of those physical and psychic territories appropriated from Black Americans by racist terrorists: school kids, police, lynch mobs. "This is the borderline," one character, alec, claims in identifying himself and his dreams, "this is our space / we are not movin." The only safe territory, the characters reveal, is segregated space where magic rules and masks come off. But even a protected haven from which to speak cannot offset the daily horrors these unemployed performers face. Lily wishes for just one decent part, like lady macbeth or mother courage, only to be reminded by eli that she can't play lady macbeth when "macbeth's a white dude." Bettina's show remains open, "but if that director asks me to play it any blacker / i'm gonna have to do it in a mammy dress." What white audiences want is what they get, the actors bitterly remind us, and even selling out to racist taste doesn't pay the bills. Near the end of the play, alec offers one powerful suggestion that would make him less tired. A gong would sound for three minutes, all over the world, while "all the white people / immigrants & invaders / conquistadors & relatives of london debtors from georgia / kneel & apologize to us." This is not impossible, he insists; this is Black magic.

Mary K. DeShazer, "Rejecting Necrophilia: Ntozake Shange and the Warrior Revisioned," *Making a Spectacle: Feminist Essays on Contemporary Women's Theatre*, ed. Lynda Hart (Ann Arbor: University of Michigan Press, 1989), pp. 93–94

DEBORAH R. GEIS   Ntozake Shange's works defy generic classification: just as her poems (published in *Nappy Edges* and *A Daughter's Geography*) are also performance pieces, her works for the theater defy the boundaries of drama and merge into the region of poetry. Her most famous work, *for colored girls who have considered suicide/when the rainbow is enuf*, is subtitled "a choreopoem." Similarly, she has written *Betsey Brown* as a novel and then again (with Emily Mann) in play form, and her first work of fiction, *Sassafrass, Cypress & Indigo*, is as free with its narrative modes—including recipes, spells, letters—as Joyce was in *Ulysses*. Perhaps more so than any other practicing playwright, Shange has created a poetic voice that is uniquely her own—a voice which is deeply rooted in her experience of being female and black, but also one which, again, refuses and transcends categorization. Her works articulate the connection between the doubly "marginalized" social position of the black woman and the need to invent and appropriate a language with which to articulate a self.

In their revelation of such language, Shange's theatrical narratives move subtly and forcefully between the comic and the tragic. A brief passage from *for colored girls* underscores the precarious path between laughter and pain which Shange's characters discover they are forced to tread:

> distraught laughter fallin
> over a black girl's shoulder

> it's funny/it's hysterical
> the melody-less-ness of her dance
> don't tell nobody, don't tell a soul
> she's dancing on beer cans & shingles

These images associated with the word *hysterical* in this passage show the multilayered and interdependent qualities of the "black girl's" experience: *hysterical* connotes a laughter which has gone out of control, a madness historically—if not accurately—connected with femaleness. Moreover, the admonition "don't tell nobody, don't tell a soul" suggests the call to silence, the fear that to speak of her pain will be to violate a law of submission. The onlooker will aestheticize the dance or call attention to its comic qualities rather than realize the extent to which the dance and the laughter are a reaction against—and are even motivated by—the uncovering of pain.

The key here is the complexity, for Shange, of the performative experience. In her plays, especially *for colored girls* and *spell #7*, Shange develops her narration primarily through monologues because monologic speech inevitably places the narrative weight of a play upon its spoken language and upon the performances of the individual actors. But she does not use this device to develop "character" in the same fashion as Maria Irene Fornes and other Method-inspired playwrights who turn toward monologic language in order more expresssively to define and "embody" their characters both as women and as individuals. Rather, Shange draws upon the uniquely "performative" qualities of monologue to allow her actors to take on *multiple* roles and therefore to emphasize the centrality of *storytelling* to her work. This emphasis is crucial to Shange's articulation of a black feminist aesthetic (and to the call to humanity to accept that "black women are inherently valuable") on two counts. First, the incorporation of role-playing reflects the ways that blacks (as "minstrels," "servants," "athletes," etc.) are expected to fulfill such roles on a constant basis in Western society. Second, the space between our enjoyment of the "spectacle" of Shange's theater pieces (through the recitation of the monologues and through the dancing and singing which often accompany them), and our awareness of the urgency of her call for blacks/women to be allowed "selves" free of stereotypes, serves as a "rupturing" of the performance moment; it is the uncomfortableness of that space, that rupture, which moves and disturbs us.

Deborah R. Geis, "Distraught Laughter: Monologue in Ntozake Shange's Theater Pieces," *Feminine Focus: The New Women Playwrights*, ed. Enoch Brater (New York: Oxford University Press, 1989), pp. 210–11

PINKIE GORDON LANE   This collection of prose and poetry
⟨*Ridin' the Moon in Texas*⟩ calls forth so many images that the reader will
see him/herself in every page. It becomes an exposé of the reader's psyche.
Now that's saying a lot for a slender volume that takes "old wine and puts
it into new bottles." That is, Shange has employed the technique of using
visual art as a takeoff for creating the substance of her verbal images. Thus,
the book also contains color reproductions of exciting contemporary art in
various media: painting, sculpture, and photography. ⟨. . .⟩

These short, disconnected pieces (unlike ⟨Shange's⟩ earlier, loosely joined
narrative) contain lyricism, metaphor, and verbal subtleties (even elitism)
that range from the vernacular to the linguistically sophisticated. The book's
subjects range from a eulogy for a friend to social criticism. "Somewhere in
soweto there's a small girl / she's grown thin & frightened." These lines
from "Who Needs a Heart" allow us to experience what it is like living
under apartheid in South Africa as seen from the perspective of a black
child. ⟨. . .⟩

The book rocks, it rolls; but it also soars ethereally, shifting gears with
dizzying speed. Breathless in its Joycean stream of consciousness, it just as
quickly plummets to mother earth, its choice of style being adapted to the
mood and subject.

Pinkie Gordon Lane, [Review of *Ridin' the Moon in Texas*], *Black American Literature Forum* 24, No. 3 (Fall 1990): 578–79

EILEEN MYLES   All of the poems in *The Love Space Demands* take
up with the world. The riveting "crack annie" takes on the news. A crack
mother sacrifices her seven-year-old's pussy to her dealer, and the lead poem
of the book, "irrepressibly bronze, beautiful & mine," was written to work
with ⟨Robert⟩ Mapplethorpe's *Black Book*. It dives in unabashedly: "all my
life they've been near me / these men / some for a while like the / friend
of my father's who drove / each summer from denver to / st. louis / with
some different / white woman." The abandonment of the black woman by
the black man is the bold angle from which Shange broaches Mapplethorpe's
portraits. She looks at these men with admiration and lust. "look at me
pretty niggah," she says. Is it whiteness *and* homosexuality he's leaving her
for? Is that what she's saying? She moves on to "even tho' yr sampler broke

down on you," a poem that mumbles in your ear as its eye grazes the rushing landscape: "(you know where my beauty marks are / all / over / HARLEM)."

In "intermittent celibacy" she rears up with "all i wanted / was to be / revealed." "abstinence / is not / celibacy," she explains, "cuz / when you filled with the Holy Ghost / every man / in the world / can smell it." "if I go all the way without you where would i go?" is as formidably persuasive on sexual abstinence as it is wildly Whitmanesque about its opposite. "i open / deep brown moist & black / cobalt sparklin everywhere." In "chastening with honey," she further expounds wiseguy spirituality: "like the Passion of Christ / which brought us Lent & we give up meat." Who are we? Whose poetry is it, so supremely confident, that its "I" or "we" can finally vanish into the nightmares of the urban landscape, from there smiting the reader's sensibility with simple reportage. Ultimately, she's taken on the work the media won't do. And she's written an unconditionally sex-positive book which suggests that having control of both the yes and the no switch constitutes real power.

> Eileen Myles, "The Art of the Real," *Voice Literary Supplement* No. 98 (September 1991): 13

GETA LeSEUR   Ntozake Shange strives to fill a void in the female literary canon. With novels such as *sassafrass, cypress and indigo* in 1982 and *Betsey Brown* in 1985, and her dramatic choreopoem *For Colored Girls Who Have Considered Suicide/When the Rainbow Is Enuf* in 1977, she has joined the ranks of prominent black women who are giving a voice to their sisters. Through her works, the audience is exposed to the issues facing black women as they develop into adulthood. Issues of racism and sexism must be addressed in order for her characters to grow. Although each of her characters finds a definition of herself as a black woman, the paths taken are unique to the individual. Each woman fulfills herself with a particular interest from which she derives power, be that interest music, dancing, or weaving cloth. These women must also learn to relate to and separate themselves from the men in their lives. With strength of character, Shange's women imprint themselves permanently in our memories. Shange wrote in *sassafrass, cypress and indigo* that the novel is dedicated to "all women in struggle." Within that statement lies the power of her writing. Her works are about black women, but they are indeed for ALL women.

She uses Ebonics in a manner that does not exclude any gender, class or culture. Rather it invites all readers to enjoy as well as understand and confront issues facing us.

Shange said in a 1987 interview with Barbara Lyons for the *Massachusetts Review* that "unless black women are writing the pieces we're being left out in the same way we used to be left out of literature. We don't appear in things unless we write them ourselves." This oppression of black women is addressed by the characters in her writings. Black women are often deprived of their sense of childhood because they must immediately begin striving for recognition in the home and community. In *For Colored Girls . . .* one of the dancers, a lady in brown, sings solemnly "dark phrases of womanhood / of never havin been a girl" and continues with the realization that the invisibility of black women is like death. ⟨. . .⟩ As the choreopoem continues and with the heroines of her novels, Shange sings the black girl's song. Betsey, Sassafrass, Cypress, and Indigo tackle the invisibility of black women and carve their own places in society along with the nameless women dressed in the varied rainbow colors of *For Colored Girls. . . .* This play also explores the never-ending experiences of women—rape, abortion, abuse, love/hate relationships, mothering, death, formulating philosophies of life, third world concerns, what it means to be an Egyptian goddess, and "being colored and sorry at the same time."

Geta LeSeur, "From Nice Colored Girl to Womanist: An Exploration of Development in Ntozake Shange's Writings," *Language and Literature in the African American Imagination*, ed. Carol Aisha Blackshire-Belay (Westport, CT: Greenwood Press, 1992), pp. 167–68

⊞ *Bibliography*

Melissa & Smith. 1976.

Sassafrass. 1976.

For Colored Girls Who Have Considered Suicide/When the Rainbow Is Enuf: A Choreopoem. 1977.

Nappy Edges (Love's a Lil Rough/Sometimes). 1978.

Three Pieces. 1981.

Some Men. 1981.

Spell #7. 1981.

A Photograph: Lovers in Motion. 1981.

Take the A Train. c. 1981.

Sassafrass, Cypress & Indigo. 1982.

A Daughter's Geography. 1983.

From Okra to Greens: A Different Love Story: Poems. 1984.

See No Evil: Prefaces, Essays & Accounts 1974–1983. 1984.

*From Okra to Greens: A Different Kinda Love Story: A Play with Music and
        Dance.* 1985.

Betsey Brown. 1985.

Ridin' the Moon in Texas: Word Paintings. 1987.

*For Colored Girls Who Have Considered Suicide/When the Rainbow Is Enuf: A
        Choreopoem; and Spell #7.* 1990.

The Love Space Demands: A Continuing Saga. 1991.

Plays: One. 1992.

I Live in Music. 1994.

Liliane. 1994.